D1738008

PRODUCTIVITY AND PUBLIC POLICY

SAGE YEARBOOKS IN POLITICS AND PUBLIC POLICY

Sponsored by the **Policy Studies Organization**

Series Editor: **Stuart S. Nagel,** *University of Illinois, Urbana*

Books in this series:

Volume 12. Sage Yearbooks in Politics and Public Policy

PRODUCTIVITY

AND

PUBLIC POLICY

MARC HOLZER
and
STUART S. NAGEL
Editors

SAGE PUBLICATIONS
Beverly Hills   London   New Delhi

For information address:

SAGE Publications, Inc.
275 South Beverly Drive
Beverly Hills, California 90212

SAGE Publications India Pvt. Ltd.
C-236 Defence Colony
New Delhi 110 024, India

SAGE Publications Ltd
28 Banner Street
London EC1Y 8QE, England

Printed in the United States of America

Library of Congress Cataloging in Publication Data

Main entry under title:

Productivity and public policy.
   (Sage yearbooks in politics and public policy ; v. 12)
   Includes index.
      1. Industrial productivity—Addresses, essays,
lectures.   2. Government productivity—Addresses, essays,
lectures.   3. Welfare state—Addresses, essays, lectures.
I. Holzer, Marc.   II. Nagel, Stuart S., 1934-   .   III. Series.
HC79.I52P77   1984   338.9   84-4862
ISBN 0-8039-2129-2
ISBN 0-8039-2130-6 (pbk.)

FIRST PRINTING

CONTENTS

SERIES EDITOR'S INTRODUCTION

Productivity and Public Policy is Volume 12 in the Sage Yearbooks in Politics and Public Policy. Previous volumes have covered a wide variety of topics that cut across numerous policy problems. The volumes have also been oriented toward public policy, as contrasted to topics in which governmental activities have relatively little actual or potential significance. The subject of *Productivity and Public Policy* is particularly relevant to both those characteristics of the Yearbook series.

This volume is concerned with productivity improvement from a societal or national perspective, rather than from the perspective of a business firm, an individual, or another type of producing entity. Societal productivity improvement can be defined as doing activities that enable a society to obtain more benefits at constant costs, the same benefits at lower costs, or, best of all, more benefits at lower costs. These alternatives thus refer to activities that enable a society to come closer to maximizing societal benefits minus societal costs in (1) making choices, (2) arriving at an optimum level for various societal activities, and (3) allocating scarce resources. The term "societal benefits" refers to effects of governmental or private actions that are considered socially desirable. "Societal costs" refers to effects that are considered socially undesirable, or to expenditures of dollars or effort. This concept of productivity can be distinguished from concepts that emphasize output per work-hour, regardless of how useless the output and how costly the hours might be, including the opportunity costs of neglecting more beneficial outputs. Some people might object to the concept of societal productivity as being more difficult to measure than labor productivity, but societal productivity may be substantially more important.

The subject of *Productivity and Public Policy* is especially relevant to the Yearbooks in Politics and Public Policy series, because societal productivity affects every policy problem, and because public policy is so important to the substantial improvement of societal productivity. A typical list of the top five societal policy problems might include defense, inflation/unemployment, crime, civil liberties, and health; other lists might concentrate on other areas. The important point is that societal productivity is relevant to whatever policy problems might be included. For example, a key problem in the realm of defense policy is how to develop more effective defenses for the United States at reduced costs. Both liberals and conservatives question how effective our defenses are, and they both question even more the extent to which we are efficiently buying defense. Increased productivity in that context does not just mean having an MX missile system at as low a cost as possible. It also means making the right decisions in terms of benefits minus costs in choosing the MX system over alternative defense systems. On an even higher level, one can talk about how wasteful any defense expenditures are in comparison to using the money for societal goods and services if we could develop alternative means of decreasing the probability of an attack on ourselves or our allies.

Rising prices and wages would be no problem if productivity were increasing simultaneously, so that people would be receiving more benefits for the increased prices and so that workers would be producing more output for the increased wages. There would likewise be no unemployment problem and a substantial reduction in poverty if we could arrange for people to be employed more productively in a more organized economy. Such an economy would see to it that all people who wanted to work had jobs, including older people, women, minorities, handicapped people, less educated people, and others. There is also much waste due to crime, not only in direct costs, but in the waste of society's resources on prisons, police activities, and losses due to crime that could be prevented through more productive societal anticrime programs providing productive alternatives to crime. Productivity in the civil liberties context especially refers to how to stimulate more freedom of speech and unconventional advocacy, which would encourage the development and diffusion of innovative ideas. On the matter of health, a key problem is how to enable society to be more productive through the distribution of better health care in order to prevent and cure ailments that decrease societal productivity.

On the point that public policy is important to the substantial improvement of societal productivity, even conservatives recognize that without an appropriate public policy environment, business would be unable to innovate and improve its ability to produce. Appropriate public policies from a conservative perspective might emphasize the following:

(1) police protection of property
(2) enforcement of contract rights through the courts
(3) maintenance of a money system
(4) limited liability for corporations
(5) protection of patents, copyrights, and trademarks
(6) uniform standards concerning weights and measures
(7) census and other statistical information
(8) good roads, harbors, airports, and other infrastructure transportation facilities
(9) protection of U.S. business activities abroad
(10) loans to various business activities, including housing, farming, exporting, and small business
(11) special rates for business bulk mail
(12) business bankruptcy proceedings that allow creditors to collect something and businesses to get a fresh start
(13) special tax treatment in terms of business deductions
(14) government purchases from business
(15) government policy that benefits the economy as a whole, including monetary and fiscal policy

Appropriate public policy for stimulating societal productivity from a liberal perspective might emphasize the need for the government to:

(1) encourage international competition by refraining from adopting tariffs or other restrictions on international trade;
(2) play a greater role in long-term societal investment decisions in partnership with business and labor, as Japanese government does;
(3) stimulate better relations between business and academia by subsidizing two-way exchanges of personnel, relevant conferences, midcareer training, and information systems whereby business is better informed of relevant developments in academia and academics are better informed of business needs;
(4) help pay for the dismantling and replacement of obsolete industrial equipment;
(5) put more emphasis on positive incentives to get business to perform socially desired activities instead of relying on regulation, litigation, and negative sanctions that generate negative relations between business and government;

(6) provide job security, retraining, and loan programs to start new businesses/jobs, to lessen the anxieties of American workers who feel threatened by technological innovation; and

(7) pursue means for reducing arms expenditures between the United States and the Soviet Union in order to free billions of dollars in potential capital for implementing productive new ideas.

Instead of talking about public policy toward increased productivity from conservative and liberal perspectives, one could discuss the subject in terms of the key elements of productivity, as this book does. Those elements are generally referred to as land, labor, capital, management, and the organization of those elements. *Land,* or natural resources, is an important element, but it cannot be improved much through public policy, although the government can encourage conservation and the development of synthetic natural resources. On the matter of *labor,* some of the productivity improvement suggestions have included the following: (1) the need for more education, especially with regard to technical skills; (2) the need for more worker input into making management decisions; and (3) more sensitivity to worker morale among public employees. It is, however, often felt that workers can be more productive with good technology or *capital* equipment with which to work even if they lack strong motivation, compared to strongly motivated workers who lack good technology. To stimulate good technology, both liberals and conservatives endorse tax-break incentives. Conservatives may, however, have more faith in across-the-board tax cuts, such as the 30 percent tax cut of the Reagan administration. Liberals tend to advocate earmarked tax breaks that must be earned through specific productivity-increasing activities. A key problem in American technology may be the need for business to improve in the area of implementation of innovation. The United States does seem to do well on creativity, especially in university research, but may not be as efficient as the Japanese in implementing new ideas.

Good *management* and leadership are important in the decision making that leads to maximized productivity. There may be a need for better training of both public and private managers with regard to practical decision-making methods. On the matter of stimulating more productive *organization,* that may mean stimulating more competition in the private sector especially, where business units can be relatively small and efficient. The matter of having a more productive organization of labor, capital, and management often raises the issue of governmental versus private implementation. In the past this issue has taken the form of emotional disputes over socialism versus capitalism. In recent years there has been a movement on the part of socialists to concede the need for more decentralization of decision making and to show more concern with increasing national income as a way of reducing poverty, rather than emphasizing income redistribution. Likewise, there has been a movement on the part of capitalists to concede the need for more governmental coordination, at least in the ways mentioned above, and to show more sensitivity to the need for equality of opportunity, with both coordination and equality directed toward increased productivity.

The next volume in this series will be devoted to the topic of comparative resource allocation, and will be edited by Alexander Groth and Larry L. Wade. It will add an important cross-national dimension to the Yearbooks in Politics and Public Policy. Such a dimension can provide helpful insights into all fields of public policy, in the area of productivity, where we have much to learn from the diversity of national public policy across such places as Japan and West Germany, and the historical experiences of the United States. Generating such insights has been an important characteristic of this Sage Yearbook series.

— *Stuart S. Nagel*
Urbana, Illinois

VOLUME EDITORS' INTRODUCTION

The impetus for this book was simply that our standard of living is a direct function of our society's productivity. The answer to the question that statement stimulates, "How can we improve our low rate of productivity growth?" however, is not simple. Elected policymakers often propound quick fixes such as technological leaps and capital formation, less government and fewer regulations, more labor-management cooperation and labor retraining. They did so most recently at the White House Conference on Productivity (September 1983). But, had busy policy-level officials lingered at the conference (instead of making cameo appearances) to listen carefully to their academic colleagues, they would have had to conclude, perhaps reluctantly, that productivity improvement, public sector or private sector, is a complex, systematic, and painstaking process. This volume is very much a manual for productivity-oriented policy and implementation, a conceptual blueprint for a more productive, more affluent society. More specifically, the volume defines key questions or considerations, explores the subtleties of derivative productivity improvement programs, and offers conclusions as to pragmatic policy development and implementation.

In Part I, Ellen Doree Rosen, in her chapter, "Productivity: Concepts and Measurement," argues that successful productivity improvement depends upon a good productivity measurement system, one that is understood and accepted by everyone concerned, because productivity measurement can be used as a means of identifying problem areas and exemplary operations, of revealing trends, and of testing management policies and decisions. Policymakers, managers, and workers need to understand the measurement process so that they can be intelligent consumers, users, and subjects: If measures are clear, valid, and regarded as fair, they can be put to constructive use. Rosen also draws attention to the "politics" of productivity measurement and the need for sensitivity and tact, as well as full commitment and technical expertise. In Chapter 2, "National Productivity: A Comparative Perspective," Howard Leichter examines, from a comparative perspective, the national debate over the declining rate of productivity growth in this country. Subsequent to an examination of Japanese and Western European policies, he argues that other nations assume a positive relationship between national welfare policy and national productivity, while current conservative U.S. policies are predicated on a negative relationship.

In Part II, Marc Holzer (in Chapter 3, "Public Administration Under Pressure") holds that the relatively recent prominence of the words "productivity," "productive," and "produce" in the vocabulary of public administration must be understood against a history of government's failure to gain public confidence in its performance. But he concludes that pressured public administration is now responding to a century of criticism in pragmatic, productive terms. The most prominent characteristics of the new public management system include, but are not limited to, productivity measurement and auditing, joint labor-management cooperation, incentives tied to performance, training for productivity, information resources and microcomputer applications, and new means of financing productivity investments. In "The Private Sector Workplace," Daniel Mitchell's thesis is that since much of the industrialized world exhibited slower productivity growth than did the United States in the 1970s, it is apparent that the causes were not confined to the U.S. economy. It appears that part of the problem stemmed from worldwide "stop-go" macroeconomic policies aimed at restraining inflation. Hence innovations such as gain-sharing wage-setting plans, which would permit more efficient macroeconomic regulation of the economy, can be expected to produce productivity gains.

In Part III, F. Stevens Redburn and his colleagues, in "Federal Economic Development Investments," argue that comprehensive evaluation can contribute to the productivity of federal economic development investments through improvements in program design and project selection and through wiser allocation of public dollars among varied programs and approaches. The elements of such an evaluative framework are specified and illustrated. The authors recommend that evaluators look beyond the first wave of benefits, that measures of benefit should be discounted for substitution and leakage, that trade-offs among multiple program goals should be identified and measured, and that comprehensive evaluation should seek to capture the full effects of sequences of public investments as well as the separate effects and interactions of nearly simultaneous public investments in the same region, community, or neighborhood. In Chapter 6, "Investment Subsidy Programs in Comparative Perspective," Raymond Duch takes a comparative approach to investment subsidy programs and suggests which subsidy strategies are likely to be effective and which should be discarded. He defines three different strategies for allocating subsidies and argues for realistic, contingent, and selective programs. Irwin Feller and Irene Johnston, in "The Innovation-Productivity Connection," argue that productivity change and innovation are two concepts that have been imprecisely linked in discussions of the performance of state and local governments. They find a propensity of city officials in the mid-1970s to adopt service-enhancing innovations, but that the deteriorating fiscal conditions of state and local governments since the mid-1970s are likely to alter bureaucratic behavior and to increase the attractiveness of cost-reducing innovations.

In Part IV, Eli Noam utilizes the case of cable television franchises to broaden hypotheses about productivity and monopoly in general in his chapter, "Private Sector Monopolies." He concludes that there may be a policy-oriented need to lower entry barriers and encourage competition. In Chapter 9, "Public Sector Monopolies," Jeffrey Straussman and Alexander Rosenberg assert that current discussions about improving productivity in the public sector often confuse normative preferences about the desirability of productivity gains with descriptive presuppositions that would enable their attainment. They clarify necessary presuppositions, particularly the link needed between maximizing behavior of bureaucrats and normatively inspired productivity objectives. The justifications for four market-based reforms in the public sector are then advanced, along with some obstacles to their implementation. In "Productivity Improvement, Management Science, and Policy Evaluation," Stuart Nagel defines policy evaluation as a set of skills associated with deciding which of various alternative public policies will maximize or increase benefits minus costs in achieving a given set of goals. He then argues that policy evaluation is especially capable of furthering productivity improvement by emphasizing management science methods as applied on a societal or public policy level. Those policy evaluation methods may be even more important than worker motivation or technological innovation in productivity improvement, to the extent that hard work means little if the wrong products are being produced in terms of societal benefits and costs. Likewise, the right policies are needed to maximize technological innovation, which is not so likely to occur without an appropriate public policy environment. Therefore, what may be especially needed are more government people who can understand and apply policy evaluation methods, and thereby aid in achieving productivity improvement in the 1980s. Finally, Rupert F. Chisholm, in "A Systems Approach to Organizational Productivity," describes a sociotechnical systems (STS) approach to designing the workplace that can achieve improved integration of the technological and social subsystems of the organizations. The approach involves a detailed analysis of technology and the social/psychological requirements of employees to generate a new workplace design. STS design also includes linkages between the immediate workplace and the surrounding organizational environment. A recommended implementation process and experience with the STS also are covered. The approach holds considerable promise for improving organizational effectiveness and employees' work experiences.

The production of this volume required an integrated effort by many professionals. Our appreciation must be extended to the authors, for the quality of their work and their commitment to meeting deadlines; to the staff of the National Center for Public Productivity, particularly Connie Siebke, for their technical support; to the members of the Policy Studies Organization; and to our friends at Sage Publications for their faith and constructive criticism.

— *Marc Holzer*
New York, New York

— *Stuart S. Nagel*
Urbana, Illinois

PART I

DEFINING THE PRODUCTIVE SOCIETY

1

PRODUCTIVITY:
CONCEPTS AND MEASUREMENT

ELLEN DOREE ROSEN

John Jay College of Criminal Justice
City University of New York

The term "productivity" seems to produce either resistance or inspiration. In some people, it evokes distaste: visions of layoffs, exploitation of workers, and everybody playing games with simplistic and unfair measures. To others, the productivity movement represents the exciting opportunity for a happier, more successful society, with less waste of expensive resources and improved quality of goods and services. It means workers who are more skilled and who have "bought into" the undertaking, making their work more effective and themselves more personally committed and proud. In short, the organization becomes more efficient and effective while the workplace becomes more humane.

Of course, neither perception is entirely true: the productivity effort is not a gateway to Hell or to Heaven. But elements of both perceptions are valid. As in any undertaking, there are opportunities and there are potentially dangerous pitfalls. The difference between success and failure depends almost entirely upon the degree to which those who are responsible for the effort really understand what they are doing. Are they asking the right questions? Do they understand what productivity is? Whose productivity will be the object of attention — society as a whole? an entire organization? an office or other work unit? Are they interested in improving the productivity of the labor force? of equipment? of all resources at once? Do they know how productivity is measured? What the "dimensions" of productivity are? Ways of measuring each element, and which ways are best for which purposes? What makes a measure "good"? Are they aware of the "politics" of measurement? What policies prepare the way for a reasonable, useful measurement system? The uses — and potential misuses — of productivity measures?

Success will also depend upon awareness of such matters as the array of approaches and techniques available for improving productivity, what principles can guide the choice of target for initiating the effort, and the choice of strategy for dealing with the "politics" of administering projects. These will be sketched briefly here, but will be dealt with in detail in other chapters. This chapter will be devoted to establishing what productivity is and how it can be measured.

WHAT IS PRODUCTIVITY?

"Productivity" is simply a convenient term for summarizing and expressing a relationship. It captures one relationship between outputs (goods or services produced) and inputs (the resources used to produce those services). "Net profit" answers the question: By how much does output exceed input? Profit = output − input. "Productivity" answers a different question: How efficiently are inputs utilized in the production of output? Put another way: What is the output produced per unit of input? (How many miles per gallon, or how much bang for the buck?) Productivity = output/input; $P = O/I$.

Productivity, then, is not measured directly; it is determined by first measuring output and input, and then calculating the ratio. Outputs are usually measured by counting units of goods or services produced, or, particularly in the private sector, in terms of the dollar value of the goods or services produced. Inputs consist of such resources as labor, equipment, space, and energy, and may be expressed as units of these or, particularly in the private sector, in dollar terms. Since it is misleading to draw comparisons between outputs of different or fluctuating quality, considerations of quality also enter into the measurement of productivity. The next section will deal with measurement procedures, techniques, and considerations, but two distinctions should be made at this point.

First, productivity is not the same as productivity improvement, although in popular usage the two are often confused, as in: "We need some productivity around here!" "Productivity" expresses a relationship between effort and result. It reveals just how efficiently the inputs are being utilized in the production of output. It expresses a level. The "productivity movement" is fundamentally concerned with "productivity improvement," with raising that productivity level, by improving output quantity and quality while conserving or diminishing resources.

The major approaches to productivity improvement cluster under three rubrics: improving the work process, improving the worker, and improving the management. Changes in the work process are achieved in several ways. The process of reorganization improves routines by such changes as adding a specialized unit, centralizing an operation, or eliminating a level in the hierarchy. Operations analysis reveals bottlenecks, delays, time lost in the transit process, or periods during which people or equipment are idle. Demand analysis helps in making optimal deployment of resources to meet fluctuations in demand, or suggests the need to "level" the demand to a more constant flow. The introduction of new technology is another major avenue to achieving productivity improvement through changes in the work process.

Changes in the workers center on improving skills and motivation, so as to improve work quality and reduce worker alienation, absenteeism, and turnover. Training is the major instrumentally for improving the worker's knowledge, attitudes, and behavior. Improved motivation is achieved through rewards, summed up as a better quality of working life. Among these are bonuses, safety improvements, career development opportunities, more variety and autonomy in the job itself, and labor participation in decision making about the work — identifying problems and suggesting ideas.

Productivity improvements are achieved also by inducing change in management's knowledge, attitudes, and behavior. Managers learn how to obtain and use productivity measures, so that they can assess performance and evaluate the impact of policies upon it. Managers often need to be made aware of more options, and of the need to reevaluate the old ways from time to time. Their perceptions of the nature and needs of the present-day work force are often outdated. Productivity improvement through management includes improved skills in areas such as fiscal management, evaluation, and human relations. It includes enhanced awareness of options: sources of financing for productivity improvement, alternative delivery modes (such as contracting out or coproduction), alternative work schedules (such as flexitime), new technology, and human interaction techniques (such as quality circles).

The distinction between productivity and productivity improvement has been drawn. There remains the distinction between productivity and program evaluation. Here the line is not so well established in the literature of the field, but it merits attention. Productivity addresses the question of how efficiently resources are being used in the production of goods and services. Goods that are inferior and services that are slow, grudging, and full of error are clearly less valuable, and so the question of quality or effectiveness becomes germane in assessing productivity levels. Effectiveness enters into the productivity consideration in terms of the efficiency with which (effective) work is produced. Essentially, productivity assessment takes the program for granted, and focuses on the efficiency issue. Program evaluation, on the other hand, addresses the question: In terms of the impact desired, is this the best program? To take the example of an in-service training program, productivity assessment would analyze the amount and quality of training delivered as against the resources used. Productivity improvement would be directed toward getting more and/or better training using the same or fewer resources: it might include comparison of alternative training modes as to their relative efficiency. Program evaluation, however, might go a step beyond, to assess whether training or some other program, such as wage increases, would be more effective, cost considered. There is overlap between program evaluation and productivity; program evaluation has concern for the benefit/cost ratio, and productivity has concern for outcome and impact, but the emphasis is different. Program evaluation reflects upon choice of enterprise, while productivity relfects upon the efficiency with which the enterprise is conducted. Policymakers have an interest in both questions, but it is important that they be clear about which one they are asking in a given situation. The focus here is, of course, the productivity issue.

USES OF PRODUCTIVITY MEASUREMENT

All measurement is arbitrary. Most of the world measures length in meters, but a meter is nothing more than the length of a bar of metal lying in a vault in Paris. Shoe sizes go up by the length of three barley corns. The cost of living or the stock market level is obtained by using a set of typical items as indicators. Measures are imperfect. They may not be entirely valid: Does the set of "market basket indicators" really convey *the* cost of living for everyone? Measures may not be entirely reliable: Barley corns vary in size, and different shoemakers undoubtedly arrived at different readings. But even relatively crude measures are better than no measures, or intuitive judgments. The human being is a notoriously unreliable instrument. We tend to color observation by prejudice and expectation. The power that underlies science inheres in the principle of careful attention to measurement according to specified standards. Productivity measurement brings some of that scientific power into the management of production. It is a tool, to be used or misused according to the training of the user. Properly used, productivity measurement can provide useful and dependable information.

One productivity measurement alone is of no use. In itself, the knowledge that a factory produces X widgets per machine-week, or that an agency processes X applications per worker-year, tells nothing about whether that level is good or bad. The significance of a productivity figure emerges only when productivity levels are compared. To be comparable, productivity measurements must be made according to the same measurement system. That is, the indicators, units, and standards must be uniform, or at least convertible to each other. For example, the input of labor, expressed in "worker-days," can readily be converted to "worker-years." But output expressed as "number of clients interviewed" cannot be converted to "number of referrals made" — unless, of course, the same number of referrals is invariably given at every interview. Also, for comparison to be valid, the quality of the output must be the same in both units, or else the quantity must be "corrected" so as to reflect the difference in quality. This is as true for services (such as application processing) as it is for goods. The ideal of a uniform set of measures and standards for each kind of work, making comparison simple across the nation, is probably utopian, as of now. But even if different organizations measure in different units, useful comparison of some kind can probably be achieved — as long as the measurement system of each has been spelled out clearly for others to understand. One of the many misuses of measurement takes place when decision makers are unaware that they are comparing figures generated in different ways.

Productivity measurement can be used as a means of identifying problems and solutions. When comparison is made between the productivity levels of work units engaged in creating the same kind of output, it is clear which ones are performing poorly. An agency that is processing X/2 applications per worker-year is clearly making less productive use of its labor. It is probably a good candidate for improvement. On the other hand, comparison reveals exemplary performance. An agency that is processing 2X applications per worker-year may be a model for others. Once the measurement figures are in, and the comparisons made, it is possible to examine the operation of the low-productivity unit and of the model, to determine where the secret of better performance lies. It may be a matter of technology, job design, worker skill, morale, or scale of operation. Comparisons among numerous units can be used to assess the effect of variables, such as size of operation, and then to determine optimal arrangements. The comparisons discussed thus far may be called "interunit," "interorganizational," or "cross-jurisdictional." Comparison within the same work unit, but across time, can also reveal useful information. It can spot problems; a sudden drop in productivity suggests the need for study and intervention. It can be used (as it is currently by the General Accounting Office) to establish targets (Usilaner, 1983). The "historical best" performance level suggests the line of reasoning, "We know we can do that well because we have done it in the past. Why are we not performing at that level now? What needs changing?"

Comparisons can, and should, be used to test management policies and decisions. A large corporation or public agency contemplating one or more innovations would do well to experiment, introducing the change(s) in a few units and then making cross-unit comparisons to determine precisely the impact of the innovation upon productivity. Changes yielding only marginal improvements are probably not worth the effort, and counterproductive changes on a large scale can be avoided. For smaller organizations, or where experimental projects are not feasible, simple pre/post comparisons can be used to make summary evaluation of innovations. If productivity has not been improved, an alternative project may be warranted.

With productivity measurement, then, decision makers can gain efficient, effective control over production weaknesses. They can determine whether or not (and where) a productivity problem exists, rule out the nonproblem units, and concentrate on the problems. The depth of a problem can be ascertained. Models, in the form of other units or the subject unit's previous performance, can suggest target levels and types of change to be made. Interunit or pre/post productivity levels can be compared to provide feedback into the assessment of productivity improvement projects or programs.

Productivity measures have additional uses in personnel, budgeting, and purchasing decisions. For legislators and program evaluators, productivity, as well as impact, is a vital criterion in deciding whether (and how) a program is to be continued, expanded, or retrenched. Information on the productivity of labor makes possible the optimal deployment of a work force, both among locations and among shifts, so as to match labor to work or to distribute the workload evenly. The (productivity) relationship of outputs to other resources, such as equipment or fuels, informs the purchasing process. The budget system can use productivity information. It can also encourage productivity improvement, insofar as economies and efficiencies are rewarded in the budget process rather than penalized, as is so often the case. A policy that permits managers discretionary use of a portion of the funds remaining at the end of the budget period will encourage economy and the search for efficiency; a policy of reducing future budgets because allocations were not entirely expended will encourage the spending of every cent.

WHO IS INVOLVED IN MEASUREMENT?

Although policymakers, managers, labor leaders, and other actors concerned with productivity and its improvement may not need to learn detailed particulars about productivity measurement, it is vital that they understand it.

Policymakers are fed productivity figures. If they are to be intelligent consumers making independent use of those figures, they need to have a basic understanding of what the figures represent and how they were derived. They need to understand the measurement process, so that they can judge what resources and arrangements are (or are not) necessary for a successful productivity measurement system.

Top managers make general use of productivity figures for goal setting, planning, and other decisions. More immediately, they facilitate and oversee measurement programs, and are often the ultimate providers of the personnel, production, and other records upon which productivity measurements are based. They, too, need to understand both the measures and the measurement process.

Both management and labor find their performances reflected in productivity figures. They have a stake in the measures — and their perceptions of the measures (as reasonable, realistic, and fair or as simplistic, biased, and unfair) will color their behavior. If the measurement system is perceived as realistic, fair, and permanent, labor and management will tend to accept it as legitimate. If it is perceived as unrealistic, unfair, and ephemeral, they will attempt to manipulate it by playing games with the numbers. This, of course, not only invalidates the measures themselves but undercuts true productivity.

Because understanding and perception are so important to the success of a measurement system, the involvement of all relevant groups in the development of a productivity measurement system is often recommended. Measures developed in a participatory fashion tend to be less misunderstood and less suspect, and the measurement system is therefore easier to institutionalize properly. In addition, the measurement system is probably more valid, since many viewpoints and types of expertise are incorporated into the measures that emerge. The problem with a system based upon broad participation is that it is time-consuming; it may also arouse sleeping dogs in the form of touchy subjects and unresolved conflicts. Alternatively, the choice of measures can be made unilaterally, by a "measurement person" or "measurement group." This avoids confrontation and the need to share decision power, but results in losses in validity and facility of installing the system. For any specific measurement project, the method or approach selected should suit the particular context.

Responsibility for the design and day-to-day conduct of a measurement program requires expertise. It requires one person (or a group of people, depending upon the size of the organization and the scope of the project), a "measurer," who understands measurement in general and productivity measurement in particular, and who understands the operations of the organization. The organization may already contain one or more people with the appropriate expertise. It may contain people who possess the potential, in the form of analytical talent and background, but who lack specific training in productivity and perhaps even in measurement itself. Such people can be given appropriate training, such as productivity workshops or other courses, or they can work for a time under the tutelage of expert consultants. One common arrangement is the hiring of an outside expert to develop and begin operating the measurement system, and teaming that expert with an in-house person with aptitude, so that an internal measurer is trained and able to assume responsibility for the measurement program when the consultant leaves. One way or another, analytical capability in the form of a trained "measurer" is an essential requisite for a successful, meaningful productivity measurement program.

The measurer may be located organizationally somewhere outside the subject work unit, perhaps in the budget office or in an evaluation unit. This keeps the measurer professionally "pure," less likely to "go native" under pressures from the operations people. On the other hand, the measurer can be located within the work unit. This arrangement lends better understanding to both the measurer (who is close to the work and the workers) and the workers, who are less apt to see the measurer as an alien force. As before, the choice of arrangement should be made in light of the particular organizational situation.

However developed and wherever located, the measurer is in a "staff" capacity — on tap but not on top. Although much can be achieved informally in tactful negotiation with the subject work force, the measurer must be backed up by serious, continuing support from the top of the line. Without such support the program becomes an exercise in window-dressing. Even the best, most fair measurement system will almost inevitably engender resistance from most parts of the organization, because it is new and represents change. There are misgivings to overcome and misconceptions to remove. For example, productivity figures are not inevitably punitive; they can (and should) be used constructively, as feedback on performance so that both the individual member and the organization as a whole can be more successful. The productivity mesurement process itself makes changes in the routine. And the measurement process is meant to serve the productivity improvement process, which means further change. But it is a rule of nature that entities seek homeostasis and resist change. Therefore a visible, continuing commitment from those in authority is needed.

MEASURING INPUTS

Productivity expresses a relationship between the work accomplished and the effort invested in its accomplishment; that is, between output and relevant input. $P = O/I$, and P is therefore measured indirectly, by measuring O and I. Let us start with I.

Every organization exists for some purpose: to manufacture, heal, lend, transport, advise, defend, negotiate, entertain, or fulfill some other function in society. Indeed, it is a prime characteristic of modern society that so many functions are fulfilled through specialized organizations. Each organization achieves its purpose by putting forth goods or services of some kind. Each organization requires resources in order to operate: labor, space, equipment, supplies, fuels, and so on. These resources constitute the input. For purposes of productivity measurement, these input factors may be dealt with in a variety of ways. They may be used selectively, so that, for example, only labor is counted, while all other input factors are disregarded (that is, are regarded as constant). This is appropriate for a situation where the facilities and equipment are not being changed significantly, but an innovation (training program, job redesign, gain-sharing program, or the like) is expected to increase the productivity of labor. Decision makers simply want to know whether the output per unit of labor has gone up.

For labor-intensive organizations (such as public sector agencies and private firms engaged in the production of services), improving the productivity of labor constitutes a prime target; in the measurement of public sector productivity, input has been expressed predominantly in terms of labor alone. There are also situations where some other input factor is of exclusive interest. For example, managers of a railroad may be introducing new passenger cars, or simply experimenting with new train lengths, and they want to know whether the output (expressed perhaps as number of passengers carried) per railroad car has gone up. They can measure the productivity of equipment and make the simplifying assumption that labor, space, and other input factors have not varied significantly. In another case, a business undertaking a fuel conservation program will be interested in the productivity only of fuel, and will express input only in units of fuel. The advantage of dealing with the productivity of only one resource or input factor at a time is simplicity.

There are situations in which more than one kind of resource enters into the picture. For example, a new piece of equipment, such as a word processor, is expected to save labor. Both equipment and labor are significant variables here, and they have to be aggregated somehow. Or a new management may introduce radical change in operations, affecting space, personnel, and technology, so that the total input becomes relevant. The obvious, and usual, method of aggregating different types of resources is to translate each factor into dollar terms and find the total. It should be noted that the dollar value can also be used to measure a single input factor as well.

The dollar value measure must be used with caution; for example, in comparing productivity over time, the dollar must be adjusted to a constant value, to correct for inflation or deflation.[1] The dollar is of limited use in measuring public sector productivity, for several reasons. With regard to output, it is difficult if not impossible to determine dollar value, because the services produced are not sold and often have no private sector "shadow" counterpart. What is the value of the services produced by the Department of Defense or the State Department? With regard to input factors, public sector managers often lack control over dollar values, so that "productivity" trends expressed in dollar terms are invalid. For example, salaries in the public sector are determined at least in part by seniority in a civil service system, which is beyond the control of a work-force manager. If two comparable organizations vary in age, so that one has a senior work force while the other is composed of new hirees, then even if they turn out the same amount of work per worker the agency with the younger work force will appear to be more productive if productivity is measured as output per dollar of labor. If the older agency loses several workers to retirement, and hires replacements who are at the bottom of the civil service ladder, it will appear, spuriously, that productivity has jumped.

Labor is by far the most commonly considered input factor, in both the private and the public sector measures of productivity. In any work organization, a skilled labor force, socialized to the job, represents an asset. Labor becomes relatively even more important in those organizations dedicated to the production of services rather than goods. Since public sector organizations are of this nature, the productivity of labor is the object of considerable attention.

Labor is usually measured in terms of worker-time: worker-hours, worker-days, worker-years, and so on.[2] A "worker-hour" represents one worker working one hour. "Six worker-years" represents the work of one worker for six years or its equivalent: six workers, working one year each; three workers, working two years each; and so on. "Output per worker-time" expresses the productivity of labor and is also a workload measure. When a given amount of labor can be made to yield more work, or when the same goods or services can be produced using less worker-time, then the productivity has been improved: The O/I ratio is larger.

It should be noted that this method of measuring labor does not take into account the differences among workers: It neglects education, experience, and other such considerations in the interest of simplicity. This can be a virtue: Comparisons of the productivity of labor between organizations producing the same kind of output can disclose whether or not variables such as education are indeed significant factors in the job, and can suggest interventions (such as training) where differences in productivity are found to be tied to specific variables (such as education).

In practice, measurements of worker-time are not derived uniformly. Some measurement systems count all time paid for; others subtract vacations and holidays. Still others subtract time lost to illness and personal leaves. Any of these methods is permissible, but care must be taken in making comparisons between labor productivity figures arrived at in different ways. The figures should be corrected to a common, and therefore comparable, form. Choice of method of counting worker-time should be based upon the use to which the measures will be put. If vacation and holiday time off is immutable, there is little point in including it in the total; it is a given, a constant. But if absenteeism is a problem and a target of a productivity improvement project, then all (nonholiday) time must be counted, or the impact of the project will not be evident in the calculations.

The data source for measurements of worker-time is generally already at hand, in the form of personnel records. For those organizations that do not have useful attendance records, the beginning of managing for productiviy may be the undertaking to gather such information.

Labor can also be measured in terms of its cost, rather than worker-time. Some of the considerations and limitations of using the dollar have been mentioned. Here, too, the choice of a labor input measurement unit should depend upon the use to which the measures will be put. Where the cost of labor is essentially fixed, as in civil service salaries, output per (labor) dollar cannot be improved. On the other hand, that figure is very relevant if, for example, an agency head is considering contracting out to the private sector as a possible alternative. In the private sector, productivity expressed in terms of the cost of labor forms the basis for personnel policies (aimed at lowering labor costs) and technological decisions (whether or not to automate, for example). Data on the cost of labor are also readily available from organizational records.

The input factor of equipment can be measured in terms of each item or in terms of cost. The productivity of a CAT scanner can be measured in terms of "number of patients examined per scanner" or "number of patients per dollar." When considering ways to make fuller use of an existing piece of equipment, the first method would be preferred; when considering the choice of which scanner to purchase, the second is more useful.

In similar fashion, fuel may be measured in units (gallons, cubic feet, kilowatt hours, and so on) or in dollar terms. So, too, supplies, space, and other relevant input factors can generally be measured in units (reams of paper, cubic feet) or in terms of dollar value.

Organizational records generally can provide data on equipment, supplies, space, and their cost. The use made of these may not have been analyzed and documented, but it can often be reconstructed from existing records.

Although it is generally quite feasible to collect the data and calculate the productivity of any one input factor, such as labor or equipment, the aggregation of any two or more factors presents problems, as has been discussed. The trade-off between equipment added and labor saved, or labor added and energy saved, cannot be expressed in the terms by which either is measured. Instead, both must be translated to the medium of exchange, money, with the limitations we have seen.

To summarize, inputs are the resources (labor, equipment, space, materials, fuels, and so on) used in the production of organizational outputs (goods and/or services). Each input factor may be measured in units appropriate to it, or in dollar terms; the choice will depend upon the use to which the productivity figures are to be put. Productivity measurement is most commonly based upon one input factor at a time (usually labor). To aggregate two or more input factors, they are expressed in dollar form. Data on input factors are usually available from existing organizational records.

MEASURING OUTPUT QUANTITY

The work done by an organization can be defined in more than one way, and measured accordingly. One way might be to count as "work" all the activity taking place within the organization, including internally consumed, intermediary processes as well as the final product. This approach is not used in productivity measurement, because the goal is to find out how much result, not how much action, is produced from a given set of resources.

The word "result" hides another ambiguity, and another measurement choice: outcome or outputs? Organizations produce goods and services; that is one result of their operations. They also produce an impact upon society. This ultimate result is their reason for being; the goods or services are justified by their appropriateness to the achievement of that impact. Thus a cannery preserves food as a means of preventing societal hunger in the winter. A police department mounts patrol and makes arrests as a means of minimizing the amount of crime that takes place. Would-be profit makers invest in the cannery because they recognize that a market exists for the product; political decision makers authorize and fund the police department because they recognize security as a political demand. It is attractive to look at the outcome (impact) per unit resource as a way of measuring productivity. It gets to the heart of maximizing benefit compared to cost. But outcome is seldom used in productivity measurement, for two reasons. The first goes back to the issue of what questions we are asking.

The question of whether an undertaking (canning or patrol/arrest) is the most effective way to achieve the desired societal impact is certainly an appropriate one for the policymakers who decide upon programs (Should we have a canning factory or police department, and, if yes, what kind?). It is an appropriate question for program evaluation. The appropriate productivity question for an extant cannery or police department, however, is this: How efficient is the use being made of the allocated resources in the effective production of the mandated goods or services? This question addresses the process and the performance of management and labor. For such an objective, the measurement of outputs (goods and services) rather than outcomes (impact) is relevant (Ross and Burkhead, 1974: 53).

The second problem with using outcome in measuring productivity is the fact that outcomes are affected by many factors other than the work of the organization. It becomes difficult, if not impossible, to isolate the impact of that work. The work of a doctor or a hospital, for example, might be measured in terms of number of people treated (service produced) or in terms of health level (outcome). But health level is also affected by other factors, such as immigration, sanitation, and changing sexual behavior patterns. Unless such other variables can be controlled for, productivity figures based upon outcome will be useless. There are exceptions, in which outcome is an appropriate measure of work — where impact is closely, directly, and almost exclusively linked to goods and services. An example might be the incidence of child abuse where little else changes except the intervention of a counseling service.

In general, then, the measurement of organizational work focuses upon neither process nor outcome, but rather upon output — the goods and services that are delivered at the boundary of the organization to the outside.

The quantity of output is generally measured as "number of" appropriate units, which will vary from one type of organization to another. This is true for both the public and the private sectors. The output of a bank might be measured in terms of "number of checks processed" or the output of a fire department as "number of fires suppressed." The output of the cannery might be measured as "number of cans" or "number of tons of produce" processed. Note that there is usually more than one way to measure the quantity of any given output. Most organizations, moreover, engage in the production of more than one output. Hospitals offer in-patient treatment of various kinds, out-patient clinics, emergency treatment, medical research, and the training of new doctors. Banks make loans and perform other functions, in addition to processing checks.

This complexity is dealt with by selecting and simplifying. This makes measurement feasible and valid, but it is important that those making use of the measures remain aware of their limitations. For many organizations, the production of one or two outputs is of major importance and takes up most of the resources. The production of each output can be seen as a "function" and, by relating that output to the resources used in producing it, the productivity of that function can be measured. In this way, the work of a fire department can be broken down into fire-suppression and fire-prevention functions, or that of a bank into savings, loan, or other functions.

Typically, the measurement of output begins with the dominant, most visible, and most improvable function, and the productivity of that function is calculated by relating the output to relevant resources. Later, the system can be made more sophisticated by including more functions. As more and more functions are included, the inputs begin to add up to the total organizational resource of that kind.

The aggregation of different kinds of output presents some problems, however. In the private sector, the dollar value of each kind of good or produt is commonly used as the basis. In the public sector, market values are usually unknown or irrelevant, but aggregation can be done on the basis of the relative portion of the budget each function commands, or the relative amount of time each requires (when the input measure is labor). Thus for a pretrial intervention service that produces both investigatory and counseling services, one investigation may be found to consume, on the average, as much time as overseeing one counselee for one month. By the creation of a common unit (one investigation = one counselee-month = one standard unit of work), it becomes possible to combine the two activities into one output measure.

A similar tack can be taken for handling the problem of how to deal with work units of different levels of difficulty. There are large, difficult fires, and there are trivial, simple fires. One can make the assumption that, over a long enough time and a large enough number of fires, the mix of the two types will turn out to be relatively constant, so that the differences can be ignored. Whether comparing different fire companies or the performance over time of one fire company, as long as the mix of difficult and easy fires is constant, "number of fires suppressed" can be used as an output quantity measure. On the other hand, it may be necessary to take differences into account, perhaps by grouping all fires into "major" and "minor" categories, and then weighting the "major" as equal to two or three "minor" fires. In that way, work of varying difficulty can be reduced to a common unit and aggregated. In the private sector, both this approach and the dollar-value approach can be used to aggregate unequally difficult outputs of the same kind.

As is the case with measuring inputs, the needed data for measuring outputs are usually available from existing organizational records, although they may need to be reclassified or otherwise adapted for use. Private organizations maintain production records that document the number of units of goods produced. For service organizations, whether in the private or public sectors, records are kept of clients examined or counseled, haircuts given, or applications processed.

To summarize, output (rather than process or outcome) is generally measured and related to input to derive the productivity figure. There is no universal measure of output quantity; each kind of good or service is measured in units appropriate to it. Choices are made by measurers: which good or service to count, whether to differentiate levels of difficulty of work, how to aggregate different kinds of output.

Productivity = outputs/inputs. Productivity can be determined by measuring number of units of output produced per unit of resource. For example, the typing pool produces thirty letters (or, alternatively, thirty pages) per worker-day. Its productivity can now be compared with its own performance last year, or with that of another typing pool. But what if one pool produces clean, accurate, attractive copy, while the other produces messy, error-ridden work? Before these outputs can be compared usefully, the quality of the work must be considered (Hatry and Fisk, 1971: 3ff.).

MEASURING OUTPUT QUALITY

What makes for quality in goods or service? For private sector products, market value might be an indication. Ostensibly, the more expensive computer or pair of shoes commands a higher price because the quality is in some way better. But price is determined largely by supply and demand — whether the demand is spontaneous or is created by advertising. Economists equate higher quality with the use of more inputs, such as the labor in hand finishing, but this definition is obviously of limited use for the measurement and improvement of productivity, the goal of which is to maximize output while minimizing input. The measurers of public sector productivity, deprived of useful economic criteria, have taken the lead in seeking other ways of dealing with the question of quality in quantitative terms. The discussion here will be concerned with these noneconomic (but not uneconomical) approaches.

Quality can be defined in terms of attributes: comfort, promptness, accuracy, durability, safety, courtesy, speed, reliability, and so on. This is equally true of goods and services. A good pair of shoes is comfortable, attractive, and durable. Good mail service is fast, accurate, and courteous. Good counseling is correct, prompt, and considerate of the client.

As these examples make clear, while all outputs can be assigned relevant quality attributes, the particular attributes that are relevant will differ from one kind of output to another. This means that a choice of attributes, to be used as quality indicators, must be made for any particular kind of output being used in productivity measurement. How are these relevant attributes to be specified? Usually there is no preexisting, authoritative specification (although in some fields existing work standards include quality criteria, and these can be adopted and applied to productivity measurement). As before, a choice must be made, involving perceptions and judgments. To one person, promptness and accuracy of service constitute the criteria by which a payment office's output should be judged. To another, courtesy/consideration is an essential criterion as well. And, as before, the judgment of what criteria to include may be made unilaterally or in some participatory way. In the interests of expediency, the measurer (whether individual or group) may unilaterally specify the criteria that will pertain for a given kind of output. Alternatively, a group or panel may be used to generate such a judgment. The group might be specific to the organization being measured, and could include workers, managers, and even users of the good or service. It might, on the other hand, consist of professionals working to produce the same kind of output, but in many organizations (such as a national association task force). The unilateral decision mode is fastest. Using an intraorganizational group adds new and varied perspectives, and helps legitimize the measurement system throughout the organization. Using an interorganizational task force or panel adds the advantage of a standardized measurement system, facilitating interorganizational or interjurisdictional comparisons of productivity, but at a loss of relevancy to the individual organization.

The simplest measurement system is the best, as long as it is valid. In some situations, one criterion may serve, at least at the start, as indicative of the quality of an output. As a beginning, for example, the quality of an ambulance service might be indicated simply by the speed with which calls are responded to. Other criteria might be disregarded, in a trade-off between keeping measurement feasible (not too costly or time-consuming) and fine tuning to gain greater validity.

Or a more complex system may be called for. Perhaps a "fair" picture of output quality can be gained only by using three criteria. And, further, perhaps they are not of equal importance — again, in the judgment of the individual or group charged with that decision. In that case, criteria can be assigned unequal weights in the calculation of an overall quality average.

Any reasonable choice in number, weight, and nature of criteria is all right — as long as those who are concerned with the measures keep the limitations in mind. This includes people involved in developing measures, being gauged by measures, or using measures to gauge others.

The importance of considering quality as well as quantity of output has been established for a decade now. Criteria have been suggested for many kinds of output, and techniques have been worked out for determining quality. Speed can be determined from direct observation or from written records. Accuracy can be determined from work sampling, as when a batch of delivered mail is examined to see what percentage has been misdelivered, or from records, as when track is kept of errors and redone work. Courtesy and consideration can be determined by surveying the users of a service and either asking them to rate it on some arbitrary scale or constructing a scale oneself from the answers to a set of questions. Observation of cleanliness can be improved by a guide in the form of a set of pictures, showing an office or street or park in various degrees of cleanliness. Instruments such as X-rays or "roughometers" can reveal defects in metal products or bumpiness of streets. In general, quality criteria are amenable to quantification in one way or another.

We have seen that quality is a vital consideration in the comparison of productivity; "output per unit input" can be compared fairly only if "output" is of standard or somehow comparable quality. We have seen also that quality levels can be established — by selecting certain attributes of outputs and using them as indicators. These designed criteria can be weighted and quantified. Here we come to the present state of the art in productivity measurement, for there is more unanimity in the field of productivity measurement about how to measure inputs and the quantity of output than there is about how to utilize quality measures.

Most productivity measurement today simply assumes, as the federal government does in much of its measurement, that quality is essentially constant (Kull, 1978: 6). Other measurement experts advocate eliminating from the "number of" units of output all those units that fall below some minimal standard (Hatry, 1976: 22f; 1980: 317; Hatry et al., 1979). In this way, all work found to be defective, erroneous, or reversed in some way would be omitted from the count. Thus one would not count the misassembled product, the wrongly written check, or the arrest that failed to survive a first screening. A third approach to handling the quality issue is to include all output (all work done), but to "discount" it for any substandard quality (Rosen, 1981). By this method, an expected standard is specified for each criterion: a 99 percent defect-free rate, or a 98 percent on-time record, or a 4.5 rating on a 1-6 user rating scale. Next, the actual quality achieved is determined and compared to the specified standard. This "achieved/standard" becomes a coefficient of quality, called "K," and is introduced into the productivity formula to correct for quality level: $P = OK/I$. For example, if a typing pool produces 150 letters per worker-week, but achieves a 95 percent error-free record although 98 percent is desired, its coefficient of quality is 95/98, or .97, and its productivity, quality considered, is $150 \times .97$, or 145.5 letters per worker-week.

When quality achieved is compared to a standard, the necessity arises for still another choice or judgment: What should the expected standard be? That judgment can be made in the same way and by the

same people who are involved in deciding which criteria to include
and what their relative weights should be.

THE PRODUCTIVITY INDEX

The point has been made that a single productivity measurement
or "reading" holds no significance by itself. The significance emerges
only when readings are compared; a productivity level is only relatively low or high — compared with previous levels, some standard or
expected level, or the level achieved by another work force. A productivity index facilitates the first kind of comparison, in which trends
in productivity level are tracked over time.

A productivity index is created by taking some one productivity
level as a base. Usually, the base period covers one year's average
performance. That productivity level, however calculated (8000
widgets per worker-week or 50 claims processed per worker-month,
for example), is arbitrarily given the value 1.0. For every succeed-
ing comparable period, the productivity level is calculated by the
same method and in the same units as were used for the base period. If
the productivity level for a given period is the same as it was during
the base period, it, too, will have the value 1.0. If productivity has
gone up 20 percent, the value becomes 1.2; if it has gone down 10
percent, it becomes .9. The index number means "compared to the
base period, productivity is up or down by a certain percentage." It
provides a clear and simple track record, revealing "historical best"
performances and descents into lower productivity. Correlating these
trends with changes in personnel policies, technology, or other factors
can disclose which policies and procedures enhance productivity and
which inhibit it.

EFFICIENCY AND EFFECTIVENESS

Almost all the writing on productivity suggests that productivity
involves both the efficiency and the effectiveness of performance.
The writing also links effectiveness with quality; they are often
treated as interchangeable. However, work to date in this field has not
produced any definitive consensus on how these are to be defined or
exactly how they are related. Some things do appear clear, however,
and they are offered here, although it should be understood that
opinions differ as of now.

Efficiency reflects a relationship between outputs and inputs. Efficiency is concerned with how much of the input is translated into output, and how much is being wasted. Productivity is basically an efficiency measure, in that it analyzes the output-to-input relationship. But productivity measurement does not attempt to express input and output in the same units so as to determine what percentage of the input is converted into output, and what percentage is lost in the "heat" and "noise" of operations.

Effectiveness reflects the ability to produce impact; effectiveness induces impact, much as stress induces strain. It is therefore related more directly to outcomes than to outputs. From the productivity point of view, effectiveness becomes important because it is patently nonsense to credit as "output" goods and services that are useless, such as erroneous instructions, post facto announcements, or fire ropes that cannot support a person's weight. The issue of quality emerges here: Accuracy, timeliness, and strength are criteria and indicators by which the quality of the respective outputs would be judged.

The question, What makes for effectiveness? is helpful in suggesting just how the question of effectiveness is related to the assessment of productivity. Clearly, both amount of output and quality of output, working together, make for impact (and for its mirror image, effectiveness). Neither a very small amount of perfect output nor a vast amount of garbage will make for effectiveness. Quantity and quality are codeterminants. Effectiveness = quantity × quality, and if either is zero, there is no effectiveness. This assumption underlies the use of a quality coefficient, K, to correct gross quantity of output. Where achieved quality is absolutely zero, K is zero, and there is no productivity.

THE POLITICS OF
PRODUCTIVITY MEASUREMENT

There is a technical side to productivity measurement. Despite the lack of total consensus on all factors, there are accepted general formulas for calculating productivity. There is a scientific "due process" to be observed: sampling, confidence in and generalizability of results, and so on. There are tools and techniques for collecting data: observation, content analysis, survey, and the like. Responsibility for this technical side generally is placed into the hands of a professional "measurement person" or "measurement team."

But productivity measurement also has a political side, insofar as it imposes a new unit and new procedures upon the life of an organization, and especially insofar as it generates "authoritative" statistics, which endow power and can be used to the advantage and disadvantage of interested actors — individuals and groups both within and outside the organization.

These two parameters must guide decisions about whether to measure, who will measure, what will be measured, and how it will be measured. Neither can be disregarded. The measurement people will fail if they are insensitive to the interests, attitudes, and expectations of those upon whom they must ultimately rely for data. Unless they understand, accept, and respect the measurement system, workers and managers will falsify logs and records, displace work priorities, and run equipment into the ground, playing to the statistics and the measurement system to the neglect of real productivity — and the measurers will not have valid measures; they will not "get at" what they are trying to assess. On the other hand, the purely political, window-dressng, give-the-boss-what-he-wants-to-hear system, in which scientific standards are totally subordinated to people's wishes, is also a failure. It is shortsighted and counterproductive, giving rise to cynicism and making future attempts at measurement all the more difficult, and it provides no usable information on productivity.

Since productivity measurement involves organizational change of some kind, it will encounter resistance. This can be overcome by attention to several things. Perhaps the most important factor is that everyone in the organization be made aware, on a continuing and persistent basis, that the measurement effort has top management commitment behind it. A pro forma memo will not suffice; people need to be convinced by involvement and activity from the top — appearing at meetings, setting deadlines, requesting and using the data constructively. The process of open communication, involving patient explanation and a lot of listening to misgivings, can minimize misapprehensions and uncertainties. Limiting the scope of the first measurement projects, so that only a small number of "measurees" is involved, will limit urgent opposition to fewer people. It will also provide the opportunity for a "pilot project" to demonstrate success, reassure that the dreaded need not happen, and, incidentally, to "de-bug" the system before expanding it.

In like manner, limiting the depth of the early projects so that only a small number of activities or behaviors are affected permits people to change a little at a time and to accustom themselves slowly to the idea of change itself. Involving as many people and groups as possible in the development and installation of the measurement system, consonant with organizational need for speed and other possible constraints, produces a better and more workable measurement system. To proceed along the lines suggested above, it is important that the "measurer" be knowledgeable about the organization's goals and operations and possess sensitivity to people's feelings.

On the other side, it is important to keep the measurer from "going native" and the measurement system from degenerating into an invalid political exercise. It is necessary, to begin with, that those in effective control of the organization really want valid measurement. If they do not want it, it will not take place, despite perfunctory assertions to the contrary. The commitment should be communicated, and the measurement unit should be positioned so as to report directly or almost directly to the top, even though its activities may take place near the operations themselves. When productivity figures are to be used as feedback — at the organizational, subunit, small work-force, or even individual level — they are less subject to politicization. When the underlying premise is that everyone wants to perform successfully, and that there is no certainty beforehand of what behaviors will be most successful, then it becomes natural to keep monitoring performance and making improvements as one proceeds. In such a climate, productivity figures are regarded as useful information, and there is general interest in having figures that are really valid. On the other hand, when, as is so often the case, productivity figures are to be used punitively or to serve another agenda, they are readily politicized, with everyone interested only in "looking good." In traditional, predictable, bureaucratic organizations, workers are expected to behave "correctly" and decision makers are expected to make "the correct" decision. The norms engendered in that context have carried over in today's organizations, which are attempting to function in an atmosphere of uncertainty and rapid change. It is often difficult to change the organizational climate. Under these circumstances, productivity measurement should be begun by addressing relatively neutral, general aspects of operation, and not sensitive units, even though they might be in most need of improvement. Laying a foundation makes way for future work. When productivity information is seen to be used in a constructive, nonpunitive way, attitudes begin to change.

In beginning productivity measurement, then, it is wise to consider beginning modestly, without arousing expectations that are too high. In moving piecemeal and slowly, those responsible for the measurement effort can feel their way, adapting the methods to the organization, achieving modest but visible successes, and building people's confidence in the system. Based upon this foundation, more pervasive and rapid progress can take place later.

It is important that decision makers, such as legislators and other initiators and consumers of productivity measures, have an understanding of the productivity measurement process, as well as productivity measures. Both their insistence and their forbearance will be more appropriately applied, in the light of their awareness of the power, limitations, and dynamics of productivity measurement.

NOTES

1. For example, see Siegel's (1980) discussion of the hazards of using deflation to derive a measure of output.

2. The term "worker-hour" or "employee-hour" is superseding the traditional, but sexist, "man-hour."

REFERENCES

HATRY, H. P. (1980) "Performance measurement principles and techniques." Public Productivity Review 4: 312-339.
——— (1976) "Approaches to productivity measurement and program evaluation." Public Productivity Review 1: 22ff.
——— and D. M. FISK (1971) Improving Productivity and Productivity Measurement in Local Government. Washington, DC: Urban Institute.
HATRY, H. P. et al. (1979) Efficiency Measurement for Local Government Services: Some Initial Suggestions. Washington, DC: Urban Institute.
KENDRICK, J. W. (1977) Understanding Productivity: An Introduction to the Dynamics of Productivity Change. Baltimore: Johns Hopkins University Press.
KULL, D. C. (1978) "Productivity programs in the federal government." Public Administration Review 38: 6.
MARK, J. A. (1981) "Productivity measurement in government: federal, state, and local." Public Productivity Review 5: 21-44.
OSTROM, E. (1977) "Multi-mode measures: from potholes to police," in M. Holzer et al. (eds.) Local Government Productivity. Washington, DC: Georgetown University Graduate School, Academy in the Public Service.
ROSEN, E. D. (1981) "O.K. work: incorporating quality into the productivity equation." Public Productivity Review 5: 207-217.

ROSS, J. P. and J. BURKHEAD (1974) Productivity in the Local Government Sector. Lexington, MA: D. C. Heath.

SIEGEL, I. H. (1980) Company Productivity: Measurement for Improvement. Kalamazoo, MI: W. E. Upjohn Institute for Employment Research.

USILANER, B. (1983) Productivity measurement and auditing workshop presentation at the Second National Public Sector Productivity Conference, New York, March 25.

WASHNIS, G. J. [ed.] (1980) Productivity Improvement Handbook for State and Local Government. New York: John Wiley.

2

NATIONAL PRODUCTIVITY:
A COMPARATIVE PERSPECTIVE

HOWARD M. LEICHTER
Linfield College

National productivity has become a national preoccupation in the United States. A prominent liberal economist, Lester Thurow, has described the U.S. decline in productivity growth as the "moral equivalent of defeat" (Thurow, 1981). On the opposite side of the political spectrum, Ronald Reagan referred to productivity, on three occasions in his inaugural address, as part of our national economic crisis — and created a National Productivity Advisory Committee to deal with the problem. In Congress, one senator told his colleagues that "productivity is golden" and warned that the United States was slipping further and further behind other major industrial nations (Garn, 1981: S12156). A *Saturday Review* editorial (January 5, 1980) identified the productivity decline as "one of the starkest problems facing the nation," and Buehler and Shetty (1981) called it "one of the most alarming trends that has emerged in the United States in the past few years." Over the past few years literally hundreds of newspaper and magazine articles, scholarly works, and political speeches have manifested the "productivity anxiety" (Henrici, 1982) that afflicts the nation today. What is all this national agonizing about?

The purpose of this chapter is to examine the national debate over the declining rate of productivity growth in the United States in a comparative context. Indeed, it is my position that productivity and the national debate over it are quintessentially comparative phenomena. Thus virtually every discussion of productivity involves references to other places and, often, other times. The term "comparative" then is used here to denote a primarily cross-national but also a cross-temporal perspective. A comparative approach to an understanding of the issue of productivity recommends itself not only because it reflects current discourse on the issue, but also because it is to other places and, occasionally, other times that we look for solutions to our currrent woes.

More specifically, the main section of this chapter examines those *public* policies in Japan and Western Europe that deal with labor and industrial productivity — such as governmental assistance to industry, industrial democracy, and productivity bargaining. These policies are discussed in terms of their purposes, accomplishments, and relevance to the United States. In addition, the relationship between national welfare policy and national productivity will be discussed. I will argue that in most Western European nations public policy has been predicated on the assumption that a positive relationship exists between the two — that is, welfare policies contribute to increased worker productivity — while in the United States the current conservative wisdom is that the relationship is a negative one.

The chapter begins by establishing the context of the national debate over declining productivity. Here the problem, its implications, and alleged causes will be identified. This discussion will underscore the essentially comparative nature of the productivity debate. In addition, it will reveal the lack of consensus among economists concerning the causes of the problem. This lack of consensus is important because, in the absence of agreement on the causes of U.S. productivity decline, it is difficult to fashion appropriate policy responses to remedy the problem.

Before proceeding it is necessary to submit two disclaimers. First, I am not an economist and, therefore, will not engage in an analysis of the technical facets of the productivity issue. As a political scientist concerned with comparative public policies, my interest lies in explaining the similarities and differences in policy responses among nations. I will leave it to others in this volume to explain the frailties of the "productivity index" or the relationship, for example, between real capital inputs and real stocks of capital and other mysteries of the universe.

Second, my concern is exclusively with potential *public policy* solutions to the declining rate of productivity. Thus, while the introduction of "quality circles" — an American innovation that the Japanese have adopted successfully and that American corporations are rediscovering — may be an important answer to our productivity problem, it is essentially a private solution and will not be addressed here.

THE CONTEXT OF THE DEBATE

THE PROBLEM

Private sector productivity is commonly measured in terms of output per hour of work.[1] Table 1 documents the nature of the problem from both cross-national and cross-temporal perspectives — and reveals the basis of concern with our productivity performance. For the two-decade period covered by the table (1960-1981), annual percentage changes in U.S. manufacturing productivity were the lowest of all eleven countries listed.[2] U.S performance in this area looks especially anemic and troublesome when it is compared to that of our major industrial competitors — Japan and West Germany. Thus for the period 1960-1981 U.S. manufacturing productivity increased at an annual average rate of 2.7 percent, compared to the Japanese rate of 9.2 percent and the German 5.2 percent.

In addition, not only are we not "keeping up with the Joneses," we are not even keeping up with ourselves. U.S. productivity declined from 3.0 percent from 1960 to 1973 to 1.7 percent from 1973 to 1981. And, while it is true that productivity has declined in *all* the countries in the table, it has been more precipitous in the United States than in, say, Japan or West Germany. The persistence and intensity of our declining productivity growth, as well as our own position relative to other nations, has raised the specter of serious economic decline in America. Indeed, if one looks at overall productivity and not just manufacturing, the United States actually experienced negative productivity growth in 1974, 1979, 1980, and 1982.

THE IMPLICATIONS

What does all this mean? The first thing that it does *not* mean is that American workers are less productive than workers of other countries: "It is a simple statistical fact that the United States leads the world in productivity. If we assign 100 to the United States to set a standard, then next in line is Canada with 91.6, France with 84.7, West

TABLE 2.1 Annual Percentage Changes in Manufacturing Productivity, 1960-1981

Output per Hour	United States	Canada	Japan	France	Germany	Italy	United Kingdom	Belgium	Denmark	Netherlands	Sweden
1960-1981	2.7	3.6	9.2	5.5	5.2	5.8	3.6	7.2	6.1	7.1	5.0
1960-1973	3.0	4.5	10.7	6.0	5.5	6.9	4.3	7.0	6.4	7.6	6.7
1973-1981	1.7	1.4	6.8	4.6	4.5	3.7	2.2	6.2	4.1	5.1	2.2
1974	-2.4	2.2	2.4	3.5	5.4	4.9	.8	5.8	3.3	8.3	3.6
1975	2.9	-2.6	3.9	3.1	5.3	-4.4	-2.0	4.4	10.4	-1.8	-.4
1976	4.4	5.3	9.4	8.2	7.1	8.6	4.0	10.4	3.8	12.8	1.0
1977	2.5	4.0	7.2	5.1	4.9	1.1	1.6	6.5	2.1	4.1	-1.5
1978	.9	1.6	7.9	5.7	3.3	3.0	3.3	5.0	2.4	6.6	4.3
1979	.7	1.7	8.9	4.9	4.9	7.3	3.3	6.5	5.8	4.9	8.4
1980	.2	-3.3	6.8	1.6	1.4	5.8	.6	3.1	1.4	1.3	1.2
1981	2.8	.3	3.2	1.6	2.7	3.4	5.9	7.3	5.6	3.1	.1
1982 (prelim)	-1.0	-2.8	1.0	6.9	1.7	1.3	3.4	-	-	-	-

SOURCE: *Monthly Labor Review*, Department of Labor, Bureau of Labor Statistics, December 1982.

Germany with 79.1, Japan with 63.2, United Kingdom with 55.1, and Italy with 54.3" (Tyler, 1982: 9). Nevertheless, the concern persists that if other nations continue to increase their productivity at a rate faster than ours, at some point in time they *will* be more productive. Thus we return to the question, So what?

Perhaps the most fundamental implication of the decline in productivity growth relates to our own standard of living. Increased productivity makes possible national economic growth and an improved individual standard of living. Healthy productivity gains mean more and better health care, education, a cleaner environment, consumer goods, new houses, and so on. Thus the recent slowdown in productivity threatens the economic well-being of the nation.

In addition, productivity is related directly to inflation. During periods of high inflation, such as our nation went through in the late 1970s and early 1980s, increased productivity enables employers to pay for increased wage demands without raising prices and, thereby, fueling inflation. Thus one contributing cause of our recent bout with inflation was declining productivity: Wage demands had to be satisfied by increasing prices rather than increased output per worker.

But perhaps the most ballyhooed facet of the productivity issue is the implications the decline has for our ability to compete, economically and politically, with other nations. Because productivity in countries such as Germany and Japan has been increasing more rapidly than in the United States, these countries are able to sell products more cheaply in the world market. When the price advantage of German and Japanese products is combined with an advantage in quality and craftsmanship, the result is devastating for the competitive position of American products in foreign and domestic markets. The huge trade deficits we have amassed over the past five years or so — about $150 billion — testify to the problem we face in this area.

Some observers have suggested that the consequences of this loss of economic competitiveness extend beyond increased deficits and declining economic growth. Such scholars as Lester Thurow (1981), Immanuel Wallerstein (1980), and Moses Abramowitz (1981) have drawn the chilling comparison between the United States today and Great Britain at the turn of the century. Great Britain was at that time the world's premier military and economic power; however, by the outbreak of World War I it had lost its leadership in both areas. As Abramowitz (1981: 10) warns us:

> The experience of Britain from 1870 to 1913 presents this country with a worrisome historical question mark. As Britain's basic industries lost their leadership and markets to the United States, Germany, and other countries after 1870, Britain's labor productivity growth rate was halved compared with previous decades, and her average total factor productivity growth during the forty years after 1870 fell to zero. The question is: Can we mount a more energetic and successful response to the challenge of newly rising foreign competitors after 1970 than Britain did after 1870?

The message is, of course, clear. Declining productivity threatens to transform the United States, as it did Great Britain, into a second-rate power. References to "America's setting sun" (Brockway, 1982) haunt American policymakers.

THE CAUSES

Who or what is responsible for our productivity decline? Unfortunately, nothing approaching a consensus exists among the experts concerning the causes of declining growth in productivity. The best we can do here is briefly review the often conflicting assertions as to the causes of our current economic malaise. The following are the most frequently cited causes of — one is tempted to say contributing factors to — the recent slowdown in productivity growth.

At the top of many lists, particularly those of conservatives, is *government regulations*. The claim here is that government regulations, but particularly those dealing with environmental standards and health and safety rules, have drained resources from otherwise productive purposes — purchase of new machinery, plant expansion, and the like. Edward Denison (1978), in an often-quoted study, estimated that diversion of resources to deal with environmental regulations, health and safety rules, and dishonesty and crime resulted in a reduction of productivity by 0.2 percent from 1972 to 1973; by 0.4 percent from 1973 to 1974; and by 0.5 percent from 1974 to 1975 — the latest years for which he had data. Based upon his data, Denison argued that the "drag" of government regulations on productivity was going to continue to increase. In addition, businessmen often claim that EPA and OSHA regulations not only force costly production changes but that the indecisive way in which they are administered exacerbates the direct and indirect costs of the regulations.

Finally, it should be noted that not all observers are willing to accept the indictment against government regulations. Thurow (1980: 48), for example, argues that "government regulation is hardly a major factor in the general decline of productivity." And William Tabb (1980), writing in the liberal journal *The Nation,* not only debunks the notion that occupational, health, and safety regulations or environmental laws are "the true villains in the declining productivity of the U.S. economy," he charges that "regulation is outrageously inadequate." The weight of opinion, if not of evidence, favors some degree of culpability on the part of government.

A second category of factors concerns certain macro-level economic changes in the country. In this regard, the two most frequently cited are changes in the *labor force* and increased importance of the *service sector.* Beginning in the mid-1960s, the composition of the labor force changed with the introduction of a large number of women and of youths born during the postwar baby boom. These two groups, it is argued, were less skilled and experienced and, therefore, less productive workers. The Council of Economic Advisers under the Carter administration estimated that use of new workers from these groups lowered productivity by one-third of a point per year. Here, too, however, Thurow (1980: 48) demurs: "If inexperienced workers were at the heart of the problem, the biggest productivity declines should have occurred in the industries that hire the most women and young workers. The industries with sharp reductions in productivity growth are not, however, the industries that hire a lot of women and young people."

The American economy over the past 30 years has shifted from an industrial to a service-oriented base. Thus in 1950 services accounted for 31 percent of the GNP, while in 1980 they accounted for 46 percent. Because productivity in the service sector is lower than the national average — about 40 percent lower, in fact — and it is harder to increase the productivity of a banker or a nurse or a police officer than that of an assembly-line welder, this shift has been translated into lower overall national productivity.

The third set of factors relates to the *condition of the American worker.* Here the evidence moves from being empirical to being downright mushy. One facet of this alleged cause is the decline of the "work ethic" among American workers. The evidence for this assertion is found in high absenteeism, work stoppages, and shoddy products. The problem is typically highlighted by references to the dedication and sense of pride characteristic of German and Japanese workers. Although many dispute this claim, it is nonetheless part of the folklore of American industry.

A second dimension of the "condition of the American worker" issue is the nature of the workplace and the worker's place in it. The typical American workplace, so the argument runs, is characterized by (1) a lack of cooperation between labor and management, (2) a high sense of job insecurity, and (3) little sense of or opportunity for worker satisfaction or commitment. As a result, not only do workers not work as hard as they can, but they often resist the introduction of productivity-improving equipment and techniques for fear that they will result in the loss of jobs. Here too the problem tends to be discussed in terms of, and underscored by, comparative references. Robert Reich (1981: 23), the director of policy planning at the Federal Trade Commission, has noted: "Citizens of Sweden, West Germany, and Japan appear to have more of a shared commitment to productivity. . . . the extent to which all segments of the work force — blue-collar, white-collar, management, government — take responsibility for improving industrial output is impressive. Indeed, blue-collar employees in these countries are among the most vocal proponents of new productive investment." How unlike the United States!

Still another explanation for our declining productivity growth involves the other half of the labor-*management* equation. Critics claim that the fault for our productivity problems lies not with labor but with management. "We do have a productivity problem but there is nothing wrong with the workforce. Any crisis of reduced output is directly caused by the poor management that has characterized our organizations in recent years" (Hall, 1981). Specifically, American management has been charged with failure to provide inspired leadership, create a sense of esprit de corps, and adopt policies and procedures to improve productivity. All the things, in other words, in which their German and Japanese counterparts excel.

The next set of factors deals with money — how much is available for *investment* and how much is devoted to *research and development*. First, investment in new plants and equipment supporting each worker-hour has declined from 3 percent from 1948 to 1973 to 1.75 percent since 1973. Nationally about 10 percent of the GNP in the United States goes into investment, compared to 20 percent in Japan. Of course, given the size of our GNP this still represents an absolutely larger sum of money, but it is still used to illustrate the relatively stronger commitment of the Japanese to future economic growth.

Related to the problem of inadequate investment is one of a decline, relative to our own past efforts and to those of other nations, in resources devoted to R& D. The problem was summarized in the 1978 "Final Report of the National Center for Productivity and Quality of Working Life," a government agency set up by President Nixon: "Since the mid-1960s, the United States R& D effort has been declining relative to that of other industrial nations. . . . R& D outlays as a percentage of GNP have been increasing in the USSR and Japan, while ours have declined since 1964" (quoted in Tyler, 1982: 12). The generally accepted figure on this point is that current U.S. R& D spending amounts to about 2 percent of the GNP, while in the mid-1960s it was about 3 percent. Here too it must be remembered that in absolute dollars, the United States continues to spend more on R& D than Japan.

Another factor that has been identified as contributing to our productivity problem is the alleged tendency for government, through import quotas, tax benefits, and "bailouts," to *protect backward or obsolete industries* rather than encouraging new ("sunrise" as opposed to "sunset") industries. Once again the Japanese are seen as providing the model to which we should aspire — and to which we shall turn shortly.

The final explanation for our productivity problem involves macroeconomic cycles. Thus, according to Tyler (1982: 11), "The empirical evidence is clear: productivity follows the 'business cycle.' In times of stagnation it goes down; in times of recovery it goes up." John Kendrick (1982: 25), one of the foremost authorities on productivity, agrees. Thus he predicted an increase in productivity beginning in 1983: "Productivity always picks up during recoveries." It should be noted that Kendrick's prediction appears accurate. While productivity actually declined by 1.0 percent in 1982, it rose by a healthy 8.3 percent in the first quarter of 1983 as the nation began emerging from the recession.

SUMMARY

These, then, are the major explanations for America's recent productivity slump: (1) excessive, counterproductive government regulations; (2) changes in the labor force; (3) increased service orientation of the U.S. economy; (4) decline in the work ethic; (5) worker resistance to innovative equipment and practices; (6) poor management; (7) inadequate investment; (8) inadequate resources devoted to R& D; (9) government subsidization of "sunset" industries and lack of ecouragement of "sunrise" industries; and (10) economic cycles. Although there are few economists who are willing to cite one factor as the villain, most contend that a combination of these have contributed to our productivity problem. And, just as the problem is often defined and illustrated in comparative terms, so too do we seek solutions to the problem in other countries.

LESSONS FROM ABROAD

Economists, politicians, and the news media have focused attention on the practices, both public and private, of Japan and Western Europe in the hope that we might learn from the apparent productivity successes of these countries. Of the nations studied, Japan has clearly captured most popular attention. However, in the 1950s and 1960s, it was Western Europe, with its experiments in industrial democracy, that engaged academic minds.

In this section the Japanese "miracle" will be discussed, as well as the currrently less celebrated cases in Western Europe. To anticipate the discussion, I will show that conservative Japan has relied on public policies that (1) focus on corporate, rather than worker, behavior; (2) rely on informal, voluntary, and cooperative arrangements among government, business, and labor; and, (3) maximize free-market opportunities. Western Europe, on the other hand, has generally favored public policies that (1) emphasize encouraging worker input; (2) have taken a more formalistic or legalistic approach; and (3) have been more willing to compromise the free market.

JAPAN, INC.

In June 1980 NBC-TV broadcast a special program the title of which conveyed the essence of our orientation toward Japan on the productivity issue: "If Japan Can, Why Can't We?" Indeed, analyzing the Japanese success has become one of the most productive areas of academic, as well as media, inquiry. Such books as Vogel's (1979) Japan as Number One: Lessons for America, Pascale and Athos's (1981) The Art of Japanese Management, and Ouchi's (1981) Theory Z: How American Business Can Meet the Japanese Challenge have been both academic and popular successes. For Americans, but especially American businesses and government, the Japanese record of high productivity growth, high quality, and comparatively lower prices has become the standard of our aspirations and the source of frustrations. How *do* the Japanese do it?

Japanese productivity success can be attributed to two broad factors: (1) the internal structure and operation of the Japanese corporation and (2) the highly supportive economic and political environment within which the corporation operates. The first of these has received the most attention in this country. Scholars and business people have flocked to Japan and returned with glowing reports of Japanese manufacturing techniques (such as "just in time" delivery of parts, heavy reliance on automation and use of robots, emphasis on defect prevention rather than detection), labor-related policies (such as lifetime employment, strict adherence to seniority in promotions, quality circles, job rotation, and minimizing pay and salary distinctions between white- and blue-collar workers), and personal/cultural differences (such as loyalty, diligence, and a sense of community). These factors, which are undoubtedly important to the Japanese success, are, of course, private practices. And at least some of them (quality circles, job security) are being introduced into American companies.

It is the second set of factors, however, that is of concern here. What *public* policies have the Japanese adopted that have nurtured their economic success? In the beginning of this century, emulating countries in Europe, Japan introduced a series of health protection and promotion measures, culminating in a Health Insurance Law (1922), that were aimed at improving the health and hence the productivity of the working class. Of particular concern to the Japanese government was the high incidence of tuberculosis in the critical textile industry (Leichter, 1979: 241-244).

Today, however, the public policy emphasis in Japan is on maintaining the economic health of industry. The guiding bureaucratic hand orchestrating the economic policies that are the envy of most of the industrial world is the awe-inspiring — and often ire-inspiring — and elitist Ministry of International Trade and Industry (MITI). MITI attracts the finest graduates from Japanese universities and views itself, and is viewed by others, as the elite of the Japanese bureaucracy. Although at one time MITI, and its prewar predecessor the Ministry of Commerce and Industry, played a direct and intrusive role in guiding and protecting Japanese industry, today its role is mainly supportive and low key. MITI works its wonders largely through maintaining close and cooperative relationships between itself and other government agencies, on one hand, and Japanese industry on the other. It is this relationship, which is mainly voluntary and noncoercive, that gave birth to the term "Japan, Inc."

The main thrust of MITI's efforts is to identify or target industries that are either new or promising (sunrise industries) or less competitive, productive, and promising (sunset industries). In the case of the former, MITI helps encourage and support creation and/or expansion of the industry. It does this by providing start-up and development funds, and by helping to secure tax breaks, needed technology, scientific information, protection from international competition, loans, licenses, access to markets, and even property. One recent case in point involved the computer and communications industries. In 1971, at the initiative and urging of MITI, the Japanese Diet passed the Temporary Law for Strengthening Selected Electronics Industries and provided $1.7 billion — supplemented in 1976 by another $1 billion — for research and development (Stursberg, 1982: 8).

In addition, MITI helps to coordinate the efforts of various companies and government agencies in order to facilitate the development of targeted industries. A recent illustration of this involved a major cooperative effort initiated, supervised, and partially funded by MITI from 1976 to 1980 among five semiconductor companies to develop large-scale, integrated circuits. The companies, with joint MITI and industry funds, set up a cooperative research laboratory that ultimately produced 1000 patents and, allegedly, Japanese leadership in various areas of the semiconductor market. Current targeted sunrise industries include large-scale integrated circuits, biotechnology, artificial intelligence, robotics, and supercomputers (see Lohr, 1983b).

MITI also targets less productive industries:

> MITI officials consider it their responsibility to assist companies in declining industries to merge or go out of business while encouraging new ones to move into the localities and employ the personnel who were laid off. If conditions are not serious enough to shut down a whole industry, they work out a "depression cartel": agreement among companies in a depressed sector to reduce production capacity, with the reduction distributed relatively equally among the companies [Vogel, 1979: 71].

An illustration of this occurred recently when the twelve major petrochemical producers reached an agreement, under MITI tutelage, to cut their production by 36 percent by 1985. The petrochemical indus-

try and coal mining, shipbuilding, and textiles have been identified as
sunset industries because of high energy costs or high labor costs
relative to other countries (Lohr, 1983b).

By weeding out less productive enterprises — yet being solicitous
and helpful in finding employment for those affected — MITI has
contributed to its own reputation and Japan's productivity success.
What Herman Kahn (1971: 81) had to say about an earlier period in
Japanese history is equally as relevant today: "It is, of course, exactly
this transfer [of human and material resources] from less efficient to
more efficient sectors that facilitates rapid economic growth."

Finally, we must reemphasize that much of what MITI does is
achieved through voluntary cooperation, guidance, and moral suasion, rather than coercive governmental action. As Sadanori
Yamanaka, the currrent head of MITI, put it: "MITI works in an
indirect fashion. When it guides industry, it is with soft hands. It has
no real coercive power anymore. The main player is private industry"
(quoted in Lohr, 1983a). Another MITI official echoed this point:
"MITI is now a kind of co-pilot. At some crucial point, when the risk
is very high in new industries, or for the adjustment of ailing industries, Government support is sometimes required and business and
Government must cooperate. To harmonize these actions is the reason MITI exists" (Lohr, 1983a).

How does MITI get such good cooperation from industry? Vogel
(1979: 74-75) suggests that MITI has done the following: (1) convinced
industry that its well-being is MITI's primary concern; (2) provided
first-rate information and analysis; (3) maintained a high level of
interaction with industry; and (4) made it clear that MITI rewards
cooperative behavior, granting licenses, giving tax breaks, and so on.

In summary, most observers agree that Japan's success in maintaining high productivity growth is the result of combined private
practices and public policies. From a public policy perspective, the
key element has been the performance of the Ministry of International Trade and Industry, which has created a political and economic
environment conducive to growth and productivity. Through a variety
of supportive, noncoercive practices, MITI has nurtured productive
industries while easing the traumas associated with disbanding or
reducing nonproductive industries. The partnership between public
and private institutions (that is, Japan, Inc.) and the compatibility
between public and private practices and values (for example, "What
is good for SONY is good for Japan") clearly have contributed to
Japan's remarkable performance over the past few decades (see Table

2.1). Whether any of this can be imported by the United States is an issue to be discussed later.

The current American preoccupation with understanding and emulating the Japanese is of relatively recent vintage, for it was not that long ago that the term "Made in Japan" was a derisive one. During the 1950s and 1960s, attention, especially scholarly attention, was focused on Western Europe and its economic miracle. Although the number of countries involved precludes either a definitive characterization or detailed analysis, the major — but by no means exclusive — emphasis in Western Europe is clear. Beginning even prior to World War II, but accelerating thereafter, the main vehicle for achieving greater productivity has been some form of industrial democracy. Although the definition, motivation, and manifestation of this approach have varied from country to country, the theoretical assumption has been the same: Workers will be more efficient and productive if they are allowed to participate in the industrial decision-making process.

That industrial democracy should thrive in Western Europe rather than in, for example, the United States or Japan, is clearly attributable to the influence of social democratic parties and socialist thought in the politics of Western Europe during the twentieth century. For social democrats, industrial democracy, whatever else it may accomplish, has been viewed as the complement to political democracy.

Some of the earliest efforts to tie the movement for social justice to increased productivity occurred in Western Europe in 1920. In that year, the first Swedish social democratic government appointed a commission to study job satisfaction and productivity. The commission recommended creating consultative factory committees composed of workers and mangement "to afford the workers a deeper insight into production and a better capacity for active participation in the promotion of the same" (quoted in Ryden, 1978: 93). For a variety of reasons that need not concern us here, the recommendation was not implemented.

In the same year, Norway went one step further when its Parliament passed legislation that created "work councils" made up of labor and management, which had as their purpose to work on productivity problems. However, as Bolweg (1976: 19) reports: "Despite the fact that more than 100 such councils were established and that the new law remained on the books until 1963 these work councils never achieved any real importance in Norwegian industrial relations."

Finally, Weimar Germany adopted a work council law in 1920 that allowed labor some limited influence over various management decisions, including those dealing with productivity. Like its Scandinavian counterparts, the German law had little practical effect. Industrial democracy was an idea whose time had not yet come.

Industrial democracy did "arrive," however, following World War II. In some instances joint worker-management arrangements came about without direct government intervention. Such was the case in 1945 with the creation in Norway of the production council agreement between the Federation of Trade Unions and the Norwegian Employer's Federation. The agreement allowed for the creation of production councils in all companies with more than 25 employees (Bolweg, 1976: 19). Ultimately, however, in Norway and other countries industrial democracy was secured through formal legislation.

The most celebrated and studied of these laws was the 1951 German Codetermination Law. The German law drew immediate and sustained interest in this country (see McPherson, 1951, 1955; Fisher, 1951; Shuchman, 1957; Spiro, 1958; Hartmann, 1970; Monissen, 1978). Interestingly, the motivation behind the law was not primarily one of improving German industrial productivity — although this was recognized as a potential by-product. Probably the most immediate motive behind the introduction of this form of industrial democracy was the concern to forestall Allied dismantling of German industry and especially the critical coal and iron and steel industries. These industries had played a vital role in the Nazi rise to power. "Never again should industrialists be allowed to support or subsidize a nationalist, let alone a Nazi, party" (Hartmann, 1970: 140). The assumption on the part of the German trade union movement was that labor representation on management boards would prevent such a reoccurrence.

There were a variety of other forces behind the introduction of codetermination in West Germany. These ranged from the apparent failure of nationalization in Great Britain (and, therefore, the tarnishing of that model) to the "Christian" obligation of management to recognize workers' claims for more responsibility (Spiro, 1954: 1119). But, from the perspective of this chapter, although not from that of its architects, the most noteworthy justification behind the codetermination movement was its contribution to worker productivity. For German industrialists and politicians, the expectation was that codetermination would buy industrial peace, stability, and, hence, economic growth. For German workers, particularly those who identified with the Social Democratic Party, codetermination was a way to reduce worker alienation. Workers who are allowed to participate in decisions affecting their working lives are going to be content — and more productive. As one contemporary American observer at the time noted: "It seems likely that employees will come to have at least more of a proprietary feeling toward the company" (McPherson, 1951: 28).

The 1951 law originally was limited to workers in the mining and iron and steel industries, and only to those companies with more than 1000 employees. Each eligible company is required to establish an eleven-member supervisory council or control board consisting of five members chosen by labor, five chosen by management, and one "neutral" member chosen by the board itself.[3] The council has the dual responsibility of setting broad corporate policy and selecting a management board that directs the day-to-day operations of the company. The management board consists of a labor manager responsible for personnel decisions, a commercial manager in charge of sales, finances, and purchasing, and a production manager.

One year after passage of the Codetermination Law, the West German Parliament passed the Works Constitution Act (1952), which gave employees outside the coal and iron and steel industries participatory rights. However, this law did not go as far as the 1951 legislation. The act provided, at the plant level, for a works council to be chosen by all employees. In addition, at the firm or company level, employees were given the right to choose one-third (not one-half, as the 1951 law allowed) of the members of the supervisory council. As Hartmann (1970: 139) described it: "But, if the Works Constitution Law produced codetermination outside of the coal and steel industries it was a highly diluted version of employee control."

Finally, in 1976 Parliament passed another Act of Codetermination of Employees, which extended the principle of *equal* employee representation on supervisory boards to joint stock companies employing 2000 or more persons. Although there are some minor differences between this law and the original act — for instance, there is no neutral member, but rather a chairman who has a double vote — the principle of codetermination clearly has been extended to cover a wider portion of the German industrial work force.

Has codetermination contributed to industrial productivity in Germany? While there have been few empirical studies to determine the relationship between productivity and codetermination,[4] there is virtual agreement among scholars with the conclusion reached by Hancock (1978: 18): "By providing regular channels for direct consultation and participation in decisions on company policy among the partners in the productive process, codetermination contributed directly to long-term industrial peace and economic growth, thereby fulfilling the expectations of its original supporter" (see also King and Van de Vall, 1978; Hartmann, 1970; Monissen, 1978).

Other countries in Western Europe, including France, the Netherlands, Sweden, Norway, and Luxembourg, have adopted some form of state-sponsored industrial democracy. In some instances labor's role is merely consultative, while in others it more closely resembles the German codetermination model. In addition, as in Germany, the tendency in much of Western Europe has been to increase the number of industrial enterprises covered by participatory plans.[5]

GREAT BRITAIN: PRODUCTIVITY BARGAINING

It may seem strange to look to Great Britain for guidance in solving our productivity problems. As has been noted, it is with the British economic experience in mind that many have viewed our declining productivity with such alarm. In addition, Britain's recent overall economic performance hardly inspires confidence. Nevertheless, there has been both scholarly (Gershenfeld, 1977) and governmental (McKersie et al., 1972) interest in this country with one particular British experience with productivity improvement. The approach is called "productivity bargaining" and it involves an agreement between labor and management in which the former agrees to accept certain changes in production and work practices in exchange for increased wages and other benefits (see Stettner, 1969: 1-3). Workers, in other words, are rewarded for accepting productivity-enhancing changes.

Productivity bargaining was first introduced in 1960 in a highly celebrated labor-management agreement involving the ESSO refinery at Fawley, England. "Briefly, the company agreed to provide large increases in its employees' rates of pay — of the order of 40 per cent — in return for the unions' consent to certain defined changes in working practices that were hampering a more efficient utilization of labour" (Flanders, 1964: 13). From 1962 until 1966 there were about 70 privately arranged productivity agreements reached in Great Britain. However, in 1966 the Labour government harnessed productivity bargaining to an income-policy program.

In the 1960s Great Britain faced increasingly severe economic problems — rising wage demands, declining productivity, and loss of markets resulting in a balance of payments deficit. In 1966, following a brief period of a freeze on wages, the National Board for Prices and Incomes (NBPI), which had been created to administer the Labour government's wage policy, "fixed on productivity bargaining as the principal escape valve for employees and unions seeking to bypass the tight wage norms of the period" (Gershenfeld, 1977: 58). NBPI established a 3.5 percent annual ceiling on wage and salary increases. However, this ceiling could be exceeded for, in the words of a government white paper, "agreements which genuinely raise productivity and increase efficiency sufficiently to justify a pay increase above 3½ per cent" (Stettner, 1969: 30). These agreements had to be approved by the Department of Employment and Productivity. Between 1967 and 1969, when the incomes and wage policy was abandoned, there were over 4000 productivity agreements approved by the government, involving over one-fourth of the British labor force.

The obvious question, did productivity bargaining work? is easier asked than answered. There are several reasons for the uncertainty surrounding analysis of the British experience. First, as one study done by the U.S. National Commission on Productivity (McKersie et al., 1972: 9) found: "One must concede that it is difficult to assess the impact of the agreements because they were so enmeshed with the prices and income policy." In other words, it is difficult to disentangle the economic impact of the productivity and incomes facets of the Labour government's policy.

In addition, it is difficult to assess the macroeconomic consequences of productivity bargaining because no more than 20-25 percent of the work force during the period was covered by productivity agreements. And, even among those that were, there is substantial agreement among observers that toward the latter part of the period many of these were "phony" agreements. These phony agreements were entered into by unions and management "simply to get a given wage increase past the prices and incomes policy [board]." Such agreements tended to dilute whatever positive results were realized from genuine agreements.

Despite these problems, American reaction to and evaluation of the British experience with productivity bargaining generally has been positive, although reserved. Thus Gershenfeld (1977: 70) concluded his study by noting: "Productivity bargaining is only one of a variety of possible solutions. It is not a panacea, but it can be a valuable helper. For approximately twenty percent of British work-ers, and their organizations who have been able to use it effectively, productivity bargaining has been a valuable source of productivity improvement and income."

Similarly, the McKersie et al. (1972: 17) study done for the U.S. National Commission on Productivity found much to praise in the principle and practice of productivity bargaining. However, where the commission-sponsored report parts company with the British experience is over the issue of the role of government. Thus the report states: "We should make our position clear on the limits of govern-ment involvement. An organization like the Board [i.e., NBPI] can be helpful as a spotlighting organization. Anything that goes beyond and begins to establish norms or standards is likely to be counterproduc-tive. This certainly was the experience with productivity bargaining under a formal prices and incomes policy in Great Britain."

The issue raised here by a U.S. government commission concern-ing the appropriate role of government in spurring productivity growth gives one some insight into the difficulty in adopting, as public policy, some productivity growth models discussed here. A look at the question of the importability of these approaches will conclude this chapter.

CONCLUSION

Since the issue of declining productivity captured the attention of government and the media in the early 1970s, the main American public policy response has been to "appoint a commission" — the National Commission on Productivity (Nixon-Ford), the National Productivity Council (Carter), and the National Productivity Advi-sory Committee (Reagan). Yet, despite all the reports, media atten-tion, and national agonizing, no administration has yet proposed a productivity policy. While the report of President Reagan's advisory committee has yet to be submitted (as of this writing), it will *not* recommend government-supported productivity bargaining; it will *not* recommend legislation for worker participation in management decisions; and it will *not* recommend the creation of a single executive agency to be responsible for industrial forecasting, coordination of information, technology, and R&D support for industry. In other words, it is highly unlikely, under a conservative administration, that any of the state-supported or directed policies used in Western Europe or Japan would find favor.

The creation of a national agency similar to MITI would face not only the traditional American philosophical antagonism toward economic planning and government interference in the marketplace — which is not limited to hard-line conservatives — but also the reluctance of bureaucrats in such agencies as the Departments of Labor, the Treasury, Commerce, and the Interior, all of whom would view such an agency as a threat to their own power. There is, one might add, some precedent in this country for centralized, government-managed productivity growth. This, of course, was the War Production Board set up during World War II, which, among other things, "encouraged employers and unions to set up joint management-labor production committees. The aim of these committees was to promote greater efficiency through consultation on absenteeism, health and safety, waste reduction, transportation, training, and other personnel matters" (Derber, 1970: 388-389). It sounds like just what the doctor ordered — but it is hardly likely in peacetime.

Thus one cannot be terribly sanguine about the prospects of the United States adopting the public policies our Japanese and Western European competitors have used, and with apparent success, in achieving and sustaining high productivity growth. Are the experiences of these countries then to remain of academic interest and public envy, but largely irrelevant to Americans? There is one dimension of the Western European experience to which I have alluded that is relevant here: the relationship between social welfare (or social justice) and productivity policy.

As noted earlier, much of the social legislation introduced at the end of the nineteenth and beginning of the twentieth centuries in Europe and Japan had as one of its purposes to improve the condition of the working class and, hence, national efficiency. In fact, the term "national efficiency" was widely used in Great Britain during the first decade of the century both to express the concern of the British for their declining world position and as a desired goal of public policy. In particular, the press and politicians viewed the German and Japanese as models of national efficiency worth emulating. Thus, for example, Searle (1971: 57) describes "an extravagant cult of Japan in Britain" that would be easily recognizable to current American readers of the business pages of the *New York Times* or the *Wall Street Journal*.

But it was the Germans who the British most envied and feared. Germany, with its material achievements, discipline, ruthlessness, and cunning, threatened to wrest the reins of political and economic leadership from Great Britain. " After all, Britain, for all her 'personal liberty', boasted nothing that could rival Germany's model army, the Bismarckian network of social insurance, or the highly organized educational system, with its organic links to the expanding science-based industries" (Searle, 1971: 55). The national efficiency movement was, to be sure, more broadly defined than our own current concern with productivity, but it is similar.

For many in Britain and other European countries, part of the German success lay, as the above quotation suggests, in the German "network of social insurance." As noted earlier, the deplorable physical condition of the British working class lay in stark contrast — or so it seemed — to the superior condition of their German counterparts. And many in Great Britain believed that state intervention in the form of health, safety, welfare, and education legislation was needed for the nation to recapture its place of primacy. As Hay (1975: 31) has observed: "The idea of national efficiency became part of the political language of the time, and many found it reasonable to express their support for social measures in such terms."

It would be absurd to suggest that the position, condition, and circumstances of the United States today is identical to that of Great Britain in 1910 or 1915. Nevertheless, one wonders whether the relationship the Germans, British, Japanese, and others discovered 80 years ago or so is not still relevant. As Reich (1981: 23) recently asked: "Is social justice essential to productivity in an advanced industrial economy?" He thinks it is, and I agree. Here is what Reich has to say about the relationship: "A narrower differential between the highest- and lowest-paid employees; more generous Social Security, unemployment, and health insurance; a greater degree of job security and job safety; cleaner and healthier environments; broader participation in management — these factors may account for the greater shared commitment to productivity in Sweden, Japan, and West Germany."

The current conservative wisdom is that government concern (that is, interference) with health, safety, and environmental regulations diverts resources from productive purposes and that overly generous social welfare programs discourage work, contribute to deficits (which affect business confidence and investment), and adversely affect productivity. The irony, of course, is that the governments of those nations with which we compete and that we envy most are more actively involved in regulation, economic planning, and/or providing social legislation than we are. It may very well be that the United States must first recognize, as our Western European competitors have, that there is a positive relationship between socially supportive policies and increased productivity.

I am not claiming here that the adopton of national health insurance or the expansion and stricter enforcement of health, safety, and environmental laws will spur U.S. productivity to new heights. However, it would probably help. It is likely that such policies, along with a variety of steps already being taken by private enterprise (such as quality circles, participative management, lifetime employment, and increased use of robots), will lead to improved productivity growth. And such measures are more likely to be adopted since they are more in keeping with the American political culture than a centralized economic planning agency such as MITI or government-sponsored industrial democracy or productivity bargaining. Europeans have shown that social justice and productivity are positively related. As Reich (1981: 23) notes: " In an advanced industrial economy like ours, and like those of our more productive neighbors, this is the only supply-side theory that makes lasting sense."

NOTES

1. For a criticism of this measure, see Henrici (1982).

2. Manufacturing productivity is used here because of available comparable cross-national data. It should be noted that manufacturing productivity is higher than for other sectors of the economy. Thus, for example, while 1981 manufacturing productivity increased 2.8 percent, business productivity increased 1.8 percent, nonfarm business 1.4 percent, and nonfinancial corporations 1.7 percent.

3. If a firm's capital exceeded a specified amount, the supervisory council was to be larger — for example, 15 or 21 members.

4. Cable and FitzRoy (1980: 117) studied worker participation and productivity in firms not covered by the codetermination laws. They conclude that "the firms most committed to worker participation are more efficient and apparently profitable than others."

5. In only one country, Switzerland, has there been actual voter rejection of industrial democracy (Pejovich, 1978b: 4).

REFERENCES

ABRAMOWITZ, M. (1981) "Welfare quandries and productivity concerns." American Economic Review 71 (March): 2-17.

BOLWEG, J. (1976) Job Design and Industrial Democracy. Leiden: Martinus Nijhoff.

BROCKWAY, G. P. (1982) "America's setting sun." New Leader (June 14): 8-9.

BUEHLER, V. M. and Y. K. SHETTY (1981) Improving Productivity. New York: Amacon.

CABLE, J. R. and F. R. FitzROY (1980) "Productive efficiency, incentives and employee participation: some preliminary results from West Germany." Kyklos 33: 100-121.

DENISON, E. F. (1978) "Effects of selected changes in the industrial and human environment upon per unit of input." Survey of Current Business 58: 21ff.

DERBER, M. (1970) The American Idea of Industrial Democracy, 1865-1965. Urbana: University of Illinois Press.

FISHER, P. (1951) "Labor codetermination in Germany." Social Research 18: 449-485.

FLANDERS, A. (1964) The Fawley Productivity Agreements. London: Faber & Faber.

GARN, J. (1981) "Productivity: international lessons." Congressional Record 127 (October 26): S12156-S12157.

GERSHENFELD, W. J. (1977) "Productivity bargaining: background and applications." Public Productivity Review 2 (Spring/Summer): 57-71.

HALL, J. (1981) "Inspiring workers." New York Times (September 18).

HANCOCK, D. M. (1978) "Productivity, welfare and participation in Sweden and West Germany." Comparative Politics 11 (October): 4-23.

HARTMANN, H. (1970) "Codetermination in West Germany." Industrial Relations 9: 137-147.

HAY, J. R. (1975) The Origins of the Liberal Welfare Reform, 1906-1914. London: Macmillan.

HENRICI, S. B. (1982) "How not to measure productivity." New York Times (March 7).

KAHN, H. (1971) The Emerging Japanese Superstate. Englewood Cliffs, NJ: Prentice-Hall.

KENDRICK, J. W. (1982) "The coming rebound in productivity." Fortune (June 28): 25, 28.

KING, C. and M. VAN DE VALL (1978) Models of Industrial Democracy. Netherlands: Mouton.

LEICHTER H. (1979) A Comparative Approach to Policy Analysis. New York: Cambridge University Press.

LOHR, S. (1983a) "Japan's Trade Ministry draws praise and ire." New York Times (May 17).

——— (1983b) "How Japan helps its industry." New York Times (May 18).

McKERSIE, R., L. HUNTER, and W. SENGENBERGER (1972) Productivity Bargaining: The American and British Experience. Washington DC: National Commission on Productivity.

McPHERSON, W. H. (1955) "Codetermination in practice." Industrial and Labor Relations Review 8: 499-519.

——— (1951) "Codetermination: Germany's move toward a new economy." Industrial and Labor Relations Review 5: 20-32.

MONISSEN, H. G. (1978) "The current status of labor participation in the management of business firms in Germany," pp. 57-81 in S. Pejovich (ed.) The Codetermination Movement in the West: Labor Participation in the Management of Business Firms. Lexington, MA: D. C. Heath.

OUCHI, W. (1981) Theory Z: How American Business Can Meet the Japanese Challenge. Reading, MA: Addison-Wesley.

PASCALE, R. T. and A. G. ATHOS (1981) The Art of Japanese Management. New York: Simon & Schuster.

PEJOVICH, S. [ed.] (1978a) The Codetermination Movement in the West: Labor Participation in the Management of Business Firms. Lexington, MA: D. C. Heath.

———— (1978b) "Codetermination: a new perspective for the West," pp. 3-21 in S. Pejovich (ed.) The Codetermination Movement in the West: Labor Participation in the Management of Business Firms. Lexington, MA: D. C. Heath.

REICH, R. (1981) "The liberal promise of prosperity." New Republic 184 (February 21): 20-23.

RYDEN, R. (1978) "Labor participation in the management of business firms in Sweden," pp. in S. Pejovich (ed.) The Codetermination Movement in the West: Labor Participation in the Management of Business Firms. Lexington, MA: D. C. Heath.

SEARLE, G. R. (1971) The Quest for National Efficiency. Berkeley: University of California Press.

SHUCHMAN, A. (1957) "Economic rationale of codetermination." Industrial and Labor Relations Review 10: 270-283.

SPIRO, H. J. (1958) The Politics of German Codetermination. Cambridge, MA: Harvard University Press.

———— (1954) "Codetermination in Germany." American Political Science Review 48: 1114-1127.

STETTNER, N. (1969) Productivity Bargaining and Industrial Change. Oxford Pergamon.

STURSBERG, R. (1982) "Productivity and employment: a review of the debate on the implications of information technology." (unpublished)

TABB, W. (1980) "Playing productivity politics." The Nation 230 (January 5-12): 14-19.

THUROW, L. (1981) "The moral equivalent of defeat." Foreign Policy 42 (Spring): 114-124.

———— (1980) "The productivity problem." Technology Review (November/December): 40-51.

TYLER, G. (1982) "The politics of productivity." New Leader 65 (March 22): 8-14.

VOGEL, E. F. (1979) Japan as Number One: Lessons for America. Cambridge, MA: Harvard University Press.

WALLERSTEIN, I. (1980) "Friends as foes." Foreign Policy 40 (Fall): 119-131.

PART II

STIMULATING HUMAN CAPITAL

3

PUBLIC ADMINISTRATION
UNDER PRESSURE

MARC HOLZER

John Jay College of Criminal Justice
City University of New York

Productivity is a hot topic in the public sector, one of the most recent buzz words in the vocabulary of public administration. It is a term that appears frequently in political and policy statements, government reports, and news media critiques. Beyond rhetoric, however, the term is increasingly a politically viable, visible "umbrella" covering and connecting a range of subjects and strategies, such as measurement and performance auditing; automation and robotics; Japanese management and quality circles; worker participation in managerial decisions and managerial participation in front-line work; investments in machinery and investments in people; feedback from and to employees; contracting out and contracting in.

In the public sector the term "productivity" suffers from baseless fears and myths: that outputs and outcomes cannot be measured; that labor will not cooperate; that managerial risks outweigh rewards; that the interest of policymakers will wane; that the media will be unduly critical. Because the term itself almost automatically meets with such objections, productivity programs must often operate under other rubrics, such as "performance management," "operations analysis," "cutback management," "quality of working life," or "joint labor-management committees." But under whatever name, by whatever means, programs to improve agency efficiency and effectiveness by increasing worker motivation and skills, by strengthening management and measurement, by reorganizing jobs and work processes, by technological and operational innovation, or by any of an array of approaches are, indeed, productivity programs.

Although productivity, de facto, currently pervades discussions of cutback-driven decisions, neither the concept nor the commitment are new (see Ridley and Simon, 1943). Concerns with public sector productivity have been as constant and as timeless as concerns with high taxes, corruption, or imcompetence. They have flourished in both orthodox and reform contexts, in discussions among business people and union people, in analyses by reporters and academicians. The century-old reform clamor to expunge corruption and partisan appointments, which lay at the origin of civil service, was, if nothing else, an attempt to enhance the ability of employees to carry out their policy-implementing responsibilities to legislative and judicial policymakers, and, therefore, to improve government's outputs (Wilson, 1887).

But the "right way" to build a road was simply not always self-evident, even when politicians and contractors were not being self-serving. Neutral public administration proved to be only a partial and insufficient, albeit necessary, step because "common sense," "on-the-job training," or similar informal approaches to productivity were constrained by a manager's own values, perceptions, and limited experiences. Thus turn-of-the century "good government" advocates, in further pursuit of productivity, sought a factual "science" of administration that could improve competence by tying labor inputs to the quality and quantity of service outputs in a more directive manner. Neutral "scientific" administration would presumably better serve the public than would its neutral "rule of thumb" predecessor. The public sector would presumably "profit" from specific, scientific techniques used by the private sector.

In recent decades, relatively sophisticated approaches to public sector productivity have also argued that views of civil servants as "motivated" by money, security, and very close oversight do not always coincide with the political, sociological, and social psychological reality of groups and individuals. That is, forces that are not apparent on organizational charts do indeed influence the productivity of employees' actions (Eddy, 1981; Greiner et al., 1981). Yet despite sophisticated approaches to productivity that are rooted chiefly in management science, behavioral science, and political science, the applied study of public administration has scarcely relieved the public's demands that its employees be smarter and worker harder. Thus the frustration in a hundred years of public administration's improvement is its continued insufficiency, perhaps most clearly evidenced by a Harris Poll for the National Commission on Productivity (NCOP) in the early 1970s; Harris revealed the public's perception of government workers as far less productive than almost any other grouping (Thomas, 1974: 31). Another NCOP study concluded that "there is a widespread feeling that local government productivity in the United States is dropping" (Hatry and Fisk, 1971: 73). Proposition 13 in California, Prop. 2½ in Massachusetts, and critical rhetoric of the last few presidential campaigns has underscored those sentiments. Could the quality of government have been viewed any more negatively by policymakers of the 1880s?

The relatively recent prominence of the words "productivity," "productive," and "produce" in the public sector vocabulary must, then, be understood against this history of the public sector's failure to gain public approval. Although that foundering depresses some civil servants, many other public administrators and policy participants are demanding progress on at least three broad dimensions: measurement, systematic analysis, and responsiveness.

Renewed demands for productivity, per se, grow in part from the demonstrated shortcomings of emphases on the inner workings of administration, emphases such as civil service, management systems, and behavioral science. Those techniques were developed or adapted, and then applied to the public sector, as supposedly efficient means for converting massive input expenditures into service accomplishments. Governments have not, however, consistently demonstrated that better bureaucratic infrastrucures really improved the ratios of outputs to inputs. Although some jurisdictions spent several times as much per capita for specific services as did others with similar demographic and geographic configurations, the average voter in high *or* low expenditure communities still gripes about efficiency, still complains that the streets are not cleaned, patrolled, or fixed efficiently (Thomas, 1974: 7). More easily measured in the private sector, in the absence of similar summary statistics that could document accomplishments and defend against perceived failures, public sector productivity is discussed qualitatively and subjectively, and then often in pejorative terms, by the private sector. Slowly, too slowly, policymakers and policy implementers have come to realize that the only way to verify or refute those complaints is to do a more careful, more sophisticated job of measuring the relationship of service outputs and outcomes to a government's inputs.

In contrast to the process-efficiency focus, governments have not assured citizens that an alternative emphasis on program consequences demonstrates effective use of inputs. For example, massive investments in model cities and military machines resulted in neither model neighborhoods nor a model military. Such programs were handicapped by an overemphasis on outputs and outcomes at the expense of inputs. They demonstrated that emphasizing effectiveness at the expense of efficiency was no more productive than efficiency without regard to effect. Thus the second demand is for comprehensive, systematic public administration — a systemic perspective that productivity programs can encourage.

The third demand, for responsiveness, stems from recent rounds of inflation, recession, and concomitant fiscal crises that have increasingly pressured the public sector to install productivity measurement and improvement systems. That is, budgetary pressures have forced participants in the service delivery systems, ranging from entry-level civil servants to policy-level appointees, to respond to crises of confidence in an accelerated time frame.

THE NEW PRODUCTIVITY
MANAGEMENT SYSTEM

As a function of external pressures from individual and corporate taxpayers and internal pressures from professional public administrators, productivity in the public sector has now been recognized as a legitimate expectation, as a rational and lasting emphasis insofar as it is a central assumption of public administration, and the underlying premise of a relatively loosely coordinated series of efforts to date. Pressured public administration is tending to respond to that premise in pragmatic, productive terms — fairly radically and very likely advantageously. The most prominent characteristics of the new public management system appear to include, but are not limited to, the following: productivity measurement and auditing, joint labor-management cooperation, incentives tied to performance, training for productivity, information resources and microcomputer applications, and new means of financing productivity investments.

PRODUCTIVITY MEASUREMENT AND AUDITING

The state of the art of productivity measurement is such that policymaking and policy-implementing officials no longer need bow to casual assumptions that government's productivity cannot be measured. The accelerated application of quantitative approaches to the objective evaluation of government programs is especially evidenced by the measures of the Government Accounting Office and the Bureau of Labor Statistics at the Federal level, and the Urban Institute at the state and local levels (U.S. Department of Labor, 1983; see also Hatry et al., 1977, 1979). Taken as a whole, the literature on hundreds of cases defines a compendium of sophisticated measures for public sector outputs *and* outcomes. Although multiple measures of public sector services cannot usually be aggregated meaningfully, recent research has even suggested ways to combine quantifications of quality and quantity (Rosen, 1981).

While productivity measurement is useful to the entire range of organizational actors, it is especially useful in the hands of staff analysts and auditors. Whether applied in the planning, management, or audit stages, when compared to measures in other organizations or to historical data valid measures provide multiple advantages, such as: generation of time-series data; identification of targets for improvement; delegation of greater operational responsibility to lower levels of management; avoidance of critical or embarrassing situations; increased analysis of linkages between resource allocation and policy achievement; and more sophisticated and comprehensive benefit-cost linkages.

JOINT LABOR-MANAGEMENT COOPERATION

Pressured public administration now recognizes that a prerequisite to productivity improvement, and a counterforce to negative and misleading assumptions, is cooperation between the organization's policymakers and the work force (defined as labor *and* middle management). It is by no means the traditional suggestion box. Under various rubrics such as productivity committees and councils, gain sharing, or quality circles, the premises are that productive ideas are equally distributed within organizations, that the top-down characteristics of bureaucracy must be replaced by an equal relationship that draws as much of its creative energy from the bottom as from the top, that makes innovation and risk taking possible, that rewards all members of the organization, and that gives labor and middle management a major psychological stake in organizational improvement.

In the context of this new model, civil service unions are becoming more of a partner, less of an adversary, to public management. Improved relationships are evidenced in contractual productivity clauses authorizing joint labor-management committees (JLMCs) or informal agreements to experiment with quality circles (QCs) (Blair et al., 1982). Unions still, of course, have their own particular interests, but increasingly productivity savings are to their members' advantage. As labor-management groups become a forum for discussion of mutual problems, without infringing on management or labor's contractual rights to collective bargaining or normal grievance procedures, "productivity" is less likely to be a dirty word in the labor vocabulary.

Successful cases of labor-management cooperation indicate that this tool works most effectively and credibly when management understands that it is important to recognize, and rely on, the institutional memory and experience of the unions, which may exceed that of public sector executives in politically appointed policy positions; when programs to change the organizational environment produce tangible productivity benefits for employer, employees, unions, and citizens; when functioning measurement and reporting systems are in place to document the benefits of labor-management innovations; when management commits resources to support JLMC or QC efforts through ongoing training and facilitator programs; and when programs begin voluntarily on a small scale, expand incrementally based on documented success, and are phased out if no longer useful.

MONETARY AND NONMONETARY INCENTIVES

The complex, interdependent nature of public organizations underscores the logic of group-based rewards for group-achieved increases in productivity, whether through JLMCs, QCs, or collective bargaining agreements. Governments have also experimented with individual, performance-based financial incentives, often on the model of the federal 1978 Civil Service Reform Act, which created a Senior Executive Service, the members of which can be substantially and differentially rewarded for meritorious achievements. Although the federal government has now backed off somewhat from this model under the present administration, the innovation has taken root in various other public personnel systems.

Nonmonetary incentives are surprisingly widespread. Job redesign strategies (in addition to the participative JLMCs and QCs referred to above) include approaches to team problem-solving and operations; job rotation, enlargement, and enrichment; lateral "promotions" and career ladders; awards and recognition; flexible working hours and job sharing; improved working conditions and less formal "dress codes" or expectations; and dozens of derivatives in hundreds of jurisdictions.

TRAINING FOR PRODUCTIVITY

Old assumptions as to the validity of on-the-job training are being superseded by an appreciation of the complexity of managerial skills, the trained competence necessary to the management of public services, and training's legitimate role as a nonmonetary incentive.

Although productivity-specific training, as such, is an under-utilized resource (in part because of the discontinuation of federal IPA funds), disaggregated training for public sector productivity is a multibillion-dollar effort. In traditional terms, training has included workshops on such competencies as management and supervision, leadership, auditing, EDP, MBO, project management, decision making, budget management, systems analysis, and program evaluation. Beyond such traditional investments, however, productivity-specific training focuses on components of what are defined herein as a productivity management system: measurement, auditing, joint labor-management cooperation, monetary and nonmonetary incentives, information resources, computer applications, and the financing of productivity investments.

INFORMATION RESOURCES AND
MICROCOMPUTER APPLICATIONS

There is an increasingly sizable and sophisticated body of knowledge about effective productivity improvement programs, a body that is cumulative and that dates back several decades. That knowledge is drawn from analyses of hundreds of cases, whether successful or not. Although much productivity experience has escaped national attention, there are some persistent trackers (such as the Urban Institute and the National Center for Public Productivity), and an ever-increasing number of trackable cases have been identified (Goldberg and Holzer, 1983). Some cases are reported widely (such as the use of quality circles in the Norfolk naval shipyard), but too few of the many successful projects have been widely replicated, despite one observation that, in this context, "plagiarism is a virtue" (Rosen, 1984; U.S Office of Personnel Management, 1981).

Unfortunately the fallout from fiscal crises has limited the ability of policymakers and managers to participate in information networks (and, typically, labor was never expected to participate at all) ranging across professional associations, conferences, workshops, training, journal subscriptions, and mere phone calls. Some, but very few, organizations are members of larger networks such as Public Technology or Control Data's Local Government Information Network (LOGIN, Control Data Corporation, Minneapolis). The underutilization of information is surprising, for, in comparison to other means of implementing productivity improvement policies, information is a cheap, abundant, and available resource.

One remedy for that shortfall is increasing utilization of microcomputers. Despite a scarcity of software designed specifically for application to public sector problem solving, desk-top microcomputers have available sufficient generic programs, useful to the public or private sectors, for such purposes as word processing, accounting and financial analysis, current and cumulative measures of efficiency and effectiveness, graphic representations of data bases and trends, improved speed and magnitude of access to information, training, inventory control, and a virtually limitless range of policy-relevant opportunities for planning, decision making, organizing, leading, and controlling. Futhermore, hand-held micros developed specifically for public sector applications also offer opportunities for more specialized applications in the field, such as checking for chronic violators, printing summonses instead of completing forms with often illegible handwriting, and reducing reporting requirements by recording data for paperless entry into agency data bases.

FINANCING PRODUCTIVITY INVESTMENTS

Systematic, detailed, methodical financial analysis is starting to replace the incremental crisis style of management as a prerequisite to funding productive investments. Although governments are seemingly unlikely to have funds for timely experimentation and investment in computers and other innovations, some jurisdictions reveal creative approaches despite financial constraints. They also illustrate the principle that most productivity improvement approaches can be applied to large-, medium-, and small-scale operations.

The Department of Defense, for example, allocates special funds specifically for productivity-improvement projects, utilizing the budget process as an incentive and means for productivity programs (Rosen, 1984). Dayton, Ohio, supports competitive technological improvement in which departments do not have to use their regular operating funds for the technology projects, although cost savings are deducted from operating budgets; the aggregate impact of many small projects has been substantial (Rosen, 1984). New Jersey's Productivity Investment Account is a revolving fund for projects with short payoffs (under five years); while it is independent of the budget process, proposed projects require the signed commitment of a cabinet officer (Rosen, 1984).

LIMITING FACTORS

Although the public bureaucracy is under new pressures to be productive, the same tensions that limited achievements under the old systems may tend to subvert the new. Thus it is important to analyze programs to date as much in terms of their possibilities as for their often unanticipated implications and subtleties: bureaupathologies, limitations of Japanese and business models, capital starvation, legal obstacles, and labor-management constraints.

BUREAUCRACY'S PATHOLOGICAL CONSEQUENCES

Our large private and public organizations share an underlying ill — bureaucratic stagnation — which current, technologically oriented policy and research virtually ignore. Although the bureaucracy is supposedly an efficient tool for both public and private organizations, it is increasingly apparent that unintended consequences of the bureaucratic structure have a very limiting effect on productivity. Too often bureaucracy is gripped by a mentality of mediocrity, entangled in red tape, rule ridden, enmeshed in paper, and unresponsive to its creators. The bureaucratic environment is characterized by an overemphasis on formality, rules and regulations, and security. It is epitomized by the sufficiency of mediocrity, by the adage "Don't rock the boat," by a stifling loss of independence, by a misdirection of energies to solving personal problems of promotion, to playing office politics, to abusing and discrediting fellow employees. Thus bureaucracies have simply degenerated into machines that may be too impersonal and too insensitive for effective, productive responses to public demands. Fueled by fears, such machines produce at very low levels and with many errors. Daily, the news media report examples of the unintended consequences of bureaucratic structures, instances in which our large organizations wasted not only our resources, but also our time and our lives (Holzer, 1984).

THE JAPANESE MODEL

Japanese management, one variant of which is "Theory Z," has been widely touted in the American private sector as a corrective to low productivity, and is now receiving increasing attention in the public sector (Helfand, 1983: 203-207).

Despite general agreement that Japanese-showcased participative management techniques have improved employee commitment and organizational productivity, possible limitations of the Japanese model in the American public sector may follow from recognizing that quality circles are rarely, if ever, used by the Japanese for local government; that after an initial burst of interest, quality circles are losing popularity in the U.S. private sector just as the public sector is increasing its involvement; that local government in Japan is characterized by a "union versus management" attitude rather than the more cooperative atmosphere evident in large Japanese corporations; that Japanese workers are likely to identify with their employing organizations, while American workers tend to identify with their professions or occupations; that Japanese organizations rely less upon staff departments and more upon vertical communication than do American bureaucracies (Helfand, 1983; Rosen, 1984).

THE BUSINESS MODEL

Many public sector productivity programs are heavily influenced by private sector assumptions, often emanating from representatives of business on oversight boards or executives on loan (for example, New York City's Municipal Assistance Corporation and Emergency Financial Control Board). Yet the assumed utility of a private sector model is constraining. For at least a century, "common sense" has held that the private sector offers the public sector models of management systems that can be applied easily to service delivery; that profit-driven employees are more motivated, while the civil service work ethic sags; that there is less energy and innovation in the public sector.

But government-business comparisons are not black and white. The "model" private sector has a productivity growth rate among the lowest in the industrialized world. Of late, it has more often declined than improved. It is also much more difficult to quantify, and therefore to enlighten the public as to progress about, public sector productivity. Long overdue wage comparability with the private sector has, in some jurisdictions, made it appear as though increases in government's costs are outrunning increases in output. In other jurisdictions, relatively low salaries hamper government's ability to deliver services. And in almost all jurisdictions the disparity in public-private salaries at the upper levels has often discouraged the very best policy-setting and -implementing talent from entering or remaining in government.

CAPITAL UNDERFUNDING

The private sector well understands the need for long-term investments in profit-making facilities, technologies, and human resources. But the same businesspersons who invest stockholders' billions in public organizations (for examples, see Cordtz, 1971; Haggerty, 1972; Rosenbloom, 1973; Grace, 1984). The resulting shortfall in capital funds handicaps governments, for it is now prohibitively billions in public organizations (for examples, see Cordtz, 1971; Haggerty, 1972; Rosenbloom, 1973; Grace, 1983). The resulting shortfall in capital funds handicaps governments, for it is now prohibitively difficult to acquire resources for requisite opportunities. The irony is that, while cutback management is supposed to improve productivity, that proposition is valid only in the short run. In the long run, public organizations often lack the capacity to invest in technology: computers, telecommunications, vehicles, maintenance facilities, energy-saving devices, and energy-efficient buildings; in the public sector, such purchases are more arduous because of an exaggerated fear among policymakers of misspending tax dollars. In the long run, public organizations often lack the capacity to invest in their work forces: training, education at the master's degree level, medical and psychological support services, and labor-management cooperation; typically, government civil servants spend only about one-fifth as much as the private sector on training, on their human capital. In the long run, they lack the capacity to invest in information: data bases, clearinghouses, publications, objective studies, case lessons; for every organization that attempts to improve public sector productivity, there are perhaps a dozen or more that focus on the private sector.

BROAD STATUTORY AND
PROCEDURAL OBSTACLES

Politically motivated contracts and laws that reduce management's prerogatives are, unfortunately, instruments of productivity-constraining policies. Their survival is testimony to excesses we can no longer afford, to the strength of entrenched interests, and to the inertia of the legislative process.

A related structural problem, which stems from an overemphasis on top-down oversight in fear-ridden bureaucracies, is the laborious approval process for contracts. It inadvertently delays management improvements and discourages the capacity building that policymakers often overtly demand. A burdensome contracting process also discourages true competitive bidding, as does the multiple approval process for federally funded, state-funnelled, city-administered programs that requires three sets of overseers to have their say. At each level, "watchdogs" win points for raising questions and obstacles "in the taxpayer's interest." Yet the sum of those hurdles is a failure to improve productivity. Unfortunately, their ethic is often one of minimizing expenditures (no matter the loss of necessary services caused by unnecessary delays) rather than investing in or facilitating productive actions.

DIFFERENTIAL REWARDS

Governments may not be able to tolerate a labor-management environment in which some employees are rewarded for better productivity, clearly defined and measured, while others lack the same opportunity (Hayes, 1977). What of the staff personnel who indirectly contribute to line productivity by providing excellent recruitment and selection and training, funds and evaluation systems, scheduling and computer operations? How are they to be rewarded?

Some policy-level executives sidestep this problem by arguing for the separation of productivity and compensation, by separating gain-sharing programs from collective bargaining issues. But governmentwide productivity suggests a large pool of savings into which every union leader will want his or her members to dip — and with strong justification. In the end, as has happened with the short-lived, "productivity-based" cost of living allowances (COLAs) in the 1970s, governments may be forced to share productivity savings across the board and across departments (many of which are interrelated in solving productivity problems) rather than on a specific per-shift, piece-rate basis (Hayes, 1977: 97-104). At the least, these considerations suggest that productivity cannot be contained in a forum separate from the collective bargaining process, nor can all monetary issues be moved from the productivity council to the collective bargaining arena.

The "profit motive" is often portrayed as a means with which to match the efficiencies of the private sector, but some unreasonable, yet tangible, realities may intervene. Despite promising experiments in cooperation between government and work force, voters, businesspersons, and the news media often hold biased assumptions as to "underworked" or "lazy" civil servants so strongly that "get tough" politicians almost always play to those beliefs rather than take risks. In Nassau County, contractual provisions for a joint productivity improvement plan were negated because an elected board held that employees did not deserve incentives to be productive (Hayes, 1977: 71-96). In New York City, Mayor Koch (as reported in the *New York Times*) originally rejected gain-sharing innovations in the Department of Sanitation until workers produced "a full day's work for a full day's pay." In each such case politics triumphed over productivity (at least temporarily) and century-old images of "businesslike" behavior over new antibureaucratic innovations that business itself is beginning to adopt.

CONCLUSION

The substantial research and experience with de facto public sector productivity programs in thousands of organizations is sufficient to dispel misconceptions that public sector managers care little about operational efficiency and effectiveness. It is true that some managers have given up trying to improve productivity or have given in to low expectations. But a more comprehensive view of public administrators indicates that, as policy implementers who are on board for the long term, many are professionally committed to productivity improvement. Their commitments are at least as strong as those of transient policymakers, and their innovations are at least as promising and sophisticated as those proposed by their sometimes condescending corporate critics.

If public administrators receive enlightened political support, if they are treated as administrative professionals on a par with their private sector colleagues, if they are relieved of artificial constraints on financial rewards for performance and management prerogatives, and if they are allowed to become less bureaucratic, then innovative, clearly focused programs and initiatives will more rapidly and widely be developed and implemented. And this will occur in spite of, as well as because of, budget cuts and limited resources.

Such public sector productivity programs promise to benefit all interested parties in a win-win relationship. Employees will benefit from more equitable distribution of workload and more pleasant working conditions, and sometimes by earning more money. Managers will benefit because they can produce anticipated results when they maintain improved control over workload and work levels. Elected officials will benefit from efficiently and effectively operated services, which the public expects and appreciates. Clients will benefit from improved services, reduced waiting time, and fewer frustrations related to dealing with the government. And, as the "bottom line," the general public will benefit from more efficient and effective uses of tax dollars.

REFERENCES

BLAIR, J. D., S. L. COHEN, and J. V. HURWITZ (1982) "Quality circles." Public Productivity Review 6: 9-18.

BROWN, J. C. (1980) A Selective Bibliography and Specific Bibliographies Relevant to Management Improvement and Productivity Enhancement in the United States Government. Washington, DC: Office of Personnel Management.

COE, C. K. (1981) "Problems small governments encounter with productivity improvement." Southern Review of Public Administration 5: 114-123.

CORDTZ, D. (1971) "City hall discovers productivity." Fortune (October): 92-96.

EDDY, W. B. (1981) Public Organization Behavior and Development. Cambridge, MA: Winthrop.

GOLDBERG, J. and M. HOLZER [eds.] (1983) The Resource Guide to Public Productivity. New York: National Center for Public Productivity.

GRACE, P. [chair] (1984) Final Report of the President's Commission on Economy and Efficiency in Government. Washington, DC: Government Printing Office.

GREINER, J. H. et al. (1981) Productivity and Motivation. Washington, DC: Urban Institute.

HAGGERTY, P. E. (1972) "Productivity: industry isn't the only place where it's a problem." Forbes (February 1): 43-45.

HATRY, H. P. and D. M. FISK (1971) Improving Productivity and Productivity Measurement in Local Government. Washington, DC: Urban Institute.

HATRY, H. P. et al. (1981) Practical Program Evaluation for State and Local Governments. Washington, DC: Urban Institute.

——— (1980) "Performance measurement principles and techniques: an overview for local government." Public Productivity Review 4: 312-339.

——— (1979) Efficiency Measurement for Local Government Services: Some Initial Suggestions. Washington, DC: Urban Institute.

——— (1977) How Effective Are Your Community Services? Washington, DC: Urban Institute.

HAYES, F. O. (1977) Productivity in Local Government. Lexington, MA: D. C. Heath.

HELFAND, G. (1983) "Symposium on Japanese management." Public Productivity Review 7 (June).

HOLZER, M. (1984) "Battling bureaucracy." (unpublished)

——— (1976) Productivity in Public Organizations. Port Washington, NY: Kennikat.

KENDRICK, J. W. and E. GROSSMAN (1980) Productivity in the United States: Trends and Cycles. Baltimore: Johns Hopkins University Press.

MANN, S. Z. (1980) "The politics of productivity: state and local focus." Public Productivity Review 4: 352-367.

MARK, J. A. (1979) "Measuring federal productivity." Civil Service Journal 19: 20-23.

MERCER, J. L. and R. J. PHILLIPS [eds.] (1981) Public Technology: Key to Improved Government Productivity. New York: Amacom.

METHE, D. T. and J. L. PERRY (1980) "The impacts of collective bargaining on local government services: a review of research." Public Administration Review 40: 359-371.

MIRINGOFF, L. M. [ed.] (1981) Local Government Productivity: A Report on the Proceedings of the Marist College Symposium on Local Government Productivity. Poughkeepsie, NY: Marist College.

MUSHKIN, S. J. and F. H. SANDIFER (1979) Personnel Management and Productivity in City Government. Lexington, MA: D. C. Heath.

National Association of State Budget Officers (1982) State Budget, Management and Productivity Improvement Projects: A Compilation of Projects, Studies, and Reports. Washington, DC: Author.

National Science Foundation, Directorate for Engineering and Applied Sciences (1980) Selected Reports on Public Service Delivery and Urban Problems: A Bibliography. Washington, DC: Author.

North Carolina, Department of Administration (1980) A Productive Government: Report of the Governor's Commission on Governmental Productivity, January 1979-June 1980. Raleigh: Author.

City of Phoenix, Arizona (1979 and subsequent annual reports) The Phoenix Productivity Program. Phoenix: Author.

POLLACK, N. F. (1979) "Productivity in the public sector: the impact of collective bargaining and other considerations." Public Productivity Review 3: 4-16.

Price Waterhouse (1980) Productivity Improvement Manual for Local Government Officials. New York: Author.

RIDLEY, C. E. and H. A. SIMON (1943) Measuring Municipal Activities: A Survey of Suggested Criteria for Appraising Administration. Chicago: International City Manager's Association.

ROSEN, E. D. [ed.] "Proceedings of the Second National Conference on Public Sector Productivity." Public Productivity Review 8 (Spring).

——— (1981) "O.K. work: incorporating quality into the productivity equation." Public Productivity Review 5: 207-217.

ROSENBLOOM, R. S. (1973) "The real productivity crisis is in government." Harvard Business Review (September): 156-164.

City of San Diego, California (1980) Total Performance Management Project: City of Long Beach. San Diego: Author.

SCHEINER, J. I. (1981) "Productivity improvement in the Pennsylvania Depart-
ment of Transportation." Public Productivity Review 5: 14-20.
State Government Productivity Research Center (1981) Improving Productivity
Through Monetary Incentives: North Carolina's Bonus System. Lexington,
KY: Council of State Governments.
——— (1980) New Jersey's Productivity Improvement Investment Account.
Lexington, KY: Council of State Governments.
STEVENS, J. M. (1981) "A comparative and contingency approach to productivity
in human service organizations." Public Productivity Review 5: 380-397.
THOMAS, J. (1974) So, Mr. Mayor, You Want to Improve Productivity.
Washington, DC: National Commission on Productivity.
TUTTLE, T. C. et al. (1981) Measuring and Enhancing Organizational Productivity:
An Annotated Bibliography. Washington, DC: Air Force Human Resources
Laboratory.
U.S. Department of Labor, Bureau of Labor Statistics (1983) A BLS Reader on
Productivity (Bulletin 2171; prepared by staff of the Office of Productivity and
Technology). Washington, DC: Government Printing Office.
U.S. General Accounting Office (1980) Evaluating a Performance Measurement
System: A Guide for Congress and Federal Agencies. Washington, DC: Gov-
ernment Printing Office.
U.S Office of Personel Management, Workforce Effectiveness Development Group
(1981) The Quality Circle Program of the Norfolk Naval Shipyard (WPR-17).
Washington, DC: Government Printing Office.
——— (1980) Manager's Guide for Improving Productivity. Washington, DC: Gov-
ernment Printing Office.
USILANER, B. L. (1981) "Can we expect productivity improvement in the federal
government?" Public Productivity Review 5: 237-246.
WASHNIS, G. J. (1980) Productivity Improvement Handbook for State and Local
Government. New York: John Wiley.
Wharton School, Management and Behavioral Science Center, University of
Pennsylvania (1980) Improving Productivity and Quality of Working Life in the
Public Sector: Pioneering Initiatives in Labor-Management Cooperation (final
report on "Project Network" to the U.S. Civil Service Commission, Office of
Personnel Management). Philadelphia: Author.
WILKINS, D. (1979) "A productivity program for local governments." Public
Productivity Review 3: 17-25.
WILSON, W. (1887) "The study of administration." Journal of Politics.

4

THE PRIVATE SECTOR WORKPLACE

DANIEL J. B. MITCHELL

University of California, Los Angeles

Productivity growth is generally acknowledged to be the source of rising living standards, improved real wages, and, therefore, a society with less chance for divisive arguments over dividing the income "pie." In a country where the pie is expanding and where all groups are getting at least some share of the gains, the chances for social turmoil over income distribution are lessened. But in the 1970s and early 1980s, a slowdown in productivity growth threatened these benefits.

Various hypotheses have been advanced to explain why productivity performance in the private sector deteriorated in the 1970s. Some of these propositions will be reviewed in this chapter. However, it will be argued that the stop-go macroeconomic policies that characterized the 1970s and early 1980s were not conducive to productivity growth, but that compensation systems that reward employees on the basis of employer economic circumstance — known as "gain-sharing" plans — can help alleviate the macroeconomic instability that characterized the period of productivity slowdown. Such gain-sharing plans are proposed below as a productivity-enhancement device. It will be argued that gain sharing is the natural accompaniment to other forms of quality of work life reform and that the union wage concessions of 1979-1983 have created a climate of special receptiveness to gain sharing.

THE RECENT STATISTICAL RECORD
OF THE UNITED STATES

As noted, the history of productivity in the United States over the past decade has not been one of a rapidly expanding pie. Table 4.1 shows trends in conventionally measured productivity gains — output per hour of actual labor input — over the period 1960 to 1981. For the overall economy, the annual rate of productivity improvement was 2.9 percent through 1973, but only 0.8 percent thereafter. The story is quantitatively different in the subsectors of the private economy shown in Table 4.1, but qualitatively, the same story is told. Productivity growth is dramatically lower after 1973 than before.

These trends are reflected in real-wage developments. Table 4.2 provides data for total compensation (including fringe benefits and payroll taxes) and hourly earnings (excluding fringes and payroll taxes) in real terms. The most common price deflator used in such calculations is the Consumer Price Index (CPI). However, there were various complaints about upward biases in the CPI, especially during the period after 1973 (Mitchell, 1982b). As an alternative, therefore, the table also presents real-wage data based on the implicit price deflator for the nonfarm business sector, a measure that avoids some of the difficulties of the CPI, and that more closely mirrors domestic U.S. price developments. As can be seen, the real-wage movements for nonfarm business compensation using the implicit deflator exactly parallel the productivity trends for that sector shown on Table 4.1. The productivity slowdown seems to have had a direct influence on real-wage incomes.

Various explanations for the productivity slowdown have been put forward and will be reviewed below. However, an obvious place to seek an explanation is in the capital investment area. Specifically,

TABLE 4.1   Trend in U.S. Output per Hour by Sector, 1960-1981
             (in percentages)

	1960-1973	1973-1981
Private business sector	2.9	.8
Nonfarm business sector	2.6	.6
Nonfinancial corporations	2.8	1.0
Manufacturing	3.4	1.5

SOURCE: *Monthly Labor Review* (1981: 101; 1983: 79).

TABLE 4.2   Trends in Real Nonfarm Compensation, 1960-1981
(in percentages)

	1960-1973 (1)	1973-1981 (2)
Real nonfarm business compensation per hour		
based on CPI	2.3	−.3
based on implicit price deflator[a]	2.6	.6
Real hourly earnings index[b]		
based on CPI	1.7	−1.1
based on implicit price deflator[a]	2.0	−.2

SOURCE: U.S. President (1983: 206-208).
a. Deflator for nonfarm, business sector.
b. Adjusted for overtime in manufacturing and interindustry employment shift. Applies to private, nonagricultural sector.

did a capital shortage in the 1970s produce a reduction in the growth of the capital/labor ratio, thus reducing measured productivity growth? The U.S. Bureau of Labor Statistics has recently compiled data on "multifactor" (capital and labor) productivity. These data — shown in Table 4.3 — do reveal a slower rate of increase of the capital/labor ratio after 1973 (although not in manufacturing) resulting from a slowdown of capital growth and an acceleration of labor inputs, the latter reflecting a surge of young people and women entering the labor market. However, these trends in capital and labor can explain only a fraction of the slowdown in multifactor or conventionally measured productivity (Bosworth, 1982: 284).

LESSONS FROM ABROAD

Whatever caused the productivity slowdown, its influence appears to have been international in scope. Data compiled on productivity trends for manufacturing in various countries reveal a worldwide deterioration in performance. As shown in Table 4.4, in each of the ten foreign countries in which productivity in manufacturing is tracked by the Bureau of Labor Statstics, a productivity slowdown was experienced after 1973. Even Japan and West Germany, the two economic "miracle" countries, were not immune, although in absolute terms their productivity growth rate exceeded that of the United States.

TABLE 4.3 Trends in Capital, Labor, and Multifactor Productivity, 1960-1979 (in percentages)

	Annual Growth in Capital/Labor Ratio			Annual Growth in Capital	Annual Growth in Hours	Annual Growth in Multifactor Productivity[a]
	Private Business	*Nonfarm Private Business*	*Manufacturing*	*Private Business*	*Private Business*	*Private Business*
1960-1973	2.6	2.3	1.8	3.9	1.3	2.0
1973-1979	1.3	1.2	2.9	3.2	1.9	.4

SOURCE: U.S. Bureau of Labor Statistics (press release USDL '83-153, April 6, 1983).
a. Inputs of labor and capital included.

TABLE 4.4   International Productivity Trends in Manufacturing,
1960-1981 (in percentages)

	Annual Rate of Change in Output per Hour		Mean Unemployment Rate[a]	
	1960-1973	1973-1981	1960-1973	1974-1981
United States	3.0	1.7	4.9	6.9
Canada	4.5	1.4	5.3	7.3
Japan	10.7	6.8	1.3	2.0
France	6.0	4.6	1.9	5.3
Germany (West)	5.5	4.5	.7	2.8
Italy	6.9	3.7	3.2	3.6
United Kingdom[b]	4.3	2.2	2.9	6.3
Belgium	7.0	6.2	n.a.	n.a.
Denmark	6.4	4.1	n.a.	n.a.
Netherlands	7.6	5.1	n.a.	n.a.
Sweden	6.7	2.2	1.9[c]	2.0
Ten foreign countries	6.4	4.7	–	–

SOURCE: Output per hour data from Capdevielle et al. (1962: 4); unemployment
data from U.S. Bureau of Labor Statistics, provided to author.

a. U.S. definitions.
b. Unemployment rates are for Great Britain.
c. 1961-1973.

It is interesting to note, however, that the productivity slowdown experienced internationally tended to coincide with a period of general deterioration in macroeconomic performance. As measured by the unemployment rates in Table 4.4, the post-1973 period tended to be one of international economic slackness. There is no reason to expect a priori that a slowdown in productivity growth should lead to increased unemployment. Indeed, since reduced productivity means that more people are required to produce a given output, the opposite might be expected initially. It is more reasonable, therefore, to assume that the economic slackness reflected in high unemployment contributed to the productivity slowdown.

MACRO PERFORMANCE AND PRODUCTIVITY

There is a general tendency, long noted in the literature, for years of "good" macroeconomic performance — of economic expansion — to be associated with good productivity performance. Table 4.5 makes this tendency apparent. The table examines productivity performance in each year during the period 1960-1981. On the left-hand side of the table are listed those years in which productivity growth

TABLE 4.5   Cyclical Impact on U.S. Productivity, 1960-1981
(in percentages)

Years in which Productivity Growth was greater than or equal to 2.1%			Years in which Productivity Growth was 2.0% or less		
Year	Productivity Growth	Change in Unemployment Rate from That Year to Next	Year	Productivity Growth	Change in Unemployment Rate from That Year to Next
1961	3.3	−1.2	1960	1.5	+1.2
1962	3.8	+ .2	1969	.2	+1.4
1963	3.7	− .5	1970	.8	+1.0
1964	4.3	− .7	1974	−2.4	+2.9
1965	3.5	− .7	1978	.6	− .3
1966	3.1	0	1979	− .9	+1.3
1967	2.2	− .2	1980	− .7	+ .5
1968	3.3	− .1	1981	1.8	+2.1
1971	3.6	− .3			
1972	3.5	− .7			
1973	2.6	+ .7			
1975	2.2	− .8			
1976	2.4	− .6			

SOURCE: U.S. President (1983: 199, 209).

exceeded 2 percent per annum, while the right-hand side lists those years in which productivity growth was less than 2 percent per annum. Accompanying each year is information on the change in the unemployment rate from that year to the next, an index of economic expansion (if the change is negative) or decline (it it is positive).

Thirteen years during the 1960-1981 period featured productivity growth above 2 percent. In all but three of those years, the unemployment rate was falling. In one of the three exceptions, the unemployment rate was unchanged. Eight years featured productivity growth of less than 2 percent. In all but one of those years, unemployment increased. The association of economic expansion and good productivity performance is quite apparent.

ALTERNATIVE EXPLANATIONS OF THE U.S. PRODUCTIVITY SLOWDOWN

Macroeconomic performance has not been the focus of much of the research on the productivity slowdown. Indeed, productivity researchers often attempt to "correct" for the business cycle effect in making their calculations. The analysis seems to break down into various camps. There is the Denison approach, which seeks to parcel out the "blame" for the productivity slowdown among various explanations and which concludes that much of the slowdown is unexplained. There is the Baily approach, which suggests that the sharp relative rise in energy prices played an important role in the productivity slowdown. And there is the Darby approach, which suggests that there is an element of statistical illusion in the productivity slowdown due to data distortions caused by wage-price controls in the early 1970s. Finally, there is the view, popularized by Lester Thurow, of multiple causes of the productivity slowdown.

DENISON'S MYSTERY

One of the most widely quoted analyses of the productivity slowdown appeared in 1979, authored by noted productivity expert Edward F. Denison (1979a, 1979b). Denison's analysis sought to explain the productivity slowdown by comparing sources of productivity change during 1948-1973 and 1973-1976. In previous work, Denison found that there was always a positive unexplained residual to productivity growth that might be attributed to "advances in knowledge," broadly defined. He found, however, that the residual factor in explaining national income per person employed shifted from +1.4 percent per annum to −.75 percent between the two periods. This shift in the residual or unknown factor dominated all other known explanations such as changes in demographic composition, educational attainment, and the capital/labor ratio.

Having completed his statistical analysis, Denison confronted a variety of hypotheses that might explain the residual factor. He found little that could explain a major part of it. For example, the acknowledged decrease in research and development expenditures is not found by Denison to have had a large role in the decline. Nor does he find some of the more hard-to-quantify explanations convincing, such as "People don't want to work any more." While Denison's work has been subject to rather casual criticism (Stone, 1980), it is difficult to fault the care and caution with which he handled his data.

BAILY'S ENERGY PRICE SHIFT

The conventional measure of capital is the capital stock, often at replacement value. However, the depressed stock market of the 1970s indicated that investors placed a lower value on corporate assets than the replacement cost. To Martin Baily (1981a, 1981b), this fact suggested that the actual flow of services from the capital stock might be less than indicated by the conventional assumption of stock-flow proportionality. An obvious candidate for causing a rapid obsolescence of capital was the dramatic change in energy prices. Some capital equipment might have ceased to be economically viable, if it were originally designed as a heavy energy consumer. Baily notes particularly the experience of airlines, which hastily scrapped fuel-guzzling planes once the relative price of energy rose. He also suggests other causes of abnormally fast capital obsolescence during the late 1970s.

In effect, Baily's approach is to explain the residual factor in productivity as a statistical illusion caused by the way in which capital is normally measured. To Baily, the true capital/labor ratio fell sufficiently (perhaps) to explain the poor productivity performance in conventional economic terms. But as Robert J. Gordon (1981) pointed out, although airline examples may be persuasive to Baily, airline productivity and alternative sources of data on utilization of particular plane models do not support the notion of a sudden obsolescence of capital. If the airline case — which should be a prime example — cannot be clearly documented, the evidence is bound to be even fuzzier in other sectors. Bosworth (1982), too, had difficulty in finding sectoral evidence of widespread capital obsolescence. However, Baily (1982) does find some association with the capital intensity of manufacturing industries and the degree to which the productivity slowdown affected them.

DARBY'S SKEPTICISM

A system of wage and price controls was imposed in mid-1971 under the Nixon administration in an attempt to stem inflation. The controls went through various forms and phases until they were abolished (except for oil) in 1974. If controls were partially evaded, so that official prices understated true transactions prices, then the real GNP would be overstated, thus exaggerating the absolute level of productivity in 1973. Hence measured productivity from the precontrols period to 1973 would be overstated. From 1973 to the post-controls period, measured productivity would be understated. According to Michael Darby (1982), the price-control explanation for the U.S. productivity decline is more persuasive than the oil-price story.

Darby is quite cautious in pushing this viewpoint, stating that "diverse opinions" are possible. The worldwide nature of the productivity slowdown raises a problem for Darby, since not all countries had price controls. When Denison considered the price-control explanation, he dismissed it because of the magnitude of the error in price measurement that would be required to change his results substantially. Denison (1979b: 19-20) also noted that the Federal Reserve Board index of industrial production, which does not rely on price data to measure real output, yields results similar to his GNP-based study.

THUROW'S "DEATH BY A THOUSAND CUTS"

Lester Thurow (1980, 1981) has argued that America's productivity problem is due to a convergence of many factors. The shift of population from agriculture to the rest of the economy — typically a source of productivity growth in developed countries — has largely run its course in the United States. Extractive industries are experiencing diminishing returns. The run up in energy prices led to substitution of labor for energy. Restrictive monetary policies — aimed at counteracting inflation — depressed demand and raised real interest rates, thus discouraging new capital investment. Moreover, some capital investment has been mandated to go toward pollution controls and similar purposes, uses that do not increase measured output. Finally, the baby-boom generation hit the labor market in the 1970s without a concomitant jump in the proportion of GNP devoted to new capital investment. All of these factors, Thurow believes, interacted to produce the productivity slowdown.

CONCLUSIONS FROM THE DEBATE

Although the various researchers have alternative explanations for the productivity slowdown (or, as in the case of Denison, feel they know what factors were *not* primarily responsible), recommendations for improving productivity performance tend to follow conventional lines. Even if a "capital shortage" was not a major explanation for the slowdown, encouraging increased capital investment would help in the future. Hence there is support for steps that might increase national saving (and investment) across the opinion spectrum — as well as concern about the dissaving entailed in projections of large federal budget deficits (Bosworth, 1982, U.S. President, 1983: 77-95). Even if a slippage in research and development was not a major influence on the productivity slowdown, there is widespread support for increasing R&D in the future (Denison, 1979b: 6-8). Economists have often expressed concern about the effect on productivity of newer forms of government regulation in the health and safety area, largely because such regulations are formulated without explicit cost/benefit analysis (Crandall, 1981). However, since these issues have been widely debated elsewhere, they will not be pursued further here.

THE STOP-GO PROBLEM

Evidence has already been presented that weak productivity performance is associated with poor macroeconomic performance. Michael Bruno (1982), for example, estimated that 40 percent of the worldwide productivity slowdown in manufacturing after 1973 was due to government-induced demand squeezes imposed to counteract inflation. However, even this estimate is based on output per unit of *actual* labor input. An alternative measure, output per unit of *potential* labor input, makes the need for a macroeconomic solution even more apparent.

Table 4.6 shows the significance of the alternative potential concept. Column 1 presents real GNP per actual employee during the period 1973-1981, a productivity measure that grew at a disappointing annual rate of 0.5 percent. Column 2, in contrast, shows the real GNP per potential employee, defined in terms of the de Leeuw and Holloway (1982) estimates of a high-employment unemployment rate. Potential employment represents the number of employees who would have been employed had the economy remained at high employment throughout the period. As it happened, in 1973 the economy was at high employment (which de Leeuw and Holloway estimated at the time to be a 4.9 percent unemployment rate), so that the 1973 estimates for the two columns of Table 4.6 represents the same absolute levels. Thereafter, however, column 2 remains well below column 1 since the economy does not return to high employment at any time. Thus there was considerable productivity waste after 1973.

The reason the economy did not return to its 1973 level of operation was conscious economic policy aimed at reducing and controlling inflation. During part of the 1971 and all of 1972, a system of wage and price controls was imposed to deal with what then seemed to be a totally unacceptable rate of inflation of 5-6 percent. In 1973, however, just as the Nixon administration attempted to remove the controls,

TABLE 4.6   Real GNP per Actual and Potential Employee, 1973-1981

Year	Real GNP per Employee[a] 1973 = 100 (1)	Real GNP per Potential Employee[b] 1973 = 100 (2)
1973	100.0	100.0
1974	100.0	96.9
1975	100.0	94.1
1976	103.7	96.8
1977	103.7	99.3
1978	104.4	101.1
1979	104.3	101.3
1980	103.4	99.1
1981	104.3	99.4
Annual Rate of Change, 1973-1981	.5%	− .1%

SOURCE: Calculated from data appearing in de Leeuw and Holloway (1982: 25) and U.S. President (1983: 175, 196).

a. Includes armed forces.
b. The high-employment civilian unemployment rate was used to calculate the number of civilian unemployed at high employment. This figure was subtracted from the total labor force (including armed forces) to determine the number of potential employees.

the U.S. economy (and the world economy) was hit by a sharp run-up of farm commodity prices and later a severe oil shock as OPEC quadrupled the price of crude petroleum. The result in most countries was a monetary restriction designed to contain the inflationary pressures and a sharp recession, which, in the United States, brought the unemployment rate up to 8.5 percent in 1975.

Although monetary policy was eventually relaxed to allow growth and stimulation, the U.S. economy was not permitted to return to its previous level of activity due to inflation fears. A second oil price shock, occasioned by political developments in Iran, triggered another recessionary episode beginning in 1979. Some turnaround was permitted in late 1980, but again inflation concerns led to another restriction. By late 1982, the unemployment rate exceeded 10 percent.

A substantial part of America's productivity dilemma, therefore, arises from the difficulty of using monetary policy to fight inflation and the resulting "stop-go" episodes. Macroeconomic policy in the late 1970s and early 1980s was dominated by actual inflation, fear of accelerating inflation, or simple uncertainty as to whether the low rate of inflation that emerged in 1982 was sustainable. The approach adopted by the Federal Reserve Board was to maintain a restrictive stance until it was clear that inflation had been "wrung out" of the economy, a posture that turned out to be costly and painful. If the productivity problem is viewed as one of obtaining maximum output from potential resources, it is clear that current institutions of macroeconomic performance require close scrutiny.

THE MICRO BEHIND THE MACRO

Although the distinction made in textbooks between macro- and microeconomics is convenient, in actual fact the economy is composed of myriad actors whose behavior is aggregated into the conventional macro performance measures such as the unemployment rate or the inflation rate. If there is a problem with the way in which the economy reacts to inflation or to anti-inflation policies, the solution is likely to reside at the local level. It will be argued below that reform of conventional wage-setting institutions could contribute substantially to the avoidance of painful episodes of anti-inflation policy, which in turn could lead to more steady and stable growth, and the greater likelihood of staying at high employment levels. Further, it will be argued that some of the more fashionable remedies for unsatisfactory productivity performance, such as quality of work life programs, worker participation in management, and labor-management cooperation need to be viewed in terms of their relationship to wage-setting practices.

INFLATION MOMENTUM AND PRICING FLEXIBILITY

If there has been any distinguishing characteristic of inflation in the U.S. experience, it has been the tendency of inflation to establish momentum. If inflation was high last year, the chances are that it will be high this year. If inflation was low last year, the chances are that it will be low this year. A high inflation rate can be reduced by tight money — the GNP implicit price deflator rose at about a 9 percent rate during 1979-1980, then dropped to around 6 percent in 1982 and even lower in early 1983. But much of the impact of tight money falls on real output rather than on pricing, so that episodes of anti-inflation policy are drawn out and painful. And broadly defined productivity (output per potential unit of input) suffers.

Suppose that inflation reacted more quickly to monetary policy. Anti-inflation episodes would be concluded more quickly and with less pain, since the inflation rate would quickly drop and the burden of the adjustment would be more on pricing and less on real output and employment. Productivity losses would be less. How much more pricing flexibility would be required to achieve this highly desirable institutional change?

Suppose that monetary policy during 1960-1981 had been set to produce exactly the same *nominal* GNP that actually occurred, but that pricing had been flexible enough so that the de Leeuw-Holloway level of high employment had been maintained continuously each year. For this result to have occurred, prices would have had to have been absolutely lower in any year when actual real GNP was below the high-employment level. Prices would have had to have been higher in those years (mainly in the late 1960s) when actual real GNP exceeded its high-employment level. Essentially, the ratio between the high-employment price level and the actual price level is the mirror image of the ratio of the high-employment GNP to actual GNP. That is, if actual GNP were 2 percent below high-employment GNP, and if nominal GNP is held constant, then a price level 2 percent below actual would have permitted actual GNP to reach its high-employment level.

Table 4.7 is based on such a calculation. Given the de Leeuw-Holloway estimate of the high-employment unemployment rate in column 1, the price level needed to maintain high employment has been calculated. The *change* in that hypothetical price level from year to year is shown in column 2 and is compared with the actual inflation rate (shown in column 3). Column 4 presents the difference between columns 2 and 3. Negative numbers in column 4 indicate years when lower inflation rates would have been needed to maintain high employment; positive numbers indicate that higher inflation rates would have been required to prevent the economy from exceeding the high-employment level of output.

The figures in Table 4.7 are purely hypothetical since they assume that actual, historical monetary policy was followed during the period 1960-1981. Obviously, had there been substantially greater pricing flexibility, monetary policy would have taken a different course, and — since monetary policy would have been a more potent anti-inflation device — the average inflation rate would have undoubtedly been much lower. Nevertheless, column 4 of Table 4.7 provides some insight into the need for greater pricing flexibility and responsiveness.

Column 4 indicates that to maintain high employment, inflation would have had to have been lower — that is, more responsive to

TABLE 4.7   High-Employment Inflation Rate, 1960-1981

	Assumed High-Employment Unemployment Rate (1)	Inflation Rate Consistent with High Employment[a,b] (2)	Actual Inflation Rate[a] (3)	Difference Between Columns 2 and 3 (4)
1960	4.2%	0.3%	1.6%	−1.3
1961	4.2	0.0	.9	− .9
1962	4.2	4.3	1.8	+2.5
1963	4.3	1.8	1.5	+ .3
1964	4.3	3.0	1.5	+1.5
1965	4.4	4.0	2.2	+1.8
1966	4.5	1.2	3.2	−2.0
1967	4.4	4.0	3.0	+1.0
1968	4.5	3.3	4.4	−1.1
1969	4.6	6.0	5.1	+1.1
1970	4.7	4.4	5.4	−1.0
1971	4.8	4.8	5.0	− .2
1972	4.9	6.3	4.2	+1.1
1973	4.9	4.6	5.8	−1.2
1974	5.0	7.9	8.8	− .9
1975	5.1	4.1	9.3	−5.2
1976	5.1	7.5	5.2	+2.3
1977	5.1	8.2	5.8	+2.4
1978	5.1	8.9	7.4	+1.5
1979	5.1	8.6	8.6	0
1980	5.1	5.9	9.3	−3.4
1981	5.1	8.4	9.4	−1.0

SOURCE: U.S. President (1983: 166-167) and de Leeuw and Holloway (1982: 25).
a. Measured by GNP implicit price deflator.
b. The actual GNP implicit price deflator was adjusted by reducing it by the GNP "gap," defined as the difference between the high-employment GNP and the actual GNP measured as percentage of the actual GNP.

monetary restraint — during the early 1960s. It says that following that period, except for the economic slowdown that occurred in 1966-1967, prices should have risen faster than they did. This would presumably have led to monetary restraint and the avoidance of the demand pressures that built up in the late 1960s and the ensuing inflationary pressures. But in the actual world of inflation momentum and lack of pricing responsiveness, the excessive expansion of the late 1960s did occur, forcing a delayed monetary contraction in the early 1970s. Column 4 indicates that high employment could have been maintained in that period had inflation been lower than actually occurred in 1970-1971. Similarly, column 4 suggests that if inflation had reacted (negatively) more quickly to monetary restraint in 1973-1975, and again in 1980-1981, two severe recessions — and their adverse effect on productivity — could have been avoided.

Obviously, there are many qualifications to this type of analysis. But the essential point remains. There is a connection between pricing responsiveness and the ability of a country to maintain a reasonably stable level of employment. If inflation has momentum — if it responds only slowly to monetary policy — then the potential for stop-go economic performance increases. Eventually, periods such as the 1970s and early 1980s are bound to occur, with substantial costs to society in terms of poor productivity performance and an absolute loss of potential output and employment.

Table 4.7 represents an "ideal" degree of pricing responsiveness that may well not be achievable. However, there is a spectrum of possible pricing behavior, and steps that could help approach the ideal must be considered seriously. It will be argued below that wage-setting and workplace reforms could play an important role in moving the U.S. economy toward a more desirable location on that spectrum, thereby improving productivity performance.

WAGES AND PRICES

Pricing and wage setting are intimately connected. This is not to say that all prices are merely markups over wages, or that wages merely reflect the cost of living. For example, prices of agricultural products are based largely on other factors, and can be radically affected by such exogenous influences as weather conditions. Wages are not rigidly linked to the cost of living; if they were, periods of declining real wages would never occur. In fact, such periods do occur.

But with all these qualifications, there is a great deal of wage and price interaction. And in recent years much attention has been focused on the rigidities of wage setting. In the United States, the private labor market is basically divisible into union and nonunion sectors. Studies of both sectors have revealed that the influence of demand conditions on wage determination is limited. This seems to be especially the case in the union sector, where long-duration contracts are common (Mitchell, 1978). But nonunion wage setting, too, is far removed from a textbook auction market. Indeed, because the nonunion sector seems to exhibit contractlike features of wage determination despite its lack of explicit union-type contracts, economists have begun theorizing about "implicit" contracting (Mitchell and Kimbell, 1982).

It seems to be the nature of wage contracting — both explicit (union) and implicit (nonunion) — that wage changes do not respond rapidly to the real state of the economy. This means that a restrictive monetary policy will not have an immediate effect on wage inflation. And because pricing has an important wage element, it means that price inflation will not be affected quickly by monetary restraint in many key sectors.

A demand restriction will thus fall mainly on real output (Okun, 1978). At the firm level, a decrease in demand will be experienced as a drop in orders at current prices. Some contraction of profit margins may occur as the firm attempts to remain competitive. However, unresponsive wage setting puts a floor on the flexibility of pricing. The firm's own wage costs will not be highly responsive, nor will the wage costs that are "contained" in the inputs the firm buys from its suppliers. Thus the demand drop must eventually translate into a decline in production and therefore a lower level of employment. Output per potential units of input will fall.

In short, the macroeconomic observation that demand restraint falls mainly on aggregate output, and affects inflation only gradually, is simply the sum of the behaviors of the many private employers (or unions and employers) that make up the economy. Wage unresponsiveness at the local level is an important explanation of why the use of monetary restraint to fight inflation is so painful. Such unresponsiveness contributes to stop-go economic policy, and hence adversely affects productivity performance.

Of course, the limited responsiveness of wage inflation can occasionally lead to *higher* levels of employment. In the early 1960s, for example, price inflation was quite low. The low level of price inflation was reflected in low rates of wage inflation. As demand picked up in the mid-1960s, wages were slow to respond. The impact of the demand pickup fell mainly on real output, reducing the unemployment rate below the high-employment levels estimated by de Leeuw and Holloway (1982). Profits and prices rose, eventually setting off a wage-price spiral. But, for a time, wage sluggishness allowed relatively high employment levels to persist.

Unfortunately, wage sluggishness is not likely to produce purely symmetrical effects. Periods of super-high employment are not likely to cancel out periods of economic slackness completely. There are constraints on how high the economy can be pushed on the upside, but no comparable limits on the downside. On the upside, technical capacity constraints place limits beyond which the real economy cannot go. Moreover, the inflation that eventually accompanies such pressure on capacity inevitably triggers a reversal of monetary policy toward restraint. But on the downside, capacity constraints do not apply. The limits on the downside are largely political and the experience of the 1970s and 1980s suggests a surprisingly high degree of political tolerance of economic slackness. And a slack of economy does not foster productivity improvement.

PAST EFFORTS AT CHANGING
THE MICRO INSTITUTIONS

Beginning in the 1960s in the United States, and before that in other countries, various experiments were tried aimed at influencing wage and price behavior. The Kennedy and Johnson administrations established a system of "voluntary" wage-price guideposts. Under Nixon, mandatory wage-price controls were imposed. Finally, under Carter, a system of wage-price guidelines that fell somewhere between the mandatory nature of the Nixon controls and the voluntary nature of the Kennedy-Johnson guideposts were put into place. The Carter guidelines were to be reinforced by a system of tax incentives for workers to accept the guidepost ceilings, a proposal known as "real-wage insurance." But Congress saw many defects in the real-wage insurance plan and never implemented it.

In some countries, and to a limited extent in the United States under Carter, attempts have been made to negotiate "social compacts" among business, labor, and government. These arrangements have yet to score any substantial long-term successes where they have been tried. And they are particularly difficult to implement in the decentralized and largely nonunion U.S. economy. The AFL-CIO does not have the authority to order its constituent unions to follow any accord it might reach with government. It certainly cannot influence nonmember unions such as the Teamsters. Nor can it dictate the nonunion wage-setting practices that cover roughly three-fourths of wage and salary earners.

SUGGESTIONS FOR REFORM
OF WAGE CONTRACTING

Because of the recent focus on wage contracting, it is not surprising that there have been suggestions to change the basic format of wage contracts, in order to achieve greater wage responsiveness to demand and supply pressures. Probably the most dramatic suggestion in this area was made by Barry Bosworth (1981: 21), who proposed a mandatory ban on union contracts with durations greater than one year. Such a suggestion would be strongly resisted, especially by management, since the multiyear contract is viewed as guaranteeing a period of labor peace. Although it has been argued that the lack of multiyear contracts in other countries has contributed to greater wage responsiveness than is found in the United States (Gordon, 1982: 40-41), the Bosworth proposal has virtually no chance of enactment. In any case, in the nonunion sector annual decision making is already the rule, and it is in the nonunion sector that most wage decisions were made. Banning multiyear contracts would have no effect on wage setting for the vast majority of the labor force.

HAS REFORM ALREADY OCCURRED?

The high visibility of certain wage concession negotiations has suggested to some observers that wage setting has already been reformed by "market" forces (Freedman and Fulmer, 1982). Indeed, the big union concessions negotiated in auto, construction, steel, meat-packing, airlines, trucking, and other industries did represent a form of wage responsiveness to economic slackness. However, a closer look reveals little sign that the concessions represented more than a temporary response to dire economic threats to the job security of the senior union members who exercise a strong influence on the internal politics of their unions.

Wage concessions were made during 1979-1983 to avoid bank-ruptcy, plant closings, and mass layoffs. Even so, the principles of long-term contracting and cost-of-living escalation were preserved. Job or income security guarantees or assurances for senior workers were obtained in a number of the concession negotiations in exchange for immediate wage relief to the employer (Mitchell, 1982a, 1983). In short, if there is to be reform of wage setting in a manner designed to avoid stop-go economic behavior — and its attendant waste of poten-tial production and resources — that reform will have to be induced. The big wage concessions were not reforms by themselves, although some elements included in the concession bargains could be de-veloped into fundamental reforms with government assistance.

GAIN SHARING AND PRODUCTIVITY

It has been established above that prolonged periods of economic slackness and stop-go policies are not conducive to growth of con-ventionally measured productivity. The broader measure or prod-uctivity proposed earlier — output per potential input — is even more adversely affected. Finally, the tendency to fall into the stop-go trap has been tied to institutional characteristics that give inflation its momentum. The lack of wage responsiveness to demand and supply pressure has been shown to contribute importantly to inflation momentum and to the weakening of monetary policy as an efficient anti-inflation device.

At the firm level, there are three key labor-related parameters that can be changed in response to declines or increases in demand. The firm's weekly labor compensation expense (C) is the product of the number of its employees (E), the average number of hours worked per week by a typical employee (H), and the average hourly compensation cost (W), which includes wages, fringe benefits, and payroll taxes. Since $C = E \times H \times W$, the firm in principle can adjust its compensation expenditure by varying *any* of the three parameters. But, in fact, W is seldom varied.

There is a standard pattern of adaptation to changes in demand by American employers. Consider declines in demand. Initially, the firm will reduce overtime hours and then normal hours per week. That is, H is the first parameter to be adjusted. If the demand decline persists, the firm will reduce its level of employment (E) through layoffs and attrition. But only in the most dire circumstances (such as the wage concessions of 1979-1983) is W affected. In general, changes in W seem to reflect a strong influence of price inflation, while demand for labor has little effect.

Much of the theorizing about implicit contracting, to which reference was made earlier, is aimed at explaining this form of behavior. One explanation is that leaving W largely unaffected by the business cycle caters to the income security needs of senior workers. Since seniority is an explicit factor in layoffs in the union sector, and seems to be used often in a similar way in the nonunion sector, senior workers are generally unaffected by adjustments in E. Thus their incomes are affected at most by loss of overtime opportunities and sometimes by shorter-than-normal workweeks (H). The largest burden of the adjustment thus falls on junior workers who are laid off. Wage concessions are made when seniority is no longer capable of insulating senior workers from the economic downturn.

There are some firms, however, that do have variable elements in the compensation they provide employees. Gain-sharing plans, of which profit sharing is the most common example, do provide elements of variability and responsiveness to average hourly compensation. In theory, if a firm has profit sharing, a decline in demand — which will presumably adversely affect profits — will result in a decline in the profit-sharing component of W. Similarly, an upsurge in demand will result in the bigger profit-sharing payments, that is, an increase in W. If gain sharing were more widespread, W would be more responsive to real economic conditions, the tendency toward stop-go economic policies would be attentuated, macroeconomic stability would be more easily achieved, and productivity — output per unit of potential input — would be higher. In addition, Weitzman (1983) argues that a natural tendency to remain at full employment would result.

THE FORMS OF GAIN SHARING

In its profit-sharing variant, gain sharing is an old idea that can be traced in some firms back to the late nineteenth century (Emmet, 1916). As currently practiced, profit-sharing plans are typically retirement programs in which the worker's "bonus" is placed into a fund from which a pension annuity can later be drawn. Various tax incentives promote this form of gain sharing, the most important being that the annuity payment is taxable only on receipt at retirement. Unlike conventional pension plans, which require either a defined benefit or a defined contribution, profit-sharing plans offer a great deal of flexibility to employers as well as less government regulation. It is difficult to obtain estimates on the precise extent of profit sharing. However, the Profit-Sharing Research Foundation estimates that about one-fifth of the work force is covered by such plans.[1]

A gain-sharing plan need not be linked to profits. Some plans, such as the Scanlon plan, developed in the 1930s, provide bonus payments on the basis of productivity-related measures (Lesieur, 1958). In principle, gain-sharing plans could also be based on company sales or level of output. Under current tax law, however, plans that pay a *current* bonus receive no preferential tax treatment. A current bonus is taxable when received as ordinary income.

In the 1970s, tax incentives were provided to various programs that provide forms of employee ownership, mainly employee stock ownership plans (ESOPs). In some cases, these plans have facilitated complete worker takeovers of firms (Rosen, 1982). Under those conditions, the distinction between wage and profit blurs, and total compensation (wage plus profit) received by owner-workers becomes sensitive to business-cycle pressures. Of course, worker ownership of enterprises is not a new idea either. Proposals for, and experiments with, such owndership can be traced to the nineteenth century. Worker ownership is a special form of gain sharing in which the workers receive all the gains and losses. But gain sharing need not go to that extreme.

THE ACCOMPANIMENTS OF GAIN SHARING

Although the gain sharing is often proposed as a direct stimulus to increased micro-level productivity, most compensation experts are skeptical that gain sharing, by itself, will have such an effect. For example, if a firm simply announces that it has adopted a profit-sharing plan, there is little incentive for the average employee to alter his or her behavior. The linkage between individual effort and firm profitability is tenuous and — even if the linkage could be perceived clearly — the fraction of the profit due to the worker's extra effort that would come back to that worker is typically very small.

But profit-sharing plans, and similar arrangements, are often accompanied by a variety of other "progressive" personnel practices designed to boost morale and produce an identification of the worker with the firm. In recent years, these practices have often gone under the label "quality of work life" and have included various participative arrangements such as quality circles. As in the cases of other workplace practices, the labels are new but the ideas are not. Such practices were known, and received considerable publicity, as early as the 1920s (Selekman, 1924).

Until recently, unions were not especially receptive to gain-sharing arrangements. Profit sharing, for example, was reported in only 1.9 percent of major private union agreements in 1980 (U.S. Bureau of Labor Statistics, 1981: 49). But the wage concessions of 1979-1983 sometimes contained profit-sharing programs. These were partly face-saving devices; some of the firms involved seemed unlikely to generate profits in the near term. But they also expressed the need for an automatic quid pro quo for the wage concession. Workers were sacrificing wages to help their employers regain viability and competitiveness. Having profit sharing meant that the sacrifice would be automatically recouped if and when the employer's economic health returned.

Gain sharing, especially when negotiated by a union, is bound to provoke demands for forms of union participation in management or, at least, more information from management about how important decisions are being made. Once the union has linked the compensation of its members to the economic success of the firm, it has an obvious interest in ensuring that decisions that contribute to success are being made. There are virtually no management decisions that do not fall into this category. Decisions about investments, mergers, marketing, plant locations, product lines, and so on are all critical determinants of firm profitability. In many respects, unions — because they represent a large bloc of "stakeholders" in the firm — are in a better position than the traditional shareholder to monitor such decisions.

GAIN SHARING AS AN ALTERNATIVE TO ECONOMIC CENTRALIZATION

In the 1940s, unions — especially those on the left of the labor movement — hoped that the New Deal policies that had led to social security and other forms of social insurance and welfare programs would continue to develop. They hoped for national health insurance, a more elaborate federally run pension program, and the like. When these programs did not develop, unions pushed for substitutes at the bargaining table and evolved the elaborate private pension and health and welfare programs that today characterize major union contracts.

Many unions hoped for some form of national economic planning in the 1940s. The idea still lives on today in calls for "reindustrialization" and "industrial policy." Unlike pensions and health insurance, however, no bargaining table substitutes for national economic planning emerged until recently. Now, with the participatory schemes that accompany gain sharing, unions do have a chance to influence management decisions — if not in the national arena — at least at the industry or company level.

Gain sharing, because it introduces wage responsiveness, is also a substitute for the centralized efforts at wage-price guideposts, guidelines, and controls that were tried in the 1960s and 1970s. The "theory" of such programs — to the extent that there is one — is that government will make private wage setters behave responsively, either by fiat or by "moral suasion." So far, however, the effects of the centralized approach have been transitory at best, and eventually government falls back to reliance on monetary policy, with its rather blunt effect on inflation. In a world of widespread gain sharing, however, the responsiveness that controls and guidelines seek to simulate would be built instead directly into the wage-setting apparatus. And productivity performance would be improved.

CREATING THE INCENTIVES FOR GAIN SHARING

Although the 1979-1983 union wage concessions did incorporate elements of gain sharing in some cases, it is not clear that these elements will be retained once the economic crisis recedes. There have been previous episodes of moderate wage settlements accompanied by cooperative experiments. These experiments eroded or disappeared once the crisis that triggered them faded (Mitchell, 1982a:

172-176). In one prominent case in 1983, the Chrysler settlement, the profit-sharing plan was eliminated in a negotiation, just as the firm was about to become profitable.

Thus if the losses of output per potential input are to be avoided in the future, some reinforcement of the new gain-sharing plans must be provided. And incentives to encourage gain sharing where it has not yet taken root must also be enacted. The main avenue available to achieve this change is the tax code. Obviously, other avenues of encouragement are also available. For example, the Federal Mediation and Conciliation Service and other government agencies could conduct educational campaigns to familiarize wage setters with the advantages of gain sharing. But historically the tax code has proved to be a powerful influence on compensation practices. In addition, since a major benefit of gain sharing is its contribution to general economic stability, there is a case for a social subsidy.

In some respects, the current tax incentives for gain sharing are too narrow; in other respects they are too broad. Hence a modification of the tax code is in order. The existing tax incentives are too narrow in that they apply only to plans that provide deferred (retirement) benefits. This feature reduces the attractiveness of gain sharing to workers who already have adequate retirement programs. The incentives refer only to profit sharing and do not explicitly recognize plans based on other measures of employer welfare such as sales, output, or productivity.

If gain sharing is to have any significance, it must truly share gains and losses. Yet the limited statistical evidence available suggests that existing plans often do not actually reflect employer economic conditions. Table 4.8, column 1, shows profit-sharing payments as a percentage of payroll for a sample of 175 firms. As can be seen clearly, apart from a gradual upward trend in the percentage, the payments seem to be immune from the business cycle. Column 2 shows a profit-related index for the year prior to the observations of column 1. (Presumably, firms will look at last period's profits in considering this year's bonus.) Column 2 suggests that column 1 ought to have exhibited considerable variation, if firms were actually basing their bonuses on their economic conditions. Apparently they were not.

Since gain sharing provides social benefits only if the payments do vary with business conditions, the tax code should reward just those plans that are linked by formula to measures of employer welfare. For a formula to be meaningful, it must be retained for a significant period of time, say three to five years. (A formula that can be changed annually is no formula at all!) The current tax code does not require

TABLE 4.8   Profit-Sharing Payments and Profitability Measures

Year	Profit-Sharing Payments, Bonuses as percentage of Payroll[a] (1)	After-Tax Corporate Profits Adjusted for Inflation as percentage of Employee Compensation, Prior Year[b] (2)
1961	1.8	10.0
1963	1.8	12.5
1965	1.8	14.9
1967	1.9	15.6
1969	1.9	12.4
1971	1.9	6.8
1973	2.1	8.7
1975	2.1	3.9
1977	2.3	8.4
1979	2.3	8.9
1981	2.3	5.6

SOURCES: U.S. President (1983: 176) and U.S. Chamber of Commerce (1982: 27).
a. Survey of 175 companies by the U.S. Chamber of Commerce.
b. Nonfinancial corporations, domestic income. Profits have been adjusted to remove inventory profits and inadequate depreciation allowances due to inflation.

establishment of a fixed formula; it should be amended to include such a requirement.

THE PATH TO IMPROVED
PRODUCTIVITY PERFORMANCE

This chapter began with a review of the disappointing productivity performance of the U.S economy since the early 1970s. While the debate on the causes of the productivity slowdown still continues, there is considerable agreement on measures that could help alleviate the problem. A capital shortage may not have been at the root of the slowdown. But even if it was not, a higher rate of saving and investment would help. Federal budget deficits absorb saving that could otherwise go toward investment. Thus addressing the chronic federal deficit tendency would position the private economy for better productivity performance. Similarly, although the slippage in research and development may not have been a major factor in the productivity slowdown, encouraging more R&D would help in the future.

It appears, however, that improved macroeconomic performance would be a key factor in providing a better environment for productivity growth. The stop-go behavior that characterized the 1970s and early 1980s was not conducive to productivity improvement.

Monetary policy proved to be a blunt instrument to deal with inflation — although it did eventually reduce inflation after a considerable and painful lag.

In this chapter, gain sharing has been proposed as a fundamental workplace reform that would increase the effectiveness of monetary policy, thus reducing the lag and the pain. It would do this by linking employee compensation to the economic condition of the employer. This condition would reflect the general state of the economy (as influenced by monetary policy) as well as the special circumstances affecting the firm's product market. Gain sharing fits naturally with other workplace reforms currently in vogue, especially worker and union participation in managerial decisions. But what is in vogue can easily go out of fashion in the future. If productivity performance is to be improved, it is important that gain sharing receive encouragement while the opportunity exists.

NOTE

1. Estimate provided to the author by Bert Metzger, president of the Profit-Sharing Research Foundation.

REFERENCES

BAILY, M. N. (1982) "The productivity slowdown by industry." Brookings Papers on Economic Activity 2: 423-454.
——— (1981a) "Productivity and the services of capital and labor." Brookings Papers on Economic Activity 1: 1-50.
——— (1981b) "Productivity in a changing world." Brookings Bulletin 18: 1-5.
BOSWORTH, B. P. (1982) "Capital formation and economic policy." Brookings Papers on Economic Activity 2: 273-317.
——— (1981) "Policy choices for controlling inflation." Alternatives for the 1980s (publication of the Center for Democratic Policy) 1: 16-22.
BRUNO, M. (1982) "World shocks, macroeconomic response, and the productivity puzzle." Working paper 942, National Bureau of Economic Research.
CAPDEVIELLE, P. et al. (1982) "International trends in productivity and labor costs." Monthly Labor Review 105.
CRANDALL, R. W. (1981) "Pollution controls and productivity growth in basic industry" and "Regulation and productivity growth." Brookings General Series Reprint 375.
DARBY, M. R. (1982) "The price of oil and world inflation and recession." American Economic Review 72: 738-751.
de LEEUW, F. and T. M. HOLLOWAY (1982) "The high-employment budget: revised estimates and automatic inflation effects." Survey of Current Business 62: 21-33.

DENISON, E. F. (1979a) Accounting for Slower Economic Growth: The United States in the 1970s. Washington, DC: Brookings Institution.

—— (1979b) "Explanations of declining productivity growth." Survey of Current Business 59 (Pt. II): 1-24.

EMMET, B. (1916) Profit Sharing in the United States (U.S. Bureau of Labor Statistics, Bulletin 208). Washington, DC: Government Printing Office.

FREEDMAN, A. and W. E. FULMER (1982) "Last rites for pattern bargaining." Harvard Business Review 60: 30-48.

GORDON, R. J. (1982) "Why U.S. wage and employment behavior differs from that in Britain and Japan." Economic Journal 92: 40-41.

—— (1981) "Comments and discussion of M. N. Baily, 'Productivity and the services of capital and labor.' " Brookings Papers on Economic Activity 1: 51-58.

LESIEUR, F. G. [ed.] (1958) The Scanlon Plan: A Frontier in Labor-Management Cooperation. New York: John Wiley.

MITCHELL, D. J. B. (1983) "The 1982 union wage concessions: were they a turning point for collective bargaining?" California Management Review 25: 78-92.

—— (1982a) "Recent union contract concessions." Brookings Papers on Economic Activity 1: 165-201.

—— (1982b) "Should the Consumer Price Index determine wages?" California Management Review 25: 5-21.

—— (1978) "Union wage determination: policy implications and outlook." Brookings Papers on Economic Activity 3: 537-582.

—— and L. J. KIMBELL (1982) "Labor market contracts and inflation," pp. 199-238 in M. N. Baily (ed.) Workers, Jobs and Inflation. Washington, DC: Brookings Institution.

Monthly Labor Review (1983) Vol. 106 (April).

—— (1981) Vol. 104 (December).

OKUN, A. M. (1978) "Efficient disinflationary policies." American Economic Review 68: 348-352.

ROSEN, C. (1982) Employee Ownership: Issues, Resources and Legislation. Arlington, VA: National Center for Employee Ownership.

SELEKMAN, B. M. (1924) Sharing Management with the Workers: A Study of the Partnership Plan of the Dutchess Bleachery, Wappingers Falls, New York. New York: Russell Sage Foundation.

STONE, R. (1980) "Whittling away at the residual: some thoughts on Denison's growth accounting — a review article." Journal of Economic Literature 28: 1539-1543.

THUROW, L. C. (1981) "Solving the productivity problem." Alternatives for the 1980s (publication of the Center for Democratic Policy) 2: 9-19.

—— (1980) "The productivity problem." Technology Review 83: 40-51.

U.S. Bureau of Labor Statistics (1981) Characteristics of Major Collective Bargaining Agreements, January 1, 1980 (Bulletin 2095). Washington, DC: Government Printing Office.

U.S. Chamber of Commerce (1982) Employee Benefits 1981. Washington, DC: Author.

U.S. President (1983) Economic Report of the President 1983. Washington, DC: Government Printing Office.

WEITZMAN, M. L. (1983) "Some macroeconomic implications of alternative compensation systems." Department of Economics, Massachusetts Institute of Technology. (unpublished)

PART III

STIMULATING INVESTMENT,
RESEARCH, AND DEVELOPMENT

5

FEDERAL ECONOMIC
DEVELOPMENT INVESTMENTS

F. STEVENS REDBURN
STEVE GODWIN
KATHLEEN PEROFF
DAVID SEARS

*U.S. Department of Housing
and Urban Development*

Federal, state, and local governments invest in regional economic development on a large scale, by a wide variety of means. These investments, taken together, constitute a de facto national industrial policy and a national regional development policy (see, for example, Rasmussen and Ledebur, 1983). The federal government is a key actor in shaping this pattern of public investments, not only due to the scale of its direct efforts, but also because, through national legislation, it shapes the behavior of other levels of government.

The federal government's ability to achieve national goals through investments in the development of regional or local economies depends in part on its ability to evaluate its own array of programs, both individually and collectively. For evaluation to play its proper role in guiding policy formation and improving the productivity of ongoing

Authors' Note: *The authors assume sole responsibility for the views, interpretations, and conclusions contained in this chapter.*

programs, however, there must be progress in conceptualizing and measuring program performance. The following discussion will specify and illustrate the main conceptual issues and measurement problems that must be faced in order to produce a badly needed comprehensive framework for evaluating federal economic development investments.

There are four parts to this analysis: (1) a brief look at the scale and diversity of the federal government's major instruments for promoting regional economic development; (2) an elaboration of the need for an evaluation framework; (3) a series of brief synopses of the essential elements of such a framework and the conceptual and measurement issues raised by each; and (4) a synthesis of these elements illustrating how comprehensive evaluation can provide insights regarding the relative productivity of various federal economic development investments.

FEDERAL REGIONAL DEVELOPMENT ASSISTANCE

The forms of federal regional economic development aid are numerous and diverse. Their diversity encompasses the choice of financing mechanism (direct subsidies to business, indirect business subsidies through grants to local and state governments, loan guarantees, and various tax incentives); the extent to which they are targeted to particular regions and/or to classes of governments or businesses; and the kinds of activity they support (ranging from direct capitalization of new private investment to public infrastructure or government planning assistance). Any listing of the major forms of federal economic development assistance must be somewhat arbitrary in what it includes and excludes and in how programs are grouped. Space is insufficient here for us to do more than indicate the approximate scope and scale of such efforts by (1) identifying major programs and tax incentives and (2) showing how an actual firm has made use of various public programs over a period of several years.

Table 5.1 provides a rough indication of the total magnitude and components of the federal government's efforts to foster economic development at a subnational level.[1] Not included in the table or considered in the following analysis are other means by which the federal government assists businesses but that are not in any explicit fashion aimed at developing the economies of regions or localities. Nor is there any consideration here of the often-analyzed regional development impacts of the larger patterns of federal spending, inter-governmental assistance, or tax policy.

A deeper appreciation of the number and variety of public instruments and subsidies now available to businesses can be gained by viewing these from the perspective of a single company. The Machine Company (the name is fictional, but the company is a real one) is an older manufacturing firm with about 400 employees located in a declining eastern industrial city. From 1978 through 1982, the Machine Company used state industrial revenue bonds to finance a major expansion; received state grants for site acquisition and preparation; was assisted with site assembly and household relocation by a non-profit business development corporation exercising the city's power of eminent domain; was indirectly aided by an Economic Development Administration (EDA) planning grant designating its area as a target for redevelopment; used federal Department of Labor funds for training and employment subsidies; induced use of the city's community development block grant (CDBG) funds for adjacent street improvements and landscaping; indirectly benefited from nearby neighborhood and commercial rehabilitation efforts by two separate publicly capitalized neighborhood development corporations; heavily employed federal tax credits for historic rehabilitation and energy conservation in renovating its oldest buildings; took newly strengthened federal tax credits for equipment purchases; and, finally, found itself in a recently designated state "enterprise zone," making the Machine Company eligible for a number of tax benefits and other forms of assistance in connection with any future expansion. Although this firm may not be typical, there is no reason to believe it is unusual. Such examples, which could be multiplied thousands of times with variation in the specifics, provide a better sense of the degree to which public (especially federal) funds are used to subsidize private investments, especially by firms located in economically distressed areas.

THE NEED FOR AN EVALUATION FRAMEWORK

Some people believe that public investments in the economic development of a place or region are, by definition, bad public policy. They argue that the marketplace is always a more efficient allocator of economic opportunities; that any government-directed use of capital indirectly displaces a use of that capital by the private sector that

TABLE 5.1   Major Federal Programs that Provide Regional Development
            Assistance: Budget Authority and Tax Expenditures
            (in millions of dollars)

	Fiscal Year 1982	Fiscal Year 1983 (estimate)
Budgeted expenditures		
Community Development Block Grants	$ 3,792	$ 3,525
Urban Development Action Grants	474	440
economic development assistance	224	34
rural development assistance	590	777
regional commissions	159	158
small business assistance	897	1,124
Off-budget loans and loan guarantees		
economic development assistance*	14	–
rural development insurance fund (FmHA)	1,535	1,191
small business assistance*	1,854	2,425
Tax expenditures		
exclusion of interest on state, local industrial development bonds	1,640	2,120
rehabilitation of older, nonhistoric structures	250	335
Totals	$11,429	$12,129

SOURCE: Office of Management and Budget (1984).
*New obligations or commitments.

would bring a higher financial return. On a large scale and over time,
this will in turn lower the productivity of the private economy and
thus lower our nation's rate of economic growth and its competitiveness relative to other nations. By this logic, publicly sponsored
development investments are "distortions" — which may be justified
as improving economic opportunities for a particular place or group of
people — but nevertheless should be minimized. Otherwise, a suboptimal pattern of investments will make us all losers in the long run.

To this view, there are basically two lines of counterargument.
One is that the private market[2] is not, by itself, likely to produce an
optimally productive pattern of national investment, as measured by
the long-run expansion of production and economic opportunity for
the whole society. This logic justifies investments in underdeveloped
regions either on the basis that (1) businesses and individuals of other

regions must make use of the public infrastructure, human resources, and private enterprises of the less developed regions, and through this use they also benefit from a strengthening of the economies of less developed regions or that (2) mobilizing underutilized facilities, resources, and people in less developed regions will produce a higher marginal gain in national productivity with less inflationary pressure than would the equivalent investment in more economically robust sections of the nation (House and Steger, 1982: 31-37). A second type of counterargument in favor of public investments in less developed regions attempts to demonstrate that other public goals — for example, equity or national security — justify a pattern of economic development that is admittedly suboptimal from a market standpoint.

Even those who believe that public economic development investments can be justified in theory, however, must confront the reality of actual public sector performance. That performance may depart as widely from the stated rationale for government interventions as the private sector's behavior does from the ideal of a free market. It is important, therefore, to evaluate carefully the performance of government as an investor — one that is using a varied assortment of subsidy mechanisms and other tools to stimulate certain private investments in selected regions or places.

The conceptual framework used to evaluate federal economic development investments must explicitly define the goals (potential benefits) of economic development policies and it must carefully specify the terms in which both the benefits and costs of such programs will be measured. As will be shown, the problems of conceptualization are rather complex. Perhaps as a result, few evaluations of economic development programs are comprehensive and sophisticated in their conception.

Before addressing the conceptual and measurement problems of evaluation, a word about the goals of economic development programs will be useful. Although such programs always serve other goals, they are treated here as though they can be evaluated in terms of their economic development impacts only. This helps to keep the intellectual task to manageable proportions. Even so, it is important to recognize that the goal of economic development involves more than increasing the level of private investment or jobs in a locale. There are two related but distinct goals that are nearly always implied if not explicitly stated in the formulation of an economic development program. One is that the benefits of the investment should flow to people with greater need for the resulting jobs and income. A second is that the short-term public stimulus should leverage a long-lasting or multiplying gain in economic welfare for the area and its people; this objective is implied by the word "development," suggesting institutional as well as strictly financial benefits. Specifically, development implies a lasting increase in the ability of a place to sustain itself and support future growth. If we judge economic development policies solely in terms of the short-term economic gains produced and ignore either the distributional impacts of those gains or longer-term effects, then we will arrive at judgments that are inconsistent with the usually stated goals of public economic development investments. Thus we would be using inappropriately narrow standards to evaluate such policies.

THE ELEMENTS OF AN
EVALUATION FRAMEWORK

The purpose of this section is to present, in turn, each of the major elements of a comprehensive framework for measuring the relative productivity of specific federal economic development investments or of sets of investments employing a common set of financing techniques and administrative requirements. For simplicity, individual investments are sometimes referred to below as "projects" and sets of investments are referred to as "programs," recognizing that these terms are being stretched to cover a variety of mechanisms by which federal support is given for regional economic development. The first of the following subsections deals with the problem of estimating the public costs (that is, expenditures or taxes forgone) of projects and programs. The other subsections each deal with the problem of conceptualizing and measuring an aspect of the benefits of such investments.

PUBLIC COSTS

Estimating the cost to the public treasury of an economic development investment is, conceptually, one of the most straightforward parts of the evaluation problem. However, there are some pitfalls. Most evaluations of public programs treat cost in a rather parochial fashion. That is, they generally give most attention to the portion of cost borne by the level of government sponsoring the programs being directly evaluated; not infrequently, cost is equated with the portion of cost that comes from a single agency's budget.

There are obvious advantages to thinking about the total public cost of a public investment. For one thing, this is the only approach that permits fair comparisons of productivity for programs with very different incidences of costs across levels of government. And a total public cost approach allows evaluators to combine direct outlays, the indirect costs of tax expenditures, and tax offsets (that is, new taxes generated by the investment that reduce its net public cost).

The incidence of costs can vary drastically, depending on both the nature of the public financing mechanism and the level of government providing that assistance. Table 5.2 presents a comparison of cost incidence for nominally equivalent subsidy amounts in the form of a $100,000 locally issued industrial revenue bond, a $100,000 below-market-rate loan, a $100,000 loan guarantee (with an assumed default rate of 22 percent), and a $100,000 grant for purchase of equipment.[3]

The actual public cost of seemingly equivalent-sized public investments can vary dramatically, as illustrated by the example in Table 5.2. Taxes forgone through subsidies, such as the tax-free interest on industrial revenue bonds and the additional tax benefits due to credits and accelerated depreciation for purchases of plant and equipment, are major elements of the public cost of most development projects. In the case of loan guarantees, the true cost is very difficult to project, depending as it does on the actual rate of defaults, and may vary greatly over the life of a program as economic conditions change and as underwriting practices become more or less conservative. Loan guarantees can also become a trap for public agencies — in some cases, drawing the public into deeper commitments in efforts to salvage troubled projects. In any case, the actual public cost is highly sensitive to project selection practices and future policies regarding refinancing and liquidation of commitments.[4]

Once the total public cost associated with a given program has been estimated, consideration should be given to the presence of other direct or indirect public subsidies associated with the same private investment. The earlier Machine Company example illustrates the reality that rarely do public programs work in isolation from one another. In fact, private investors who use public programs at all are often skilled specialists in combining or pyramiding diverse sources of assistance.

ASSET VALUE OF THE ASSISTANCE

Equal-sized public subsidies can have very different values to firms, depending on the form of the subsidy as well as the firm's tax

TABLE 5.2   Comparison of Cost Incidence (in dollars)

Program	Direct Outlays		Tax Offsets		Total Costs	
	Federal	State	Federal	State	Federal	State
IRB	31,591	3,601	−4,497	−1,181	27,094	2,420
BMR loan	21,276	–	−4,596	−511	16,680	−511
Guarantee	10,844	–	–	–	10,844	–
Grant	100,000	–	−13,051	−3,428	86,949	−3,428

position and investment plans. Rasmussen et al. (1982) have developed a standardized measure of the utility to firms of specified or known characteristics of each dollar of public investment, which they call the subsidy's "asset value" to the firm. While the asset value of a subsidy does not directly measure its contribution to local economic development, it should prove to be a good predictor of the extent to which a subsidy of a certain form given to certain firms can leverage new private investment and jobs (see the following subsections on leverage ratios). It is thus a useful intermediate measure of relative program efficiency.

The asset value of public assistance is the ratio of the government's cost of providing a subsidy to the benefits received by the assisted firm. The benefit to the firm is calculated as though each subsidy were given as an outright gift of an asset, with no strings attached. The asset value of assistance is always less than 100 percent of the subsidy provided; for example, an interest subsidy to reduce a firm's borrowing cost will increase the firm's cash flow subject to federal and state taxation, thereby reducing its net value to the firm. In addition, a firm incurs costs when it applies for assistance, and these costs will vary widely between, say, participating in the Urban Development Action Grant (UDAG) program and receiving tax benefits for investing in an enterprise zone. Finally, the asset value is measured at its present value; future benefits may be discounted at the rate of the firm's long-term borrowing costs. The asset value of assistance thus constitutes a measure of the "kick" provided by public subsidies; the higher the ratio of subsidies to benefits, the weaker the incentive for new private investment generated by each dollar of public cost.

A ten-year, $100,000 IRB used to aid a high-profit firm (assumed to have combined state and federal marginal tax rate of 49 percent) would cost the federal government about $24,000 in direct outlays.[5]

The firm's borrowing costs would be reduced, thus giving it more income subject to taxation, which would produce tax offsets of about $7,700, reducing the net federal cost to about $16,000. The discounted stream of benefits to the firm from the IRB will be about $7,200. Thus the ratio of federal costs to firm benefits is an inefficient 2.24. The same $100,000 IRB, on the other hand, costs a typical state less than $2,000 (in direct outlays less tax offsets). Thus, from its perspective, this form of subsidy has a highly efficient asset value ratio of .25.

The asset value of the assistance can be calculated for any form of economic development subsidy in order to compare the incentive strength of different forms of assistance. Care must be taken, however, in projecting the future tax liabilities of the aided firms and future default rates for loans and loan guarantees.

LEVERAGING

Assessing various approaches taken by the federal government or other levels of government to stimulate economic development involves an examination of several types of benefits. As the following discussion shows, some are easier to measure than others, but, even when not quantifiable, they need to be considered by policymakers. Furthermore, there is no magic formula for weighting the relative importance of different benefits in order to reach a "net effect"conclusion. Ultimately, that becomes a policy judgment. Even so, that judgment can be better informed if systematic and, where possible, empirical analysis is undertaken to clarify the full costs and impacts of different federal programs.

The effort to compare systematically across programs focuses on two basic benefits: leveraged investment and jobs. Often these go hand in hand, but not always. For both jobs and investment, direct and indirect effects should be considered.

Private Investment. Beginning with the Carter administration, federal economic development policy has increasingly emphasized a strategy of investing small amounts of public money to leverage large amounts of private money to create jobs. For instance, the UDAG program uses the ratio of total private investment to total public dollars as a selection criterion in awarding its grants. The average leverage ratio for UDAG projects has increased in recent years — probably an indication of the importance attached to it by program administrators.

Higher leverage ratios usually are interpreted as signs of a more efficient economic stimulus. However, cross-program comparisons must be done very carefully to account for differences in program design and objectives. In some cases, such ratios may not even be meaningful. Programs vary, for instance, in the type of subsidy given (that is, whether direct loans, loan guarantees, or outright grants); they also vary in the purposes for which the money can be spent, as well as the portion of the development costs covered by the subsidy. In some programs, such as EDA'S Local Public Works program (LPW), there is no direct leveraging of private investment, since all costs are covered by federal, state, or local governments. EDA's Business Development program covers, on average, one-half of any single development project's costs. At the other end of the continuum, the UDAG program is designed to provide the smallest amount needed; that is, it either finances the gap between a project's costs and the developer's private loans and equity or puts up the money to finance the necessary infrastructure for the particular development. This contribution averages about one-fourth of project costs. Therefore, by design, UDAG's leveraging ratios will usually be higher than those for projects of EDA's Local Public Works program or Business Development program.

Additionally, there is considerable evidence showing that leveraging ratios vary by the type of project funded. ABT Associates (1980) estimated an average leveraging ratio of 2.94 for EDA's Grants for Public Works and Development Facilities, which subsidize localities' infrastructure improvements to stimulate long-term development. There were wide variations, however, in leveraging ratios among different types of infrastructure: roads (5.18), water (4.62), and sewer (4.53) had high ratios compared to buildings (.80) (Abt Associates, Inc., 1980).[6] Similar variation was found in the evaluation of UDAG: while the overall leverage ratio for all the funded development projects was 5.5, commercial projects (such as hotels and shopping malls) generated less (3.9) and industrial projects more investment (6.3) (HUD, 1982).

Since times frames for the expected private investment vary from program to program, as well as from project to project within the same program, it is necessary to discount the private investment benefits (as for the public costs) to their equivalent present value.[7]

One issue in the use and interpretation of leveraging ratios concerns the degree to which a cause-and-effect relation can be inferred between a particular federal economic development program and the subsequent private investment. In many development projects at the local level, there are a variety of sources of public money. No single program can be given credit for the entire economic stimulus when other public subsidies are present — although, of course, some will be more critical than others.

To the extent that data are available, actual rather than projected private investment expenditures should be used in calculating the investment ratio. Otherwise, there is the potential for bias when using the anticipated figures provided by applicants competing in a project selection process that looks favorably on larger leverage ratios. There is some evidence in the UDAG program that the actual private investment was higher than projected; however, this appeared to be due to delays, and higher-than-expected inflation in labor or material costs, rather than larger-scale projects. In other words, no extra jobs or real increase in private investment was realized by the higher-than-projected private outlays (EDA, 1980: 46-49).

Jobs. Another common impact measure is simply the number of jobs created per public dollar spent by a federal program. The most direct approach usually taken is the count of the full-time jobs created as a result of some private investment stimulated by public dollars, or jobs completely financed by the public sector. By this measure, the higher the number of jobs per dollar, the more effective or efficient the federal program.[8] The Local Public Works program was found to cost about $65,000 (1980 dollars) per construction job, with 92 percent of the costs paid by the federal government and the remainder by other state and local sources. No private investment was involved, since the program focuses only on public facility and infrastructure improvements (EDA, 1980: 29).[9] The UDAG program creates new permanent jobs at a cost of just over $11,500 (HUD, 1982: 61).[10] Once again, substantial differences among federal economic development programs in design and objectives can create difficulties in making comparative evaluations.

One issue that complicates the use and interpretation of the jobs ratio concerns the extent to which an economic development program has the objective or effect of retaining jobs. UDAG applicants, for example, are evaluated primarily on the basis of proposed new jobs created; however, in some projects, especially industrial developments, the argument in favor of the UDAG subsidy may be that it will help retain jobs in a jurisdiction that otherwise might be lost to another area of the country, or lost because the firm would go out of business completely due to lack of the capital it needs to revitalize its operations and to make itself more competitive in the market.

Arguments as to whether retained jobs should be included in the jobs ratio depend, to a large extent, on the level of analysis — whether national or local. From a national perspective, jobs retained in one place that otherwise would be moved elsewhere do not represent a net addition of jobs. The federal subsidy is simply adjusting — some would say interfering with — market forces through a place-oriented development program. From the perspective of the locality about to lose the firm — often an economically distressed city in the north central or northeastern areas of the country — there are strong reasons for federal help to prevent economic and social disruption in the particular locality.[11]

SUBSTITUTION

The effectiveness of economic development investments is often diminished because public dollars are used for projects, or parts of projects, that would have proceeded in about the same time and place with private funding alone. When public funds are merely substituted for private funds in this fashion, no real public benefits have been created and public resources have been wasted. Determining the extent of substitution is one key to accurate measurement of the effectiveness of an economic development program. However, as pointed out by Shalala (quoted in Nathan and Webman, 1980) and Jacobs (1981), the measurement of substitution is exceedingly difficult. It requires a demonstration of what might have occurred in the absence of the subsidy — an inherently subjective judgment. For example, in their review of an evaluation of EDA's Public Works program, EDA officials claimed that in every "doubtful" case, the evaluators decided against the program, while the evaluators claimed that every doubtful instance of substitution was "settled" in favor of EDA (Centaur Associates, 1982).

The strongest tests for substitution used in any evaluation to date were devised for the U.S. Department of Housing and Urban Development (HUD) 1981 evaluation of the UDAG program (HUD, 1982). An unusually stringent test for substitution was appropriate in this case, because, by law, UDAG funds may not: (1) directly substitute for private or public (state or local government) dollars that would otherwise be invested; or (2) be granted when the private investment is not contingent on the UDAG investment.

Thus the law implies a series of tests for substitution. The direct substitution test may be failed in two ways, defined as follows: S1 =

all of the UDAG dollars invested in a project substitute for private or nonfederal funds; S2 = some (but not all) of the UDAG dollars invested in a project substitute for private or non federal funds, thus constituting "partial" substitution. The contingency test may not be met in three ways, as follows: L1 = all of the UDAG was required, but it was needed to stimulate only some of the private investment that occurred; L2 = no UDAG was needed for any of the private investment that occurred; L3 = some (but not all) of the UDAG dollars invested did not stimulate any of the private investment that occurred. For a set of projects, the calculation of the proportion of the total dollars that were unnecessary (that is, U) can be obtained by the following formula:

$$U = \frac{S1 + S2 + L2 + L3}{T}$$

where T equals the total of UDAG funds provided to the project. L1 is excluded from the formula because, in these cases, all of the UDAG was necessary, even though some of the private investment was not stimulated by the UDAG.

In its 1981 evaluation, HUD found that in nearly two out of three UDAG projects (65 percent), the Action Grant was clearly needed in order for the project to proceed. Conclusive evidence of "full substitution" was found in six of the eighty projects examined (8 percent); and ten projects (13 percent) were classified as instances of "partial substitution," in which some component of the project would have been developed without the federal funds. For instance, in a large industrial expansion, for which UDAG paid the major cost of a sewer line, there was irrefutable evidence of a commitment between the firm and the city that if the city did not receive a UDAG the firm would pay for its share of the sewer line. The UDAG was clearly not needed to leverage the private investment. As a result of such instances, it appears that 17 percent of the UDAG dollars were spent for development that would have occurred without the federal funds. For the remaining twelve projects (15 percent), no conclusion could be reached regarding substitution because the evidence was mixed and inconclusive.

The UDAG evaluation establishes the practicality of measuring substitution through a combination of careful fieldwork and expert analysis. The fieldwork involved detailed discussions with those directly involved in putting together each of the sampled projects, including the private developer, lenders, and city officials. Among the issues discussed relating to substitution were the following: the length of time the site had been available; previous investor interest; the availability of alternate financing or alternate sites; and the prospective profitability of this investment compared to similar investments. A triangulation process in which the answers of various actors were compared provided the opportunity to turn up discrepancies and to probe for differences of opinion.[12]

The rate of substitution may be used to recalculate leverage ratios in order to provide a truer measure of program benefits. The 1981 UDAG evaluation applied substitution findings by not counting any benefits associated with those projects or parts of projects that would have proceeded without federal support. As a result, the investment leverage ratio dropped from 7.1 to 5.5 private dollars for every public dollar. As a result of similar calculations, the apparent cost in UDAG program dollars of each permanent job created increased from $7392 to $9344.

Although the main focus of evaluators is likely to be on public-for-private substitution, the substitution of federal for other public dollars is also sometimes an important policy issue. One of the few studies to take this type of substitution into account was an evaluation of EDA's Local Public Works program, which estimated the rate at which federal funds substituted for local funds at less than 9 percent (EDA, 1980: 45).

LEAKAGE

The benefits of an economic development investment may "leak" away from the intended beneficiaries to other areas or people. Economic development programs are nearly always targeted to classes of places or people with special needs for assistance, typically places with high proportions of low-income or unemployed residents. But, given the complex interconnections among various components of the economic system, it would be virtually impossible to design an economic development program that did not benefit groups and areas in addition to the intended beneficiaries. Some degree of leakage is inevitable, but the extent to which it occurs depends on program design and administration.

Evaluators can measure what proportion of benefits reaches the targeted places or people and can also help to specify the conditions under which leakage is minimized. For instance, one of the UDAG program's objectives is to provide jobs for low-and moderate-income people. Necessarily, however, when a new UDAG-subsidized hotel opens, the new jobs created include not only bellhops, maids, waiters, and waitresses but also managers and chefs. The latter jobs will often be filled by people who live and pay taxes outside the distressed city. Perhaps more significantly, the hotel's owners and investors may be wealthy individuals who will spend or reinvest profits from the hotel in ways that provide no direct benefits to the distressed city or low-income people.

Enterprise zones have recently been created in several states as a means of stimulating new enterprise formation and expansion of existing business in economically depressed areas or neighborhoods. Both leakage and substitution are difficult to control in such programs because eligibility for benefits is conferred by geography alone, in many cases, and because the zones are designed to function automatically, with a minimum of administrative monitoring and control. However, one state, Connecticut, is attempting to minimize leakage of the economic benefits of its enterprise zone program by requiring that employers hire a minimum percentage of new employees from within the zones or from the city's lower-income population in order to qualify for tax benefits and wage subsidies. Since the zones are located in low-income areas, it is likely that many of the new jobs created will be filled by people who most need these opportunities.

Several measurement problems must be addressed in order to determine the extent to which the benefits of a public development investment leak away from the targeted area and population. First, program goals may not be specified clearly enough to establish precisely when benefits are or are not reaching the intended target. For instance, "low-income" jobs may be defined simply in terms of current income or in terms of attachment to a career ladder that promises substantial future income gains. Second, considerable effort may be required to trace the flow of benefits, especially the amount of profit earned by various investors and its subsequent use or reinvestment. Third, there may be circumstances where an initially high rate of leakage leads to a subsequent second round of benefits to the targeted population or locale; for example, a high-technology park that at first creates relatively few jobs for low-income residents of an area may produce a variety of subsequent opportunities for entry-level positions with training and for the creation of new service firms employing low-skilled persons. Thus the amount of leakage measured in the initial stages of a project may differ significantly from that measured later on.

OPPORTUNITY COSTS

A third way in which benefits may be reduced occurs when better opportunities for investment are lost because of a less-than-optimal expenditure of funds or use of other resources. One notion of opportunity costs prevalent in public finance theory suggests that opportunity costs inhere in any allocation of public budgetary resources. Sometimes this notion of opportunity cost is framed in terms of budgetary trade-offs, such as "guns versus butter." More relevant to this discussion are those opportunity costs that arise through the choices made about how to distribute public resources among programs or projects to stimulate local economies. Analysis of these kinds of costs involves looking at programs' efficiencies and the match between program impacts and local, regional, and national needs.

Another type of opportunity cost occurs in the choices made by the local government or developer, or both, in the type of use to be made of a particular site. For example, in a downtown revitalization project heavily supported by local CDBG and EDA funds, the city has allowed a developer to tear down a historic tavern/restaurant to allow for construction of a high-rise office building without making any effort to assess the physical and economic viability of saving the historic structure.

Once a choice is made about the type of development, other uses of the land and of the public and private resources are precluded. In real estate appraisal, the standard applied to such choices is referred to as that of the"highest and best use" of land. The analysis of opportunity costs suggested here goes beyond the usual real estate appraisal and market feasibility analysis, however. In addition to establishing the economic feasibility of a particular project, the analysis should examine whether a proposed project yields maximum possible benefit relative to the following: a community's overall economic development strategy; a local land-use plan (if one exists); and the preservation of historically valuable structures or environmentally unique areas. Opportunity cost analysis will always contain a subjective element of opinion and personal value. Even so, it is a worthwhile endeavor and should be incorporated into economic development decision-making processes at all levels.

GROWTH OR DECAY OF BENEFITS

Although most evaluations look at projects at a single point in time, it is more appropriate to consider them as producing a stream of benefits over time. The benefits of the initial public investment may remain stable or may grow or decay. A loan to a small business may trigger a growth process that produces an industrial giant. Or, more frequently, the enterprise will fail within its first few years.

Economic development programs tend to occupy a financial twilight realm between the world of bright prospects that have no difficulty attracting private investment and the underworld of financial infeasibility. Often, the risk associated with an economic development investment is a function of location, since the aim of such programs is to move private investment into territory it would otherwise not occupy. However, public financing may also attract schemes and schemers that are marginal for other reasons — blimp factories backed by foreign princes and the like. Marginality may manifest itself as lack of successful management experience, unusually complex financial packaging, dependence on untried technology, or questions regarding the integrity of principals. It is probably fair to assume that experienced private lenders have better noses for marginal proposals and are more likely to know their customers than are public agencies, but the private sector is hardly immune to error either.

In 1979, a new manufacuturing venture was started in one of the most distressed urban areas in the United States. Financed with a combination of private capital and subsidies and guarantees from three separate federal agencies, the operation promised to produce up to 300 jobs, nearly all for low-income and minority people. Despite the early loss of a major purchase contract (on which initial judgments of financial feasibility rested), the firm struggled along for nearly three years. Difficulty getting assembly-line equipment to work, a large unexplained fire, muggings of key personnel, labor problems, disputes among the investors, and a chronic shortage of working capital all contributed to its demise. By 1983, the city-owned building it had occupied was vacant. Perhaps the most visible economic development failure of recent years is not a publicly sponsored project but Ford Motor Company's Renaissance Center in Detroit.[13] Ford has provided over $300 million of the $357 million spent through the middle of 1983 to develop and finance this cluster of office and retail towers; it has also provided or recruited enough tenants to keep the Center's office space 95 percent occupied. However, Ford had originally planned to invest only $6 million in the project, which has operated with huge losses since opening. Amid the glut of downtown office space it helped to create, the Center is able to charge only a fraction of the rents it needs to cover costs. In early 1983, Ford and the other equity partners defaulted on their mortgage payments. Although the Center remains in operation and continues to provide employment and income,[14] it has generated huge losses of capital, which could have profound consequences for the investors and the city of Detroit.

Evaluators can aid policymakers by establishing the empirical relationships, for public programs, between particular project characteristics and the likelihood that benefits will be increased or lost over time. For instance, it may be found that newly organized firms that are financed from multiple private and public sources are unusually vulnerable to failure stemming from problems with management or financing. Identification of such probabilities should be a feature of any long-term evaluation effort, since results can be used to improve future project selection.

Assuming, however, that evaluations will typically be conducted fairly early in the life of a program, information can still be generated about the kinds of projects that are ahead of or behind schedule, above or below expectations regarding scale of operation, or showing other symptoms of changes that could erode or multiply their benefits over time. It may be possible to construct reasonable projections, for groups of projects, of the net growth or decay of benefits over time. Given the unreliability of economic projections generally and the discounting that always applies to benefits or losses occurring in the future, the results of such projections should not be overweighted in reaching judgments about the overall value of a public investment.

In the case of loans or loan guarantees, it should be noted that project failure or financial difficulty also affects public costs. At a minimum, default will mean a loss of repayment and/or public assumption of obligations for the project's debts. Not uncommonly, however, default will lead to deeper public commitments to bail out a troubled venture. Evaluators should look closely at this pattern, in an effort to provide better guidance on when it is better to bail out and when to go in deeper.

SPIN-OFFS

In addition to spreading through time, the effects of a public development investment move outward to influence private investments in other projects. New construction creates jobs, at least temporarily, in many trade and supplier industries. A new commercial or manufacturing operation similarly aids supplier firms and may foster the development of consumer firms, that is, operations that use its products or services as components of their own. Also, a successful commercial or housing project may change the investment climate in its neighborhood or community, leading to a self-reinforcing cycle of improvements by many property owners.

A large, successful, highly visible project such as Baltimore's Harbor Place may even influence the investment climate of an entire city. On the other hand, some projects that are internally successful will have negative spin-offs. For example, the introduction of new retail, hotel, or office space in a saturated market can lower rents and create higher vacancies, thus damaging existing investments. Detroit's Renaissance Center presents a conflicting picture of positive and negative spin-offs. Since the Center opened in 1977, Detroit has had a persistent glut of prime office space, and office rents per square foot are well below those in other cities. This strongly suggests that the project has harmed other office investments in the city (Knecht, 1983). Also, the fortresslike character and siting of the Center tend to minimize the spin-off of commercial investment to the surrounding area. Still, the Renaissance Center may have some offsetting value as a symbol — both locally and nationally — of the city's continuing vitality. Whether and how this psychological value to the city is translated into future investments may never be known.

The size, configuration, and visibility of commercial or residential investments may help to determine their influence on other, subsequent investment decisions. This is a familiar idea to specialists in neighborhood development, who often identify highly visible properties as early targets for striking exterior improvements and then seek to magnify the impact through publicity and follow-up efforts to stimulate a psychology of reinvestment. In 1979, the city of Pittsburgh began an effort to reverse the decline of six North Side neighborhoods (Reilly and Brophy, 1980). Of 5000 properties in the area, 400 were vacant and another 2000 needed moderate or substantial rehabilitation. The city's program included making below-market loans to people who would buy and rehabilitate homes in the area and providing rent subsidies for low- and moderate-income households to prevent their displacement as the neighborhood changed. This public investment generated an accelerating round of improvements, much of it privately financed. From 1979 to 1981, sales prices in the area rose 17 percent, compared to 6.5 percent in the entire city, a trend that suggests the revitalization process had become self-sustaining.

A second important determinant of spin-offs is the degree to which a development project is integrated with the local economy. This applies to industrial as well as commercial and residential investments. The effect of an initial investment is multiplied to the extent that the suppliers of the subsidized firm are local, to the extent that customers for its products or services are local, and to the extent that any profits are reinvested locally. The contrasting situation is familiar in developing countries; a foreign company sets up an assembly operation to employ cheap local labor or an agribusiness or mining operation to remove resources but contributes little more to the local economy than it pays in workers' wages.

There are two basically different approaches to estimating spin-offs. One is to gather information on the purchases, sales, and employment generated by individual development investments, then aggregate these numbers by program for evaluation purposes. The second is to use a standard nationally or regionally calibrated model to estimate input-output type multipliers of each investment across industrial sectors, again aggregating these numbers to evaluate programs or program variations. HUD has used the Regional Industrial Multiplier System (RIMS II) model, developed by the Commerce Department's Bureau of Economic Analysis, to assess the effects of various types of urban redevelopment expenditures (Cartwright and Beemiller, n.d.). This is a less expensive approach to estimating regional spin-offs than the alternate survey method, since it requires only a knowledge of the kinds of businesses being directly subsidized and the total amounts of their initial investments.

The major drawback of the modeling approach is its inability to produce information about the variation among projects, even among those involving similar industries. A second problem is that, because of the expense required for their initial calibration and recalibration, RIMS or similar models may use out-of-date multipliers or may not be calibrated at all for some regions.[15] The appeal of the project survey approach to estimating spin-offs, despite its higher costs, is enhanced by its potential for generating insights regarding the role of project design and participants' behavior in determining second and subsequent rounds of investment effects.

INSTITUTION BUILDING

Another way in which the benefits of a public development investment may be multiplied is by creating lasting local institutional capacity to support and sustain future economic development. The

importance of institution building receives great attention in the literature on developing nations (Hirschman, 1958), but is probably given
too little attention in most analyses of U.S. economic development
policy (Etzioni, 1983). Some federal programs, notably those of the
Economic Development Administration, the former Community
Services Administration, and the Small Business Administration,
have concentrated on direct efforts to develop local strategic planning
capacity, locally managed pools of investment capital, or other institutional supports for business development.

Other programs generate institutional gains indirectly, as a by-
product of the process by which development projects are created,
funded, and managed. The UDAG program, after its first three years,
was found to have increased the local public sector's economic development capacity in about 40 percent of the places where it was
used (HUD, 1982). Gains that were measured in these cities included
the first use of a particular development tool, new staff or offices, and
first instances of city leadership in negotiating development deals
with the private sector. However, the UDAG staff in Washington
continues to be a critical factor in such negotiations, since it can "play
the heavy" and thus help cities in hard bargaining with developers.
Therefore, the extent to which cities have achieved independent
deal-making capacity remains unclear.

Evaluators should look for at least four forms of institution building. First, by taking on risky projects, the public sector may demonstrate to the private capital market the financial feasibility of a
neglected category of investments. The learning generated thus
removes an institutional barrier — lack of information or experience
— that has prevented the private market from functioning efficiently
and opens the way for future unsubsidized investments of the same
general type. Second, the process of dealing with private
entrepreneurs may bring to the local public sector a new sophistica-
tion and new technical knowledge that increases not only the number
and variety of future development projects it can negotiate but also
the chances that each deal will be tailored to produce an optimal blend
of private return on capital and public benefits. This new public
deal-making ability may be acquired by existing staff or by the addition of staff or the creation of new offices or agencies. Third, the
process of project negotiation that first brings together private
entrepreneurs and investors with public agencies on an ad hoc basis
may sooner or later produce institutionalized public-private partner-
ships. This pattern of institutional innovation has been repeated over

the last two decades in city after city, producing an array of development corporations possessing delegated authority to invest public capital and manage development projects (Clarke, 1982). A fourth important form of institution building is the creation of new pools of investment capital, taking various forms. Federal economic development programs have increasingly placed the primary decision-making responsibility at the state and local levels of government, presumably encouraging them to build up a permanent capability to foster and manage economic development.

Because gains in institutional capacity may take many forms, multiple measures are required to assess this dimension of benefits. Many of the institutional gains are highly visible and readily measured; the main difficulty is in attributing them to a particular investment or program, since all but the smallest communities will be using many programs, more or less simultaneously, to pursue multiple projects. A second major difficulty lies in determining how lasting are the gains in institutional capacity; public capital aftmay be quickly dissipated through poorly chosen investments. Finally, it will be difficult to place relative values on various institutional gains, where value is conceptualized as the ability to support and sustain future development activity. Both the permanence and relative value of institutional gains can be assessed only after some period of time; thus a multiyear research design is a prerequisite for evaluations that measure this form of benefit properly.[16]

LOCAL STRATEGIC VALUE

An economic development investment's strategic value may be judged, from a local perspective, in two ways.[17] Either it is helping to create the kinds of economic development that a community determines it wants, or it is moving the local economy in a direction that is desirable by some objective standard. For instance, applying the first standard, if a local majority prefers to maintain its area's rural character and protect natural resources, it may favor investments in environmentally sound agriculture or nonpolluting industry but oppose other forms of development. Applying the second standard, it has been argued that older manufacturing centers should adapt to changes in the national economy by making themselves more attractive to emerging or rapidly growing industries; many (almost certainly too many) such communities have, in fact, decided to pursue a "high-technology" strategy. It may well be that the kind of development a community decides it wants and what it needs are the same, but this is not always the case. On the other hand, it is doubtful whether the foresight and wisdom exists in the federal government or elsewhere to override local desires and impose on a locality some development strategy that outsiders determine is in its long-run interest.

Judging the local strategic value of an investment from a subjective standpoint requires an analysis of local public opinion and the statements and actions of local government and business leadership. For example, to the extent that local leaders and public opinion are clearly behind a particular strategy (for example, exploiting the presence of certain skills in the local labor force), each development project can be examined to determine whether it is making a positive contribution to the strategy, making no contribution, or working against the strategy. Where local opinion is divided over strategy, evaluators can note the compatibility or incompatibility of each project with each strategy. The success of efforts to measure strategic value by a subjective standard depends, however, on the clarity with which local strategies have been articulated.

Judging local strategic value by objective standards requires the ability to predict the relative levels of development that are likely to be realized by pursuing one strategy or another. Savas (1983: 451) argues that, above all, the goals of a local development strategy "must not conflict with the external forces that are shaping the future," over which a locality has no control. These include technological change and trends in the national and international economies. A locality's choice of strategy must also, according to Savas, reflect the strengths and weaknesses of its location, resources, and people. Any effort to evaluate federal development investments by such a standard would be forced to break new ground in trying to operationalize objective criteria against which to measure projects and programs.

THE UTILITY OF A
COMPREHENSIVE EVALUATION FRAMEWORK

A comprehensive approach could make major contributions through improvements in program design and project selection as well as wiser allocation of federal and other public dollars among varied programs and approaches — leading to a more productive use of those public resources devoted to regional economic development. Here are three illustrations of how comprehensive evaluation leads to new insights and presumably better public policy.

ADJUSTING PRODUCTIVITY ESTIMATES

One of the payoffs of a more comprehensive evaluation approach is the ability to refine estimates of program benefits and costs, to produce more realistic comparisons across projects and programs. Because of the high rates of substitution and leakage inherent in the design of some programs, adjustments of initial leverage ratios for these benefit losses are absolutely essential for meaningful cross-program comparisons. If Program A has leakage and substitution rates of 25 percent each, then these losses will reduce *actual* benefits for the targeted area or population to about 56 cents of every dollar of *apparent* benefit. Program B, with substitution and leakage rates of 50 percent each, would generate only 25 cents of actual benefit for every dollar of apparent benefit.

Given the goals of economic development investments, however, evaluators have an obligation to look beyond the first round of benefits by estimating rates of growth or decay of benefits over time, major opportunity costs, spin-offs, and institutional effects. The adjustments to raw benefit estimates implied by these concepts can again produce sizable shifts in the estimated relative productivity of various investments.

On the cost side, an emphasis on total costs and the combined subsidies of multiple public investments contributing to the same project will often drastically alter the estimated relative productivity of apparently equivalent public expenditures. It is unlikely that the results of more sophisticated productivity estimation will consistently favor one program or approach. Rather, it is likely that different programs will present different profiles of strengths and weaknesses; and that their relative utility will vary with the circumstances under which they are applied. The relative value assigned by policymakers and citizens to different forms of benefit will also alter the perceived utility of various approaches.

ESTIMATING TRADE-OFFS

By broadening their study designs, evaluators increase the likelihood that goal trade-offs can be identified. For example, there is likely to be an inverse relationship, across programs, between substitution rates and loss of benefits due to project failures. Efforts to limit substitution by screening out projects that the private market will support will often inadvertently exclude financially viable projects that need public support. The remaining pool of selected projects will include a higher proportion of marginal projects, many of which will fail or fall short of expectations. Another example of trade-offs is that between minimizing leakage and maximizing the leverage of private investment and jobs. If public dollars are directed successfully toward the most needy areas and people, the resulting pool of eligible projects will, on average, require deeper public subsidies to attract private investment; this is a function of the higher risk and lower expected return associated with projects in the most distressed places. Comprehensive evaluations can help in determining the number and steepness of such trade-offs.

MEASURING COMBINED EFFECTS
OF MULTIPLE INVESTMENTS

A third way in which more comprehensive evaluations can lead to productivity gains is through understanding of the combined effects of multiple public investments. As noted earlier, the number of subsidies provided by various federal agencies, other levels of government, and quasi-private development corporations and the tendency for these to be concentrated in small areas lead to many instances where the interaction and degree of complementarity among public investments become paramount evaluation issues. A comprehensive evaluation frame applied to such packages of investments can be used to establish their combined effects and to identify inefficiencies due to oversubsidization or the failure of agencies to coordinate the timing and terms of their investments.

To date, few if any evaluation efforts have made a substantial effort to sort out the separate effects of and note the interactions among nearly simultaneous public development investments. Nor have evaluations been designed to capture the full effects of a series of public investments, over years or decades, in the same community or neighborhood. A casual survey of the pattern of federal investments in community development would certainly identify many neighborhoods and communities where a sequence of redevelopment efforts began with urban renewal in the 1950s and 1960s and has continued under a series of labels and with shifts of objectives and techniques up to the present time. A comprehensive approach to evaluation is essential to understanding how a sequence of investments over many years either increases or fails to increase the economic opportunities available to residents of these program-affected areas.

Debates over federal economic development policy will always be a mixture of conflicts: (1) between economic (for example, regional, sectoral, class) interests; (2) over values or objectives (for example, maximizing long-term national economic competitiveness versus preserving opportunities for established communities or expanding opportunities for the poor); and (3) over the relative efficiency of different programs (and/or the unregulated private market) in meeting these objectives. It is the last of these three aspects of the policy debate that is most subject to clarification through systematic, comprehensive evaluation of federal economic development investments. While sound evaluations of relative program productivity will not produce a policy consensus, they may lead to a better understanding of how and under what conditions public investments can lead to lasting gains in local economic opportunity at reasonable public cost.

NOTES

1. A more complex budgetary analysis would distinguish within programs between area-targeted and nontargeted expenditures; between those providing direct business aid and those providing public infrastructure and improvements; and, within programs, between expenditures closely related to economic development and those for housing, services, or other purposes. Such analysis would reduce the apparent magnitude of federal economic development activity supported by the listed programs. On the other hand, this partial listing excludes many smaller business assistance or development-related programs or program components (such as agricultural subsidies) as well as that portion of General Revenue Sharing that is used locally for economic development.

2. The reference is to the private market as it exists, not a hypothetical "free" or "perfect" market.

3. This comparison employs a methodology developed by Rasmussen et al. (1982) for comparing the net public costs of various economic development programs. In this version of their analysis, the firm is assumed to be a not very profitable one facing a combined state and federal marginal tax rate of 24 percent. Total costs are direct outlays minus tax offsets. All future costs are discounted to their equivalent present value. The assumed interest rate for the IRB and the below-market-rate loan is 9.8 percent versus a market rate of 14 percent.

4. Whenever costs and offsets are distributed over a period of years in the form of interest subsidies, tax benefits and offsets, loan repayments and defaults, or profit sharing, it is important to discount all future benefits to their equivalent present

value, so as to standardize calculations and allow for meaningful cross-program comparisons. The application of an annual discount rate to future expenditures reflects the standard assumption that dollars spent or received in the future are worth less, in today's terms, than dollars spent or received immediately. The same procedure applies to streams of future benefits as well.

5. This example employs the methodology developed by Rasmussen et al. (1982).

6. These figures are obtained by "discounting" the figures given by cities and developers for future investment plans. Investments based on rather firm plans to start within the next two years are discounted at 8 percent. As such plans extend into the future and are less firm, they are weighted less. This is a different use of the term "discounting" than elsewhere in this chapter; see Bingham and Blair (1983).

7. The present value of the expected investment should be discounted to reflect the fact that a given investment figure that will not occur until the future is worth less than that same amount if it were invested today. This notion is comparable to discounting loans to present value to reflect in current dollars the amount to be paid to the lender.

8. Part-time permanent jobs are adjusted to full-time equivalent figures such that two half-time jobs equal one full-time job. Temporary jobs, such as those in construction, should not be included in the full-time figure. For those programs that produce many temporary jobs, a separate construction/temporary jobs ratio can be calculated. This is particularly appropriate where the economic investment is in housing construction or renovation.

9. This study also estimates the overall cost of creating direct, indirect, and induced (spin-off) jobs at about $16,000 to $17,000 per year.

10. This figure reflects adjustments to account for instances where public funds merely substituted for private capital that would otherwise have been used to finance the same development.

11. If the federal subsidy is being used to prevent the loss of jobs due to the closing of operations, as in the case of the loan guarantees given to Chrysler, other policy questions arise. Should federal monies bail out firms that have not been competitive with other American or foreign firms? More pragmatically, will such federal help provide anything other than temporary retention of jobs?

12. For a random subsample of 27 projects, findings from the field research and other information on the nature and financing of the projects were presented to a panel of real estate experts. The panel included nationally recognized specialists in urban real estate finance and development. In its review, it examined such factors as projected rate of return on investment, market conditions, and development costs to reach an independent judgment on whether each project would have proceeded in the same place, at about the same time, and at the same scale without the UDAG funds. This expert review provided a check on the field study methods. The two approaches were merged in reaching judgments on these 27 projects. The inability of this method of substitution analysis to identify firmly all cases of substitution is a limitation on its usefulness; however, it represents a considerable advance over previous efforts to measure one way in which the benefits of federal economic development investments are diminished and their productivity thus reduced.

13. See the account by Knecht (1983).

14. The question of the Center's net effect on the area's economic growth is, of course, a more complex matter. See the following section on spin-offs for further discussion of this example.

15. Since multipliers are not available for separate jurisdictions, the use of regional multipliers will overstate the indirect jobs (and income) effects for any given locality. This is because supplying industries are likely to be located in neighboring jurisdictions within a region. These leakages may be exacerbated if employees spend their wages in areas other than where they work (Jacobs and Roistacher, 1980: 355).

16. See Culp et al. (1980) for an example of multiyear evaluation focusing on institutional effects.

17. In theory, the strategic value of local economic development investments can also be assessed relative to a specified national area development or industrial development strategy. In the absence of any explicitly formulated regional growth or industrial policy, however, any attempt to evaluate projects or programs in these terms would be a purely academic exercise.

REFERENCES

Abt Associates, Inc. (1980) Development of a Crosscut Evaluation System, Phase I, Draft Final Report, Vol. 4: Employment and Investment of EDA Public Works Investment and Implications for Future Evaluation Methodology. Cambridge, MA: Author.

BINGHAM, R. and J. BLAIR (1983) " Leveraging private investment with federal funds: use and abuse." Policy Studies Journal 11: 458-464.

CARTWRIGHT, J. V. and R. M. BEEMILLER (n.d.) RIMS II, Regional Input-Output Modeling System: A Brief Description. Washington, DC: Bureau of Economic Analysis, U.S. Department of Commerce.

Centaur Associates (1982) Economic Development Administration Title I Public Works Program Evaluation: Evaluation Results and Methodology. Washington, DC: Economic Development Administration, U.S. Department of Commerce.

CLARKE, S. E. (1982) "Trends toward local corporatism: institutionalizing local business/government relations." Presented at the annual meeting of the Midwest Political Science Association, Milwaukee, Wisconsin.

COOKE, P. and G. REES (1982) "The industrial restructuring of South Wales: the career of a state-managed region," in S. Redburn and T. Buss (eds.) Public Policies for Distressed Communities. Lexington, MA: D. C. Heath.

CULP, D., J. S. TILNEY, Jr., P. FINN, T. MILLER, and W. J. KNOX (1980) An Evaluation of the Community Economic Development Program: Long-Term Evaluation and Final Report. Cambridge, MA: Abt Associates, Inc. (for the U.S. Department of Housing and Urban Development).

Economic Development Administration [EDA] (1980) Local Public Works Program: Final Report. Washington, DC: U.S. Department of Commerce.

ETZIONI, A. (1983) "Reindustrialization of America." Policy Studies Review 2: 677-694.

HIRSCHMAN, A. O. (1958) The Strategy of Economic Development. New Haven, CT: Yale University Press.

HOUSE, P. W. and W. A. STEGER (1982) Modern Federalism: An Analytic Approach, Lexington, MA: D. C. Heath.

JACOBS, S. S. (1981) "Assessing UDAG as an urban economic development policy." Presented at the meeting of the Eastern Economics Association.

—— and E. A. ROISTACHER (1980) "The urban impacts of HUD's Urban Development Action Grant Program, or Where's the action in action grants?" in N. J. Glickman (ed.) The Urban Impacts of Federal Policies. Baltimore: Johns Hopkins University Press.

KNECHT, G. B. (1983) "Renaissance Center: Ford's costly failing bid to revive Detroit." New York Times (July 3).

MAY, J. V. (1981) Leveraging Performance of Federal Economic Development Programs. Washington, DC: U.S. Department of Housing and Urban Development.

NATHAN, R. P. and J. A. WEBMAN [eds.] (1980) The Urban Development Action Grant Program. Princeton, NJ: Princeton Urban and Regional Research Center, Woodrow Wilson School of Public and International Affairs, Princeton University.

Office of Management and Budget (1984) Budget of the U.S. Government, Fiscal Year 1984. Washington, DC: Government Printing Office.

RASMUSSEN, D. W. and L. C. LEDEBUR (1983) "The role of state economic development programs in national industrial policy." Policy Studies Review 2: 750-761.

RASMUSSEN D. W., M. BENDICK, Jr., and L. C. LEDEBUR (1982) Selecting Economic Development Incentives: A Cost Minimization Approach. Washington, DC: Urban Institute.

REILLY, M. K. and P. C. BROPHY (1980) Reinvestment in Pittsburgh: Three Case Studies. Washington, DC: U.S. Conference of Mayors.

SAVAS, E. S. (1983) "A positive urban policy for the future." Urban Affairs Quarterly 18: 447-453

U.S. Department of Housing and Urban Development [HUD] (1982) An Impact Evaluation of the Urban Development Action Grant Program. Washington, DC: Office of Policy Development and Research.

6

INVESTMENT SUBSIDY PROGRAMS
IN COMPARATIVE PERSPECTIVE

RAYMOND M. DUCH

University of Houston

The United States is currently debating whether or not the federal government should adopt an "industrial policy" as a solution to the serious industrial problems that confront the country (Magaziner and Reich, 1982; Bluestone and Bennett, 1982). An important part of the debate concerns whether or not government should offer investment subsidies to private industry as part of the government's efforts to promote industrial change.

The European and Japanese experiences with industrial policies indicate that investment subsidy programs are likely to be a key element of a country's industrial policy. This essay will focus on investment subsidies, suggesting which subsidy strategies are likely to be effective and which are not. The conclusions drawn here are based on the experiences of the French, the English, and the Japanese.

Governments can pursue a number of goals with investment subsidy programs: redistribution of wealth, enhancement of their chances of reelection, promotion of economic growth, and so on. An evaluation of the effectiveness of these programs depends upon what goals we assume they are pursuing. This essay is simply concerned with the effectiveness of subsidy programs in promoting economic growth. Investment subsidies represent an effort to promote this economic growth by redirecting societal resources — that is, funds available for investment — so as to affect certain industry characteristics (Stone, 1978). The recent history of Japanese and European subsidy programs suggests two fundamental industry characteristics that governments have attempted to manipulate: the nation's industrial portfolio and its industrial structure.

A nation's industrial portfolio is the mix of major industries found in a nation. Germany, for example, might be characterized as having an industrial portfolio dominated by the machine tool, steel, chemical, and automobile industries. Governments are concerned that their industrial portfolio consist of industries that are likely to experience high growth both domestically and internationally (Stoffaes, 1977). Investment subsidy programs have been designed primarily to encourage a high-growth industrial portfolio for the nation by lowering the effective costs of investing in these potentially high-growth industries.

The structural characteristics of a nation's industries have also been of concern to governments. With increasing competition for international markets and with declining protective tariffs, governments have become concerned that their national firms be of sufficient size and have sufficient resources to be able to compete effectively both in the international market and in their domestic markets. Industrial growth, of course, is predicated upon the ability of a nation's firms to maintain a significant share of the domestic market and to sell its products on foreign markets. By awarding investment subsidies, governments have reduced the relative cost of investments that contribute to the concentration and rationalization of industry.

Investment subsidies, then, are efforts by the government to reduce the actual cost of making an investment and thereby redirect the allocation of society's investment resources. Without government inducements, investment resources would seek out other investment opportunities. Governments assume that subsidies actually induce investors to make decisions they would not make if the investment subsidies did not exist. In fact, governments might offer subsidies for investments that investors or firms would make regardless of such government inducements.

There are two principal *subsidy instruments* governments can adopt. One is for governments to subsidize the cost of borrowing funds to finance investment. The market rate for business loans might be set at 10 percent, but the government, in its attempt to redirect investments, might offer or guarantee qualified firms loans at 5 percent. The second instrument is the direct subsidy. Qualified firms might receive a lump-sum payment from the government that might correspond to some percentage of the investment costs assumed by the firm. For example, the government might commit itself to subsidize 10 percent of certain types of investments; a capital investment project costing $1 million might receive a subsidy of $100,000 from the government. The effectiveness of investment subsidy programs may be influenced by which of these two instruments is selected. This essay does not evaluate the relative effectiveness of subsidy instruments. Rather, it examines the implications of adopting different allocation strategies.

The term "allocation strategies" refers to the manner in which the government selects the firms it intends to subsidize. There are three strategies that form somewhat of a selectivity continuum. Governments can offer very general investment subsidies rewarding firms that invest but that are not targeted at any particular types of firms and are not conditional on the firm's commitment to a particular investment strategy. Incentive-based investment subsidies are subsidies that are conditional on the firm committing itself to a particular investment or corporate strategy (for example, a commitment to increase exports). Finally, selective investment subsidies are those that are targeted at particular industries or particular firms. The government, for example, might target the semiconductor industry as a priority industry and therefore direct its investment subsidies to that industry.

Each of these subsidy allocation strategies has serious shortcomings. Regardless of the good intentions of senior policymakers, investment subsidy allocations are very susceptible to political pressures — subsidy programs and subsidy allocations end up furthering the short-term political interests of politicians rather than the long-term industrial health of the economy (Brittan, 1975). Moreover, the subsidies in themselves, even if they do not fall victim to political influences, are frequently allocated in such a manner as actually to harm rather than promote economic growth.

To the extent that governments insist on implementing investment subsidy programs, they should adopt allocation strategies that will inflict the least harm upon the nation's industrial performance. This essay suggests that the least harmful is the selective allocation strategy. By adopting a selective allocation strategy, governments will minimize the economic inefficiencies, and therefore economic harm, they are likely to generate.

GENERAL INVESTMENT
SUBSIDY PROGRAMS

General subsidy programs do not distinguish among industries or firms but rather provide investment subsidies for all firms regardless of what firm, industry, or activity is involved. There are many examples of these general subsidy programs. The French government, for example, has maintained interest rates on loans to business at artificially low levels, thereby subsidizing all businesses applying for loans. Governments have also been known to provide investment credits to firms that commit themselves to investments that create new jobs. These subsidies are indifferent to the kind of firm or industry undertaking the investment and therefore are general in nature.

General investment subsidies are found in almost all developed nations in the guise of regional development grants. These regional development grants are general because typically they are not awarded to selective firms or industries. Governments establish these regional development subsidy programs because they are literally desperate to attract industry — they are not particularly concerned about what kind of industry they attract.

General subsidy programs have a neutral or negative impact on a country's industrial portfolio, industrial structure, and industrial growth. Since these subsidies do not favor any particular industry, firm, or activity they will not promote industrial growth. Subsidies will be allocated to industries and firms according to their relative prominence in the economy. The impact of these subsidies might be negative in the sense that they allow marginal, declining industries to remain viable when in fact these subsidies should be promoting a shift from declining industries toward more growth-oriented industries. Consider, for example, a country with a predominance of declining industries such as textiles or steel. Since the government is not selective in its allocation of subsidies, these declining industries will be the major recipients of aid. Growth-oriented industries such as telecommunications and computers are new and therefore represent a much smaller fraction of the present industrial base. They will receive a much smaller amount of aid.

GENERAL SUBSIDIES IN THE UNITED KINGDOM

Ideally, we would like to establish an empirical link between general investment subsidy programs, industrial structure, and industrial portfolio, and industrial growth. This is beyond the scope of this essay. Nonetheless, some tentative conclusions can be drawn based on the experience of the United Kingdom.

In recent years, the United Kingdom has implemented two general subsidy programs: a jobs creation subsidy and a regional development subsidy. Three programs have been in existence that subsidize firms creating jobs: the Temporary Employment Subsidy, the Small Firm Employment Subsidy, and the Youth Employment Subsidy. These subsidies are allocated to firms in order to stimulate new employment or to induce employers to retain employees they would otherwise let go (Burton, 1979: 15). In 1975, the Temporary Employment Subsidy program alone cost £400 million (Burton, 1979: 14).

A program of this nature will negatively affect industrial growth because subsidy funds will be allocated to uncompetitive firms. The negative ramifications of such a program are numerous. First, by not selectively allocating subsidies to firms with high growth potential, the government provides the means by which many uncompetitive firms continue in business. This makes life more difficult for more dynamic, competitive firms; growth in their market share is stinted because these uncompetitive firms are kept in business by subsidies. Moreover, competitive firms are forced to compete for investment funds with firms that might have disappeared without the government's largesse. Finally, by subsidizing job creation, the government is rewarding labor-intensive firms at the expense of capital-intensive firms that are much more efficient and competitive.

The United Kingdom has made a major commitment to regional aid: Between the years 1971-1972 and 1977-1978, £5000 million (1978-1979 prices) were spent on regional policy (Grant, 1982: 54). Regional investment subsidies have been very popular in the United Kingdom and elsewhere because they generate political benefits for elected politicians. Simply from a social perspective, there are political pressures on political incumbents to respond to the plight of the less fortunate regions of the country, where one finds a high concentration of unemployment and poverty. From a more strategic perspective, politicians promote regional aid because it generates benefits for their constituents and improves their changes of reelection (Duch, 1982). Labour governments, for example, have been strong advocates of regional aid because many of their constituents are found in the more depressed areas of the United Kingdom (Grant, 1982: 57-58).

Overall, regional subsidies are unlikely to make a positive contribution to industrial growth. Much of the evidence suggests that regional subsidies do not seriously affect the locational decisions of firms. More important considerations for the firm are quality of the labor force, proximity to markets, and transportation and communication infrastructure. Econometric studies suggest that very little of the variance can be accounted for by subsidy variables (Wolkoff, 1983). Moreover, the British experience suggests that regional aid can be extremely costly, with very limited payoffs in the form of jobs or industrial activity (Grant, 1982: 60-62).

The more serious economic costs of regional subsidies are exactly the same as those outlined for job creation subsidies: Less competitive, low-growth firms end up receiving subsidies and crowd out market and financial opportunities for the more competitive firms.

There seems to be a growing awareness among governments that regional subsidies do not promote industrial growth and — to the extent that government continues offering subsidies to private industry — they should be substituted with more selective subsidy measures. In Britain, regional subsidies have been on the decline since the late 1970s. The government's 1977 white paper on expenditure stated that "the Government intend to move towards putting emphasis on selective, as against general, assistance to industry" (Grant, 1982: 59). Grant notes that total expenditure on regional industrial policy in the United Kingdom "at [1978-1979 prices] declined from a peak of 903 million pounds in 1975/76 to 854 million pounds in 1976/77 and 530 million pounds in 1977/78" (Grant, 1982: 59).

An investment subsidy policy designed to promote change in the nation's industrial structure and industrial portfolio must reward certain firms and industries over others. Such a goal is inconsistent with a general investment subsidy program such as the two described above.

INCENTIVE-BASED
INVESTMENT SUBSIDIES

Governments can take a somewhat more selective approach to subsidy allocations — they can allocate subsidies only to firms engaged in particular activities encouraged by the government. Examples of these activities might include firms engaged in exportation, firms committing considerable resources to research and development activities, or firms agreeing to mergers and rationalization. These types of subsidies are labeled here as "incentive-based" subsidies.

Most developed nations resort to incentive-based subsidies. Research and development subsidies are undoubtedly the most popular of the incentive-based subsidies. In order that their industries survive in increasingly competitive international markets, governments consider it crucial that domestic industries maintain high levels of spending on research and development. To encourage such spending, governments provide subsidies to assist firms in their research and development investments.

Another strategy for coping with this increasingly competitive international environment has been to provide direct investment subsidies to firms that export. Direct subsidization of exports is a violation of the 1975 GATT agreements. Nevertheless, governments have circumvented these regulations by including export performance as a criterion for the awarding of investment subsidies. Technically, they are not subsidizing exports, but rather are simply subsidizing the investment activities of a domestic firm as they would subsidize any firm. France, for example, includes export performance as a critical criterion for awarding all of its investment subsidies. A recent study of investment subsidies to the French food-processing industry has demonstrated very conclusively that export performance of firms was a critical criterion in deciding whether they received an investment subsidy (Duch, 1982).

Throughout the post-World War II period the Japanese have employed various forms of subsidies to support their export industries. One example described by Johnson (1982: 232) concerned the cross-subsidization of shipbuilding with the funds generated from sugar import licenses:

> Between 1953 and 1955 MITI [Ministry of International Trade and Industry] would issue import licenses for sugar to trading companies — which were then selling Cuban sugar in Japan at from two to ten times the import price — only if they had allied themselves with a shipbuilder and could submit an export certificate showing that they had used 5 percent of their profits to subsidize ship exports.

The Japanese Export-Import Bank and the Japan External Trade Organization (JETRO) subsidize exporting firms. Established in

1949, the Export-Import Bank has subsidized loans to customers of Japanese manufactured goods. JETRO collected trade and market information from its offices located throughout the world, providing Japanese firms with information that allowed them to exploit international markets more effectively.

Governments have also employed incentive-based subsidy programs in an attempt to rationalize their industry structures. Faced with the necessity that their industries compete in an increasingly competitive international market, governments have designed investment subsidy programs that encourage mergers and rationalization. Larger firms with greater financial resources and improved economies of scale are better able to compete in international markets.

Since as early as 1970, following the elimination of tariff barriers between EEC members, French authorities have attempted to encourage the rationalization of its industries by awarding investment subsidies. France was particularly disadvantaged because of the fragmentation of most of its industries (Jenny and Weber, 1974) and therefore put a high priority on the rationalization of its industry structures. In the textile industry, Berrier (1978) points out that Ministry of Industry officials adopted rationalization goals for the industry in 1965. In principle, subsidies were strictly targeted for firms committing themselves to merger and rationalization. A similar policy goal was adopted in the food-processing industry. In the early 1970s, senior planners insisted that the *Prime d'orientation agricole* favor firms engaged in merger and rationalization activities. Such firms were to receive very favorable subsidy rates (Duch, 1982).

The Japanese also conditioned their subsidies on firms' pursuit of merger and rationalization policies. In 1963, for example, the Japan Development Bank earmarked 3 billion yen for "structural credit" loans to larger firms that merged (this figure was raised to 6 billion yen in 1964). Prior to that, the bank had provided generous financing to small and medium size firms that engaged in mergers and rationalization. The Special Measures Law for the Stabilization of Designated Medium and Smaller Enterprises of 1952 authorized MITI to create cartels among small businesses as exceptions to the antimonopoly Law (Johnson, 1982: 225).

In 1961, Japan was forced by international pressure to liberalize its import controls. This liberalization brought fears that Japanese industry — especially the textile industry — would not be able to withstand the rigors of international competition. In April 1961, the Industrial

Structure Investigation Council was created in order to identify industry weaknesses compared to American and European competition. The council recommended reductions in the number of firms within particular industries and the strengthening and rationalizing of those firms left in each sector (Johnson, 1982: 253). Government subsidies designed to encourage structural rationalizations were also created as part of the 1962 Draft Law of Special Measures for Strengthening the International Competitive Ability of Designated Industries (Johnson, 1982: 258).

The effectiveness of incentive-based subsidy programs is measured by their contribution to industrial change and industrial growth. Incentive-based subsidies are likely to have neutral or negative effects because they simply treat the symptoms of industrial growth by rewarding activities that are associated with accelerated growth such as exports and research and development. These subsidies are not necessarily directed at modifying the nation's industrial portfolio and industrial structure.

A hypothetical example will illustrate this point. There are certain industries that, from both domestic and international perspectives, face very high growth potential (for example, the market for telecommunications services and hardware). On the other hand, there are industries that face relatively poor future growth prospects, such as textiles. In both types of industries, there are likely to be firms engaged in export and R&D investments. An incentive-based subsidy program would not distinguish between low-growth and high-growth industries, rewarding export performance and R&D investments in both industries. By not distinguishing between these two types of industries, the government's subsidy program is likely to have a neutral or negative impact on the nation's industrial portfolio. Assuming that the government would like to build up the nation's portfolio of high-growth industries, a strictly incentive-based subsidy program could be counterproductive. Firms in less dynamic industries could benefit from these incentive-based subsidy programs by committing themselves to exports or R&D investments. Yet, regardless of their export performance or research and development activities, these may be industries that the government ought to be discouraging rather than encouraging. The funds used to subsidize these less dynamic industries would be put to better use by the more dynamic high-growth industries.

When an individual evaluates investment opportunities using market criteria, he or she sizes up the overall characteristics of the firm: its long-range investment plans, its financial soundness, its management, its products, its markets, and so on. Incentive-based subsidy programs encourage exactly the opposite kinds of behavior. They encourage bureaucrats allocating these subsidies to focus on one or two particular characteristics: To what extent is the firm committing resources to research and development or what proportion of a firm's production is exported? Such an allocation strategy can result in the subsidization of uncompetitive firms. A firm might meet one of the government's criteria but, on many of the other evaluative grounds, might be a poor investment. These incentive-based subsidy programs might make the life of bureaucrats easier, but will hardly benefit the economy.

Unfortunately, since there are no good statistics kept on incentive-based subsidy programs, it is difficult to evaluate the impact of these subsidies on industrial growth. An examination of selective case studies provides useful insights into the effectiveness of incentive-based subsidy programs. France provides two revealing cases: subsidies to the food-processing and the textile industries.

THE FRENCH FOOD-PROCESSING INDUSTRY

Since the late 1960s, the French government has implemented an incentive-based subsidy program for the food-processing industry (Duch, 1982). With the elimination of EEC tariff barriers in the late 1960s, the French government became concerned that a very fragmented French food-processing industry would not be able to compete with the larger and more efficient firms found in neighboring countries. During this same period, American multinational food-processing firms were expanding into France by buying up small family-run firms. The French subsidy program for the food-processing industry was directed by senior planners to provide favorable subsidies to food-processing firms that were committed to mergers and rationalization of their productive facilities. This they hoped would promote larger, stronger, and more competitive French food-processing firms.

The oil crisis of 1974 produced a serious trade deficit in France. Government officials hoped to reduce the deficit by promoting French exports. In the post-1974 period, the French government directed administrators of food-processing investment subsidies to reward those firms that demonstrated a commitment to export their products. This produced a definite preferential treatment of firms engaged in export trade. Incentive-based subsidies, like any government subsidy program are vulnerable to political influences. Administrators of these incentive-based subsidies came under political pressure from professional associations representing small cooperative firms that stood to lose the most from a subsidy program that rewarded larger export-oriented firms. Moreover, members of the government's legislative coalition lobbied hard for support for food-processing firms in their districts that might close down without government subsidies. As a result, regardless of the incentive criteria established for allocating these subsidies, political considerations played an overwhelming role in subsidy allocations (Duch, 1982).

Food-processing investment subsidies suffered from another shortcoming. Bureaucratic myopia seriously handicapped the evaluation of subsidy candidates. Administrators focused on very limited criteria in evaluating applications: merger intentions, efforts to rationalize production, or export effort. They failed to take into consideration the overall quality of applicants: their management, their marketing efforts and plans, their production capabilities, and so on. As a result, subsidies were directed to many uncompetitive firms.

In the late 1970s, members of the prime minister's cabinet responsible for the food-processing industry and members of the Ministry of Finance became unhappy with the effectiveness of the food-processing subsidy program. One reason for this dissatisfaction was the misallocation of subsidies to firms with very poor economic prospects — a result of political pressures brought to bear on administrators and a result of bureaucratic myopia. In response to this dissatisfaction, the agency adopted a more selective allocation of subsidies — one that took into consideration the overall quality of applicants.

THE FRENCH TEXTILE INDUSTRY

In 1965 the French government approved its first major incentive-based subsidy program for the French textile industry (Berrier, 1978: 159). The program was designed to encourage firms to merge and rationalize their productive facilities. This and subsequent incentive-based subsidy programs were for the most part unsuccessful. It was not until the latter part of the 1970s that the industry experienced a substantial decline in the number of firms — this, though, was primarily the result of increased international competition (Mytelka, 1982: 138). Two major factors contributed to the failure of these subsidy programs: politics and bureaucratic myopia.

The Comité interprofessional de renovation des structures industrielles et commerciales de l'industrie textile (CIRIT) was established by the Ministry of Industry to allocate investment subsidies to
textile firms. It was initially to remain independent of the textile firms
and of their professional association, the Union des industries textiles
(UIT). The CIRIT did not remain independent; the UIT used its
political power to exhert its control over the CIRIT. As a result,
subsidies were not allocated so as to promote mergers and rationalization, but rather to support traditional firms that were to small and very
uncompetitive. A program initially designed to promote change in the
textile industry ended up inhibiting change. (Berrier, 1978: chap. 4).

Another serious flaw in the subsidy program was its focus on
narrow criteria for allocating subsidies. The overriding concern of
government planners was that the number of textile firms be reduced.
Little careful thought was given by the CIRIT as to what firms ought
to be merged and what commitments to rationalization ought to
accompany these mergers. A number of mergers occurred in the latter
part of the 1960s, but they were simply horizontal mergers in which a
large number of small family operations were brought under the
control of a larger firm. The factories of these smaller firms should
have been shut down and the production of the various small firms
merged into large production facilities that could benefit from scale
economies. This rarely occurred, however, and was not strongly
encouraged by the CIRIT as a condition for granting subsidies.
Horizontal mergers in fact burdened health firms with a number of
small, uncompetitive units of production.

INDUSTRIAL RATIONALIZATION
IN THE UNITED KINGDOM

In the United Kingdom, rationalization emerged as an industrial
priority under the Labour government. The Industrial Reorganization Act of 1967 established the Industrial Reorganization Agency
(IRA), which was "to undertake mergers in the interests of greater
efficiency" (Burton, 1979: 26). These mergers were promoted with
subsidized loans to firms that committed themselves to mergers and
subsequent rationalization. In 1970, the IRA was abandoned by the
Tories. A National Enterprise Board (NEB) was created in 1975 that
addressed the same problem — the need to encourage the rationalization of British industry — but channeled its subsidies to firms via
purchases of equity rather than subsidized loans.

Overall, these incentive-based subsidies were not successful. A large part of their failure can be explained by the factors outlined earlier. Bureaucratic myopia resulted in mergers that eventually failed because those responsible for encouraging mergers did not carefully consider the complex factors associated with a successful merger. Caves (1968) has pointed out that this policy of encouraging rationalization is simply a strategy of "finding the most efficient firm and merging the rest into it." As a result, the more efficient firms are burdened with less efficient firms.

A good example of failure resulting from this bureaucratic myopia is the case of the Upper Clyde Shipbuilders. In 1966, the Geddes Report on Shipbuilding recommended the promotion of mergers in the shipbuilding industry as a solution to its poor competitiveness in international markets. A number of failing shipbuilders responded to the government's rationalization priority by merging into the Upper Clyde Shipbuilder Company. It received considerable support from the IRA and kept coming back for more public funds.

In 1972, the firm went into receivership and was split into two groups: Govan Shipbuilders and Marathon. Government officials were mistaken to think that a simple merger of a large number of failing firms would result in improved competitiveness. As a number of commentators have noted, the rationalization efforts failed because they were implemented so narrowly without taking into consideration the complex mix of factors that contribute to competitiveness (Dell, 1973: 168).

The government's narrow focus on mergers and size meant that smaller shipbuilding firms, regardless of how efficient and competitive, were unlikely to receive investment subsidies. By directing public funds into the larger, uncompetitive shipbuilding firms and by denying funds to the smaller, more competitive firms, government subsidies were actually contributing to the increased uncompetitiveness of the British shipbuilding industry.

British Leyland was another creature of the Labour government's rationalization priorities. Created in 1968 from a hodgepodge of British automobile manufacturers, British Leyland has yet to integrate its various components, models, factories, and work forces. Coates (1980: 118) has suggested that British Leyland's low productivity is the result of the 1968 merger that created "the overlapping and uncoordinated range of cars and parts in over sixty geographically scattered plants, with a labour force that was as high as 200,000 in 1972-1973." Not surprisingly, British Leyland's productivity figures compare very unfavorably with those of its Japanese and continental competitors. Once again, a fixation on merger as a goal in itself without giving serious consideration to the many other complex factors that lead to an efficient, competitive firm resulted in failure.

These merger incentives were not simply based on a concern with industrial growth. Successive British governments promoted mergers such as British Leyland in an effort to save jobs. By burdening the more efficient firms with less efficient, money-losing ones, the government reasoned they could save threatened jobs. The principal attraction of merging smaller producers into a larger entity is that through the rationalization of production, the larger entity presumably can benefit from greater scale economies. But the government was very reluctant to tolerate the massive job losses that would result from such rationalization. Governments are quick to promote mergers, but are also quick to prevent subsidized firms from making the kinds of reductions in their labor force that would make the mergers work.

JAPANESE EXPERIENCE

Japan has undoubtedly implemented the most successful investment subsidy programs. Like its European counterparts, the Japanese government (in particular, MITI) was and is concerned that its firms adopt particular corporate strategies — such as concentration, exportation, or research and development. The Japanese, though, never made the mistake of assuming that by rewarding these narrow activities (such as export performance) they could improve industrial growth. Successful investment subsidy programs required that industrial planners encourage exports, R&D, and the like, but also that they selectively target subsidies to promising industries and to the most appropriate firms within an industry. This kind of synergy among subsidy allocation strategies never existed in Western Europe.

As early as 1954, the Japanese government embarked upon a program promoting exports. The Comprehensive Policy for Economic Expansion did not simply promote exports among all Japanese industry, but rather promoted exports among selective industries that the government considered particularly promising. In the 1960s, when rationalization of Japanese industry became a prime industrial goal, the government did not indiscriminantly promote mergers and rationalizations. Rather, the government selected key industries that showed economic promise: steel, automobiles, machine tools, computers, petroleum refining, petrochemicals, and synthetic textiles. It was in these selected sectors that government would promote mergers (Johnson, 1982: 278). (It should be noted that a number of the ventures — for example, petrochemicals and refining — were failures.) In promoting industrial goals, the government was not only selective in its choice of industry, but was careful about which firms received its support.

SELECTIVE INVESTMENT
SUBSIDY PROGRAMS

In the 1970s western governments experienced severe balance of payments problems associated with the oil crisis of 1974 and a general slowing of economic growth. The French and English governments were generally disastisfied with the efficacy of their industrial policies. A general consensus seems to have emerged among advocates of industrial policy that government initiatives would have to be much more selective, targeted at specific industries, specific sectors, and specific firms. They saw this as a means to get more bang from their subsidy buck.

The selective industrial policy strategy includes two basic components. Government officials select industries in which the nation is no longer competitive and provides incentives and government support for disengagement from these industries (for example, the costs of retraining and possibly relocating the labor force or the costs of attracting new firms to a particular region). A second component requires the government to support growth industries that will generate employment and export revenues for a nation. Investment subsidies are one manner in which the government can support and promote these growth industries.

A selective industrial policy places considerable decision-making burdens on government officials. First, government must identify industries that are likely to experience high growth rates in both domestic and international markets. Sometimes simply identifying industries is not sufficient — a more refined identification of growth sectors within industries is necessary. For example, the computer industry is likely to experience considerable growth potential in the next ten years but within that industry microcomputers are likely to experience a much faster growth rate than mainframe computers.

Second, government officials must determine where the country's comparative advantages lie. Is there a domestic or potential domestic market that could be exploited in order to build up production scales before the product is offered on the export market? Does the nation have the intellectual talent needed to develop the industry (such as trained computer programmers, biologists, or automotive engineers)? Are there domestic firms involved in complementary activities that might move into these industries? Can the country finance entry into these new industries?

Industries are not static; at various stages of their evolution they demand different competitive strategies (Porter, 1980; Lawrence and Dyer 1983). Solar industries, for example, are at a very different evolutionary stage than steel. Selective subsidy programs must be based on careful evaluation of the nation's industries, their stage of development, the opportunities at that stage of development, and the appropriate strategies for helping firms exploit those opportunities. Since the success of subsidy programs is so dependent upon these evaluations of competitive strategies, a brief review of the strategic considerations that governments must make in the evaluation of industries, sectors, and firms is offered.

NEW INDUSTRIES

Governments are attracted by new high-technology industries and the benefits they offer for the nation's industrial portfolio, structure, and growth. Major efforts have been conducted by governments to attract or build up such industries as robotics, digital telephone exchanges, communication satellites, and fiber optics. How does a government determine which new high-technology industries it should encourage and whether it should allocate investment subsidies to firms in these industries?

A key consideration here is the stage of innovation characterizing a new industry. Governments should promote new industries at very early stages of innovation. If an industry has experienced considerable innovative development, domestic firms may have little hope of catching up and competing in the international market. The semiconductor industry is a case in point. Japanese and American semiconductor firms have a major lead on other firms in the development of 256k semiconductor chips. It would be very risky for other nations to attempt to compete in this market. There are, nonetheless, particular niches of any market that might be exploited by a nation's firms — in the semiconductor industry, for example, such a niche might be custom manufactored microprocessors. All things being equal, though, a government is likely to have a greater chance of success if it promotes an industry that is in its early stages of innovative development.

Governments must also evaluate the costs of entry into any particular industry. Regardless of how developed the technology, the costs of developing a particular technology may be prohibitive for certain nations. Firms in a number of nations, for example, could not be expected to develop and exploit the technologies associated with space exploration, commercial aircraft production or mainframe computer development. Another consideration is whether the expertise or technologies developed in other industries reduce the costs of entering a new industry. Japan, for example, which has considerable expertise in advanced manufacturing processes and numerically controlled machine tools, was ideally positioned to enter into the robotics industry. Similarly, France's considerable expertise in aeronautics should put it in a good position for entering the space industry.

Access to markets is also an important consideration that governments must make prior to committing resources to a particular industry. How accessible are international markets to a particular product? With governments becoming increasingly protective of certain industries, governments should promote industries that are not likely to face such barriers.

The attraction of the early development of certain new technologies is that firms reap monopoly profits until other firms are able to emulate the technology or license the technology. Governments will want to promote new technologies and industries that promise considerable monopoly profits for their domestic firms. Industries in which the technological advantage can be maintained for a considerable period of time are clearly to be favored. Countries, for example, that are able to generate new products in the areas of bioengineering and intelligent computing are likely to reap considerable monopoly profits.

Having selected new emerging industries, the government must then decide how to promote firms in the industry. Investment subsidies may not be appropriate. Even if they are appropriate, they may take on a different form than subsidies administered in the mature industries. Unlike mature industries, where there may be major capital investments, emerging high-technology industries may have little need for major capital expenditures. Their major costs might consist of hiring skilled engineers and scientists, purchasing expense software, or licensing certain technologies.

HIGH-GROWTH COMPETITIVE INDUSTRIES

Governments might also consider promoting competitive industries in which the technology is fairly widely diffused and in which there are typically a number of firms competing for domestic and international markets. This category would include such industries as PBX manufacturers, manufacturers of many types of office equipment, and personal computer manufacturers.

Once again, governments are confronted with a plethora of factors to take into consideration. Cost of entry is once again a major consideration. Can domestic firms obtain or develop the appropriate technologies at a reasonable cost? What kind of marketing effort — both domestically and internationally — will be required? Do domestic firms have such a capability? How high are the start-up costs associated with a particular industry or product?

Another important consideration is the comparative advantages of the nation's firms. Will the nation's firms have reasonably easy access to the intellectual and material factors associated with the industry? If domestic firms are already present in the particular industry, the government's promotional efforts are more likely to succeed.

Competitive industries do not always remain unconcentrated industries. Industries frequently reach a mature stage in which the market is dominated by a small number of large firms. Government officials should determine the likelihood of an industry shake-out that would leave only a few dominant firms. If domestic firms are unlikely to withstand such a shake-out, it may be inadvisable to target the industry altogether.

A selective subsidy strategy requires that the government target specific firms in an industry. Government officials must decide which firms are most likely to perform well in the targeted industry. These may be firms already actively involved in the industry or they may be firms involved in related industrial activities.

MATURE INDUSTRIES

Mature industries that have moderate to high growth potential are also a possible target for government subsidies. There are two likely circumstances in which government will consider investment subsidies to mature industries. One is when the technology associated with a mature *product* undergoes major change. Government may also consider subsidies when the *process* technology of a mature industry undergoes major change (Hayes and Wheelwright, 1979a, 1979b; Hayes and Abernathy, 1980).

Products of mature industries that have experienced major technological changes would include the automobile, the telephone exchange, and the watch (Abernathy et al., 1983). Manufacturers of conventional products have been faced with a major competitive threat from producers that have incorporated the new technologies. In the 1970s the traditional American automobile was subject to very intense competition from imports that were smaller and better performing. They literally were forced to redesign a new automobile product.

For many years telephone exchanges were based on the analogue cross-bar technology. In the 1970s a new digital technology was developed that could handle voice and data communication and incorporate certain computing tasks. Market leaders such as Western Electric were caught somewhat off guard by these developments and came under intense competitive pressures from other manufacturers. Swiss watchmakers faced a similar challenge from manufacturers of digital LCD watches. They were very slow to respond to the technology changes introduced by the Japanese.

As a defensive move, governments are prone to offer investment subsidies to their threatened mature industries. Or, seeing the opportunity of challenging market leaders in a mature industry, governments will consider granting investment subsidies to domestic firms that have a chance of successfully mounting a challenge.

Mature industries can also be shaken up by radical changes in process technologies. These are the processes associated with the manufacture of a product. An excellent case in point is the steel industry, which has experienced significant changes in the technologies associated with the manufacturing operation (Lawrence and Dyer, 1983: chap. 3). The advantages of firms in these mature industries are usually considerable. They have a large proportion of the market, significant manufacturing economies of scale, and an extensive distribution or marketing network. Governments are reluctant to see such industries succumb to international competition.

Investment subsidies should be tailored to these particular circumstances. To the extent that firms must respond rapidly with new innovative products, the government should target subsidies at capital expenditures associated with such developments. Similarly, if the firms are threatened by process innovations, government should provide subsidies for expenditures associated with the development of new process innovations that will increase manufacturing productivity.

In the event that a government decides to allocate investment subsidies, a selective allocation of these subsidies is the most efficient use of its resources. Nonetheless, even this selective allocation strategy has pitfalls that might lead to failure.

In this section the factors that enter into a selective subsidy allocation strategy have been outlined. There are three types of industries that the government might subsidize, and, within each of these typologies, there are a number of unique factors that government decision makers must consider. The costs of gathering the appropriate information are high. They require extensive information regarding the domestic and international market for a large number of goods. Government decision makers must make fairly complex evaluations of the comparative advantages of the country's productive factors. A careful evaluation of the nation's industries and firms would also be required (Stoffaes, 1977).

While certainly not an insurmountable barrier, the probabilities are high that government will not commit the resources and the time required to collect the appropriate information. Most governments operate within fairly restricted time constraints that usually run around four to five years. Action must be taken before they come up for reelection, and this usually leaves little room for serious information gathering. Moreover, administrators within a government bureaucracy are, for the most part, not well equipped to gather the type of information outlined earlier in this section.

A selective subsidy program like all subsidy programs, is subject to political influences. Selective subsidies to mature industries are the most prone to political influences. They are established industries, usually with a large labor force and found in specific geographic concentrations. Governments may overlook the criteria for efficient allocation of subsidies when dealing with these industries. A selective strategy calls for subsidizing those mature industries with a significant growth potential in domestic and international markets. These criteria are frequently overlooked in response to political pressure from industry and its employees. As pointed out above, subsidies should be allocated for either developing new technologically advanced products or for funding of innovative manufacturing methods. Under political pressure, subsidies are frequently granted without any contractual arrangements that might ensure that companies put the subsidies to these proper uses.

JAPANESE SELECTIVE INVESTMENT SUBSIDIES

Japan is the one capitalist nation in which industrial policy has had some reasonable success. Its strategy of aiding selective industries is a major contributing factor to this success. The history of recent Japanese industrial policy reflects this selectivity. During the early sixties MITI targeted four key industrial sectors: electric power, shipbuilding, coal mining, and steel plants (Johnson, 1982: 211). Later in the decade, the Nakayama Committee was to focus the government's industrial assistance on seven industries: steel, automobiles, machine tools, computers, petroleum refining, petrochemicals, and synthetic textiles (Johnson, 1982: 278). Strategic industries in the post-oil crisis period of the 1970s included automobiles, semiconductors, numerically controlled machine tools, robots, and advanced consumer electronic goods such as videotape recorders (Johnson, 1982: 302).

FRENCH AND BRITISH
SELECTIVE INVESTMENT SUBSIDIES

Selective strategies do not always work. The French and British experiences with selective subsidies are evidence that such strategies can fail. Since World War II, French governments have targeted key industries as part of the French Plan. In the post-oil crisis of the 1970s, President Giscard's government targeted four high-technology industries that would form the core of French industrial policy: communication systems, aeronautics, armaments, and nuclear reactors. A review of the French experience with selective subsidies in the computer and steel industries indicates the pitfalls associated with such initiatives.

In 1967, the De Gaulle government responded to the poor competitive record of the French computer industry by instituting a selective subsidy program titled the Plan Calcul. The first phase of the Plan Calcul spanned the years 1967-1971 and received close to a billion francs in government subsidies (Le Pors, n.d.: 253-271). The principal recipient was the Compagnie internationale pour l'informatique (CII), the company designated as the French computer manufacturer that would do battle with IBM in both the domestic and the international markets. Notwithstanding the significant commitment from the French government, the plan was a commercial failure. In France itself CII was only able to gain 7.5 percent of the market compared to 19 percent for Honeywell Bull and 60 percent for IBM (Le Pors, n.d.).

The second Plan Calcul, which lasted from 1971-1975, suffered a similar fate. Once again the government committed in excess of 1 billion francs, most of which went to CII. By 1973 the market share of CII had progressed only to 10 percent. Its presence on the European and international markets was insignificant, although somewhat aided by its joint venture with Siemens and Philips.

Although selective, the Plan Calcul failed because of the efforts of politicians to impose their political priorities associated with national defense and national prestige on the investment decisions of private computer firms. De Gaulle was concerned that France have advanced mainframe computing capabilities as part of its defense requirements and also that the national presitige be upheld by demonstrating that France was not dependent upon the United States for computing technology. From a marketing perspective it was unrealistic for CII to try to support a full line of computers as the government dictated. By not identifying niches of the market where they could realistically gain an important foothold, the firm was never able to gain a major share of any aspect of the computer market (Zysman, 1977).

Until very recently, efforts by the French government to rescue the French steel industry have represented a major failure for selective subsidy programs. In the 1967-1970 period, the *convention Etat-siderurgie* committed the government to subsidies worth 2,700 million francs in an effort to "make the steel industry competitive" (Le Pors, n.d.: 214). Although the industry did experience a certain degree of rationalization during this period — the number of factories dropped from 118 in 1965 to 99 in 1970 — it actually became less competitive vis-à-vis its international and European competition. Output increased at a historic low rate and the trade balance for steel actually became worse, indicating increased imports and decreased exports (Le Pors, n.d.: 220).

During the 1970s, in an effort to promote the modernization of the steel industry, the government pumped considerable public funds into the construction of greenfield steel manufacturing facilities at Fos and Dunkirk. These facilities proved no salvation for the industry and never fit well into the integrated chain of steel production. For the most part, these selectives subsidies to the steel industry failed because the government was not willing to face the political costs associated with a massive cutback in the steel work force. In order to make the French steel industry more productive and competitive, steel firms would have to shut down outmoded production facilities and reduce their overall work force. The government never seriously pursued such goals and therefore, even with the introduction of modern steel manufacturing facilities, the overall industry remained overstaffed and burdened with outmoded production facilities.

As the financial situation deteriorated even further in the late 1970s, the Giscard government decided in 1978 to take drastic steps in order to prevent massive bankruptcy of the industry. The government in effect took over the financial and management control of the major steel firms and forced a restructuring plan that led to a cut in employment from 150,000 workers to 105,000 over a two-year period. Indications are that, confronted with a serious crisis, the government adopted a selective subsidy strategy that may actually lead to a more competitive steel industry (Cohen et al., 1982: 70-71).

The English have focused their selective subsidization efforts on the National Enterprise Board (NEB), which was established in 1975. The board's subsidies take the form of direct investments or equity financing of promising concerns. In principle, the board was to abide by normal commercial criteria when making investment decisions. NEB investments were to be confined to selected industries and firms that showed significant commercial promise.

Notwithstanding this commitment to commercially viable investments, the NEB succumbed to political pressures and devoted most of its energies and resources to shoring up prominent lame-duck firms. In its first years of operation under the Labour government, the NEB did not serve as a catalyst of private investment and growth, but rather as a nursery for sickly British corporations. Of its first £1000 million budget, £450 million went to Rolls-Royce and British Leyland — both of which were suffering from major losses. Although the Wilson government publicly commited itself to improving the performance of British Leyland by "better industrial relations and higher productivity," productivity declined, industrial relations became worse, and British-Leyland's share of the home market dropped (Coates, 1980: 122).

Under the Thatcher government there has been an effort to reform the NEB, reorienting it toward investment in selective industries that show commercial promise and that will likely contribute to industrial growth. Although it is somewhat early to evaluate the changes, there are indications that it has shaken its role of tending strictly to lame-duck firms.

Under the Conservatives, the NEB has been used increasingly as a catalyst in the field of advanced technologies. Willot has identified three major types of NEB high-technology investments: major initiatives in electronics firms such as Inmos (semiconductors and microprocessors) and Nexos (electronic office equipment), smaller ventures such as those in medical electronics and software, and rescue efforts for such firms as Cambridge Instruments, Ferranti, and ICL (Willott, 1981: 140).

CONCLUSION

Confronted by slowing economic growth, increased international competition, and failing industries, governments may include investment subsidies as one option for promoting industrial change and industrial growth. Governments should be aware that there are at least three different strategies for allocating subsidies: general investment subsidies, incentive-based subsidies, and selective investment subsidies. In the case of all three allocation strategies, subsidies may fail to promote industrial growth because of political pressures brought to bear on the government and on those responsible for administering the subsidies. There is no way of insuring against this possibility and therefore it should enter into any evaluation of investment subsidies as a policy instrument.

With respect to the promotion of industrial growth, there are more and less effective strategies for allocating investment subsidies. The least effective strategy is a general investment subsidy that does not discriminate among the types of firms eligible for government aid. General investment subsidies are likely to promote the industrial status quo if not aggrevate the industrial ills of a country.

A somewhat more effective investment subsidy strategy is one that conditions the awarding of subsidies on some aspect of the firm's corporate strategy. For example, has the firm committed itself to an accelerated program of research and development? Although ostensibly promoting a corporate activity that might contribute to industrial growth, these subsidies tend to be allocated without considering overall firm characteristics. As a result, many uncompetitive firms benefit from such a program, which in turn detracts from the growth potential of a nation's industries.

A selective subsidy investment program is likely to be the most effective strategy for subsidizing private firms. Under such a strategy, subsidies are allocated to industries and firms that the government decides will make the most positive contribution to industrial growth. These subsidies may carry contractual conditions, but what is important is that they are made available only to those firms judged likely to have a maximum positive impact on industrial growth.

REFERENCES

ABERNATHY, W.J., K.B. CLARK, and A.M. KANTROW (1983) Industrial Renaissance: Producing a Competitive Future for America. New York: Basic Books.

ALLEN, G.C. (1981) A Short Economic History of Modern Japan. London: Macmillan.

BERRIER, R. (1978) "The politics of industrial survival: the French textile industry." Ph.D. dissertation, Massachusetts Institute of Technology.

BLUESTONE, B. and H. BENNETT (1982) The De-Industrialization of America. New York: Basic Books.

BRITTAN, S. (1975) "The economic contradictions of democracy." British Journal of Political Science 5: 129-159.

BROADWAY, F. (1970) State Intervention in British Industry 1964-1968. Madison, WI: Fairleigh Dickinson University Press.

BURTON, J. (1979) The Job Support Machine: A Critique of the Subsidy Morass. London: Centre for Policy Studies.

CARTER, C. [ed.] (1981) Industrial Policy and Innovation. London: Heinemann.

CAVES, R. (1968) "Market organization, performance, and public policy," pp. 279-323 in R.E. Caves et al. (eds.) Britain's Economic Prospects. London: Allen & Unwin.

COATES, D. (1980) Labour in Power? A Study of the Labour Government 1974-1979. London: Longoman.

COHEN, S.S. and P.A. GOUREVITCH (1982) France in the Troubled World Economy. London: Butterworth.

COHEN, S., J. GALBRAITH, and J. ZYSMAN (1982) "Rehabbing the labyrinth: the financial system and industrial policy in France," in S. Cohen and P. Gourevitch (eds.) France in the Troubled World Economy. London: Butterworth.

DELL, E. (1973) Political Responsibility and Industry. London: Allen & Unwin.

DUCH, R. (1982) "Investment subsidies to the French food processing industry: industrial priorities, constituency pressures, and bureaucratic procedure." Ph.D. dissertation, University of Rochester.

GRANT, W. (1982) The Political Economy of Industrial Policy. London: Butterworth.

HAYES, R.H. and W.J. ABERNATHY (1980) "Managing our way to economic decline." Harvard Business Review (July/August): 67-77.

HAYES, R.H. and S.C. WHEELWRIGHT (1979a) "Linking manufacturing process and product life cycles." Harvard Business Review (January/February): 133-140.

——— (1979b) "The dynamics of process-product life cycles." Harvard Business Review (March/April): 127-136.

JENNY, F. and A.P. WEBER (1974) Concentration et politique des structures industrielles. Paris: Commissariat général du plan.

JOHNSON, C. (1982) MITI and the Japanese Miracle: The Growth of Industrial Policy, 1925-1975. Stanford, CA: Stanford University Press.

LAWRENCE, P.R. and D. DYER (1983) Renewing American Industry. New York: Free Press.

LE PORS, A. (n.d.) "Les transferts Etat-Industrie: evaluation et signification (1962-1974)." Ph. D. dissertation, Université de Paris.

MAGAZINER, I. C. and R. B. REICH (1982) Minding America's Business: The Decline and Rise of the American Economy. New York: Vintage.

MYTELKA, L. K. (1982) "In search of a partner: the state and the textile industry in France," pp. 132-150 in S. S. Cohen and P. Gourevitch (eds.) France in the Troubled World Economy. London: Butterworth.

PORTER, M. E. (1980) Competitive Strategy Techniques for Analyzing Industries and Competitors. New York: Free Press.

STOFFAES, C. (1977) La grande menace industrielle. Paris: Calmann-Levy.

STONE, A. (1978) "Subsidies as a policy instrument," pp. 249-256 in J. Brigham and D. Brown (eds.) Policy Implementation: Penalties or Incentives? Beverly Hills, CA: Sage.

WILLOTT, W. B. (1981) "The NEB involvement in electronics and information technology," pp. 203-212 in C. Carter (ed.) Industrial Policy and Innovation. London: Heinemann.

WOLKOFF, M. (1983) "Chasing a dream: the use of tax abatement to spur urban economic development." Public Policy Analysis Discussion Paper 8206, University of Rochester.

ZYSMAN, J. (1977) Political Strategies for Industrial Order: State, Market, and Industry in France. Berkeley: University of California Press.

7

THE INNOVATION-PRODUCTIVITY
CONNECTION

IRWIN FELLER
IRENE JOHNSTON
Pennsylvania State University

Productivity change and innovation are two imprecisely linked concepts utilized in discussions of the performance of state and local governments. This essay has three objectives: (1) to specify possible connections between productivity and innovation; (2) to review findings concerning the character of several of these connections; and (3) to present new data on one of these connections, with respect to the characteristics of innovations adopted in municipal governments.

Attention to the connection stems from a variety of themes: the fiscal crisis caused by differentials in the growth of demands for public services and politically feasible revenue bases; "Baumol's disease," which concerns the inevitable rise in the relative real cost of providing labor-intensive public services; comparative studies on the efficiency of public sector and private sector delivery of services; and econometric estimates of rates of productivity changes in state and local governments. Two propositions characterize current views of the nature of the connection. First, rates of productivity changes in state and local governments have been low, both in absolute terms and relative to private sector organizations (Spann, 1977). Second, the low rate of productivity change in state and local governments is due, in part, to their slow and low innovation-adoption rates (Urban Institute, 1970; Hayes and Rasmussen, 1972).

Several explanations have been advanced for the "recalcitrance" and "laggardness" of decision makers in state and local governments to adopt innovations. Those explanations most important to this study emphasize the absence of property rights to the gains from innovative behavior in public sector organizations; the postulated predilection for public sector managers to seek innovations that augment total budgets rather than those that minimize unit cost; and the difficulties in measuring the efficiency of public sector delivery of goods and services, whether by "traditional" or "innovative" means.

The association between low rates of productivity improvement and low rates innovation adoption has yet another "supply-side" proponent. Federal agencies, public interest groups, and firms seeking new markets each found a cause and at times a raison d'être in promoting the transfer of technologies to state and local governments. Although largely decimated by budget cutbacks during the Reagan administration, this "public technology" community played a key role in the 1960s and 1970s in advancing the view that productivity improvement in state and local governments could be achieved through the adoption of new technology (Woolston, 1981). Indeed, one such study, *Public Technology,* is subtitled *Key to Improved Productivity* (Mercer and Philips, 1981).

This essay addresses a set of issues rooted in the very definitions of productivity that are used to measure performance in the operations of state and local governments (Ross and Burkhead, 1974). Productivity is the relationship between the quantity of resources (inputs) used in production and the quantity of output (Kendrick, 1977). The displacement of partial productivity indices (such as output per worker-hour) with total factor productivity indices (such as those whose computations include *all* inputs) has clarified the difference between changes in input composition (such as changes in capital/labor ratios) and changes in total input use. With partial productivity indices, decreases in the use of one input may be offset by increases in the use of other inputs. The results of such a change is indeterminate: The total resource cost of producing the output may not have fallen as rapidly as the decreaase in the "economized" input, may have remained unchanged, or may even have increased. These possibilities were not always recognized during the halcyon days of proposals to reduce the costs of state and municipal services through the adoption of labor-saving, but capital-using, technologies.

Using total factor productivity measures, productivity improvement can be viewed either as increasing the maximum possible level of output for a fixed bundle of inputs or as reducing the minimum level of inputs necessary to achieve a fixed level of output. The analysis is most direct when the characteristics of inputs and outputs are (essentially) unchanged during the period under study. Where characterstcs change, estimates presumably can be caluclated (and adjustments made as necessary) by using market prices or incomes indicators of qualitative differences (Denison, 1979). Productivity change, however, is a much broader concept than innovation. Productivity may increase because of attainment of economics of scale, through learning by doing, and through adjustments in the use and composition of input levels so as to correspond more closely to efficiency criteria — all with existing techniques.

Adjustment procedures to account for changes in characteristics, although often complex, are standard fare in productivity studies (Hatry and Fisk, 1971). However, adjustments invariably are easier to make on the input side than on the ouput side. It is particularly difficult to make adjustments that reflect changes in the characteristics of goods or services. Even abstracting form some of these complexities, changes in productivity are not necessarily measures of technological progress. As noted by Kendrick (1977: 13), such measures (adjusted total factor productivity indices) "do reflect changes in technology as embodied in cost-reducing processes and producer goods. But part of technological advance comes in the form of new or improved consumer goods, which affect the output and productivity measures only partially and indirectly." This problem is most pronounced in the public sector, which, almost by definition, lacks "market" prices for its goods and services and thus is especially lacking in proximate indicators of changes in output characteristics.

Thus a twofold problem. First, productivity change and technology progress, the consequence of innovation, are not synonymous concepts. Second, to the extent to which a relationship between the two exists, this relationship holds most clearly for cost-reducing innovations, not necessarily for those that come in the form of new goods. But, as we suggest below adoption of innovations that have these latter characteristics is built into the incentive systems and institutional milieu of decision makers in state and local governments. Thus, even if these innovations meet effectiveness criteria ("the extent to which the stated goals and objectives of collective action are being fulfilled") or efficiency criteria ("the level of resource requirements for given levels of output"; Greytak et al., 1976: 11), they are not likely to be recorded by most measures of productivity.

CRITIQUE OF CURRENT TREATMENTS

Briefly stated, our argument is that few systematic connections exist between the analytical or empirical studies that have examined productivity change and those that have examined innovation in state and local governments. As a consequence, an association and equivalence between the two concepts has been drawn that is analytically incomplete, and, perhaps more important, is at times misleading both in policy formulation or in the design of programs to foster productivity improvement.

The larger body of empirical productivity literature employs either time-series or cross-sectional data and is directed at identifying economies of scale, the influence of comparative organizational forms, and the contribution of different independent varibles on unit costs (for example, see Hirsch, 1965; Czamanski, 1975; Savas 1977; Coulter et al., 1976). These studies do no consider directly the effects of the introduction of the new techniques on input coefficients over time. The state/local government innovation/diffusion literature (see Bingham and McNaught, 1975; Feller et al., 1976; Lambright et al., 1977; Eveland et al., 1977; Yin et al., 1977; Perry and Kraemer, 1979) has examined the rates of adoption and diffusion characteristics of innovators and has analyzed and advanced several process models of organizational behavior with regard to the search for adoption and implementation of new techniques and practices. However, it provides little in the way of direct estimates of productivity change following the adoption of an innovation. Similarly, a recent comprehensive review of this literature produced by the National Science Foundation (1983) does not treat the subject of productivity at all.

The principal connection points between these two traditions exists in the project evaluation literature (for example, in human resources scheduling) and in a series of case studies on urban technologies. The first group tends to be case specific (Mechling, 1974). Although often quite rigorous in detailing the efficiencies gained from introducing new practices, this literature seldom extends itself in its obligatory opening sections on the introduction of the innovation to consider how its narrative relates to the concurrently emerging literature on innovation processes in state and local governments. Much of the second group has serious quality-control problems (Mercer and Phillips, 1981; Szanton, 1978).

The types of conceptual and empirical problems that can be encountered in linking the two broad concepts of productivity change and innovation can be illustrated by Getz's work on the performance of urban fire departments (1979) and of libraries (1980), for he is one of the few researchers to consider formally both production relationships and innovation behavior in single studies. In his study of fire departments, Getz develops several measures of the input mix and output mix for municipal fire-fighting services as a prelude to evaluating their performance. Getz also analyzes the effects of technological change on performance. The pace of adoption of sixteen fire-fighting innovations is studied, and efforts are made to explain the rank in which cities adopted these innovations. The model resembles in many ways those used in other studies on urban innovation (Feller et al., 1976; Bingham and McNaught, 1975) and, like them, fares poorly in its explanations. As Getz (1979:139) notes:

> Overall, the discrimination of early from late adopters innovations is not very successful. The statistical significance of the relationships is low. The theoretical complexity of the adoption decisions makes empirical study difficult.

More germane to the current argument is Getz's (1979:139) further observation: "While the rate of innovation cannot be measured in a production function context and is probably slower overall than in many other sectors of the economy, the fundamental production processes do seem to be amenable to improvement."[1]

INNOVATION-PRODUCTIVITY CONNECTIONS:
FIVE PROPOSITIONS

There are five different general propositions to consider in the productivity change-innovation connection: (1) The incentive systems and institutional enviroments of public sector organizations generate a set of barriers to innovative behavior — a collection of theoretical and descriptive statements underlying the "struggle" involved in bringing new technologies to state and local governments, (2) public sector organizations have been slow and incomplete in their adoption of new technologies — "Only the color of the fire engine is different" (Frohman, 1973) — an empirical argument). (3) Adoption of new technologies and practices have contributed and can contribute to improvements in the effectiveness and efficiency of state and local governments' operations (the task is to promote additional activity — the productivity improvement approach). (4) The incentive systems and institutional environments of public sector organizations lead them to adopt innovations that serve bureaucratic ends, but do not necessarily relate to production efficiency — the "conspicuous production" argument. (5) Public sector organizations have a propensity for adopting innovations that expand their scope of services rather than reduce their unit costs.

BARRIERS TO INNOVATIVE BEHAVIOR

The first proposition, based upon the incentive system and institutional structure within the public sector, explains low levels of productivity change in state and local government in terms of impediments and barriers to innovative behavior. This proposition forms a standard part of the litany of woes of state and local governments, and, when expressed more formally in the public choice literature (Ahlbrant, 1973), constitutes one of the analytical building blocks that explain why public sector production (as contrasted with consumption) of a commodity is likely to be less efficient that in private sector production (Savas, 1982). The implicit assumption throughout this proposition is that those innovations that would be adopted would increase the organization's efficiency in delivering a specified level of a well-defined bundle of goods and services.

Despite the frequency with which this proposition is cited, it is neither analytically self-evident nor empirically valid. Roessner (1977) has surveyed the various theories that hold public sector organizations to be inherently less receptive to innovation than private sector organizations, and has found them to be lacking in unique predictions. Roessner (1977: 36) concludes from his review that "the empirical evidence concerning the relative innovativeness of public versus private organizations, coupled with numerous recent examples of improved productivity in government through innovation, give reason to doubt the validity of the hypothesis that the public sector is inherently immune to efforts to increase innovative behavior there."

Moreover, the diffusion studies cited earlier have each identified variables and relationships that directly affect processes of adoption, diffusion, and implementation, and that indirectly affect the relationships between innovation and productivity that are far more complex than the set of relationships outlined under this first proposition. Eveland et al. (1977), for example, have pointed to the iterative process by which the characteristics of an agency's "needs" both influence and are shaped by the characteristics of an innovation during a process of "matching." Yin et al. (1978) have pointed out that "routinization" is a necessary link between "innovation" and impact on agency performance. There are several phases in the life cycle by which an innovation becomes core practice, and different influences are at work at each of these phases (Yin et al., 1978).

SLUGGISH ADOPTION BEHAVIOR

The second proposition, that public sector organizations have been slow to adopt new technologies, is an empirical counterpart of the validity of the first proposition. Feller and Menzel (1978) have examined patterns of adoption for a board cross-section of urban technologies. Getz (1979, 1980) examined patterns of diffusion of fire-fighting and library innovations; Roessner (1977) compared rates of adoption of solid-waste collection and hospital technologies between public and private performers. Each found that the diffusion patterns in the nonmarket sector resembled those found for the industrial technologies.

In a sample of technological innovations in urban governments, Feller and Menzel (1978) found that the rate and extent of adoption of many techniques had been rapid and extensive, while that of other techniques was slower and limited; that there had been a pronounced acceleration in the rate of adoption of technologies in traffic control, air pollution control, and fire fighting; and that the diffusion patterns in these three functional areas indicated a continuous stream of advances. They argue that their data suggest the "need to revamp some of the most widespread ideas about the archaic nature of the technologies in use in municipal agencies" (Feller and Menzel, 1978: 479).

The relationship of these empirical findings to the productivity connection, however, is ambiguous without resolving the question of the innovations' characteristics.

INNOVATION EFFICIENCY

The third proposition that adoption of innovations enhances agency productivity constitutes the most direct link between the two concepts. New practices and techniques are adopted that permit a reduction in the inputs required to produce a specified quantity of unchanged output. Adoption results in a measurable increase in productivity (CONSAD, 1980).

Treatments of productivity measurement in the public sector contain careful statements concerning the difficulties of gauging output in terms of a single or even composite indicators of the physical dimensions of a given agency's activity (Ostrom, 1975). What is less well recognized is the difficult in relating the adoption of innovations to these measures, not so much because of the multiple characteristics of the output but because of the mutability of technologies. The productivity improvement approach tends to assume that measures are equivalent to needs for specific pieces of equipment. This approach assumes a well-defined agency production function in which desired changes in the level of output can be treated as generating a derived demand for (technological) inputs. In contrast, one can view an agency's operations as consisting of a series of activities, each subject to specific constraints or bottlenecks, and affected peripherally by the global operations of the department. Two immediate consequences of such a view are that (1) the level of agency output (and perceived "performance" gaps) need have little impact on the demand for new technologies, which serve specific, intermediate production processes; and/or (2) the adoption of any piece of equipment need not have any noticeable impact on the level of performance. Thus, for example, the relationship between fire losses or other measures of departmental performance and the adoption of a specific innovation, say lightweight hose, may be so indirect that one will find only a minor statistical relationship between the two.

Not only can output be multidimensional, but a given technology may be put to an extensive range of uses. Without knowing the characteristics of the technology and the mutability of its services within an agency, it is not possible to specify the appropriate measure of performance. For example, adoption of the minipumper was often advocated on the grounds that it provided adequate response to most fires, and could be an important source of labor savings. In some cities, it was adopted not as a labor-saving substitute for regular pumpers, but as a more effective means of combatting fires in otherwise difficult to reach areas, such as enclosed parking lots in urban areas or brush fires (Feller et al., 1976).

"CONSPICUOUS PRODUCTION"
AND INCENTIVE SYSTEM BIASES

The fourth and fifth propositions concern two hypothesized relationships between bureaucratic incentives and agency performance. They bear upon the question of whether there is a necessary association between the adoption of innovations and productivity improvement. Briefly, they relate to the contention that the environments in which decisions are made in state and local governments is such that innovations are not necessarily adopted to reduce costs but rather to (a) enhance bureaucratic well-being and/or (b) expand the scope of agency services. The two propositions derive from the same general analytical model of the behavior of bureaucratic adopters of innovations in state and local government; they differ primarily at the ex post facto level in terms of whether or not the innovation enhances agency performance, broadly defined. Moreover, as presented in the literature they have different implications for the relationships considered here. The proposition of "conspicuous production" suggests not only that "fads" can occur in public sector technologies as elsewhere (industrial technologies, consumer goods), but that the characteristics of the public sector contribute to the adoption of such innovations. The "conspicuous production" proposition asserts that independent of (ex post) validation of an innovation's impact upon performance, the characterisics of public sector organizations are such that innovative behavior or the adoption of specific technologies may increase the well-being of decision makers, even if an improvement in neither production efficiency nor in the delivery of services occurs.

The fifth proposition is dual edged. It implies that there are systematic influences on the characteristics of innovations adopted by state and local governments that will have budgetary impacts different than those presumed to follow from the acquisition of new technology. Even if these innovations meet formal performance criteria — say, yielding benefit-cost ratios greater than one — they may not contribute to improved productivity levels because of the difficulties in measuring the new forms of service. Under this proposition a positive relationship between innovative behavior and productivity improvement will not be found because the innovations adopted fail to meet the criteria that a cost-minimizing/output-maximizing decision maker would employ.

The fourth proposition can be found in Feller's (1981) application of concept of conspicuous production to public sector innovation. The incentive systems confronting public sector managers, the potential political gains from "high-tech" production of public services, and the difficulties in measuring the efficiency of production technologies, according to this view, produce an inversion of the proposition that disincentives to innovate in state and local governments exist. Rather, according to Feller (1981: 15),

> the same environmental influences which have been held to make state and local government officials risk-averse in responding to new technologies, may instead serve to induce those officials to adopt technologies that do not generate improvements in services or reductions in costs. . . . this inversion is most likely to happen when the technology under consideration has certain characteristics, principally long-term capital requirements and quantum jumps in technology and when it occurs in those functional fields, such as fire, police, management information services, where the agency bureaucrat enjoys relative autonomy or invisibility in his relationship to either elected officials of the public.

The fifth proposition, the main focus of the remainder of this essay, is rooted in the theoretically based assertion that a dichotomy exists in the reasons for and characteristics of innovation in public sector organizations.

INNOVATION-PRODUCTIVITY CONNECTIONS: SUGGESTED DICHOTOMY

Public sector organizations appear to have a propensity for adopting innovations that expand the scope of their service provision without decreasing their unit costs. Yin et al. (1977) have described two types of incentive systems at work within local governments that reflect both cost efficiency and the bureaucratic incentive system: (1) production efficiency and (2) bureaucratic efficiency. Production efficiency in the public sector resembles that found in the private sector, and is based upon the fact that a conscious decision to decrease the costs of service provision will increase the availability of slack resources (the difference between operating expenditures in a department and that department's revenues), which in turn can enable the organization and its members to reap additional benefits in the form of higher "profits" or larger operations via the reinvestment of those slack resources. In the public sector, slack resources enable the department manager to expand the scope of the department's services without decreasing existing services.

The key difference in the incentive systems in the public and private sectors is the absence of profit in the public sector. Accruing profits is, by definition, impossible; increases in slack resources through cost-efficient service production techniques therefore have no direct impact upon the personal financial well-being of the decision makers. The only way in which benefit from slack resources can be captured by an individual is when the benefit to the organizations as a whole can be transferred to an individual's specific gain.

Reflecting this nonmonetary incentive system, Yin et al.'s (1977) theory for innovation adoption suggests that bureaucrats who are considering an innovation will be motivated to accept it only if it enables them to (1) survive organizational change, (2) survive the next election, (3) increase the prerequisites associated with the decision maker's position within the organization, or (4) create a relative advantage for the innovating department with respect to other units within the city. Yin et al. further postulate that innovations that increase the department's position with respect to other organizational units can be expected to be promoted favorably by members of that department. This incentive system does not exclude the possibility that innovations that increase the individual's and organization's well-being can simultaneously increase the well-being of the citizens.

From this dichotomy has come a further one — that between service-augmenting and cost-efficient innovation. Cost-efficient innovations are innovations that decrease the unit cost of service provision, thus producing a decline in expenditures given a constant level of service. Service-augmenting innovations result in either the provision of a substantially different type of service from the initially provided or the provision of a totally new service.

The dichotomy, as recognized by those who have employed it in their work, is loosely defined (Lambright, 1979). Assignment into the cost-efficient or service-augmenting categories is on an ad hoc basis.[2] The fact than innovations cannot truly be designated as cost efficient or service augmenting *ex ante* blurs the dichotomy. Innovations that were intended to be cost saving by their adopter but that turn out to be more expensive can be labeled "service augmenting." That is, they are described in such a way as to indicate a change in the quality of service provided, resulting from the innovation's adoption. Failure to improve productivity can be transformed into program enrichment because of the difficulty of pinpointing the benefits of a service or of measuring the costs of that service's provision in the public sector (Feller, 1980). Feller does not, however, indicate that one type of innovation will be more prevalent than the other. Rather, the proposed dichotomy signifies the need to consider both innovation types when discussing and analyzing public sector innovation adoption.

In the public sector, the rewards to managers are not readily linked to efficient production of goods and services. The last large-scale study of the relationship between monetary comepensation performance in the public sector was done in 1973. This survey showed that the use of monetary incentives in state and local governments was relatively rare (Greiner et al., 1981). Only 6 percent of the local governments surveyed reported performance bonuses for their employees. The use of monetary rewards for performance does not appear to have increased much since that time. Other incentive systems, performance targeting, performance appraisal, and job enrichment are relatively more widespread, but leave open the characteristic of performance (Johnston, 1982).

A decrease in the production cost of a good or service that results from an innovation does not seem to be translated directly into a gain for the innovator or for the innovating department. In fact, it has been argued that a decrease in the cost of production in the public sector, and thus a decrease in the necessary department operating budget, is counterproductive to the department manager's well-being since the manager's salary and benefits appear to be correlated with the department's budget size. Given this argument, it has been hypothesized that during their tenure bureaucrats will seek to maximize the total budgets of their departments, constrained only by the expectations of those monitoring the departments' budgetary growth (Niskanen, 1971). If voters are assumed to be the end users of most of a department's services, then one monitoring force behind budgetary decisions is the vote. Yet, McKean (1972) was argued that voters are relatively uninterested in the efficiency of service provision since the marginal benefit to each voter is far less than the cost to that voter of monitoring the production of each service. Likewise, voters are more likely to favor increases in services, either of quality or type, if the marginal benefits exceed the marginal costs to them.

Among the ways in which an individual can accrue benefit from innovation in the public sector is when that innovation increases the relative position of the department/agency with which that individual is affiliated. Increasing the relative position of a department/agency can be accomplished, in part, by expanding its budget, its scope of services, or its level of service provision, that is, changes associated with the adoption of service-augmenting innovations. These incentives create a situation in which the adoption of service-augmenting types of innovations is highly desirable.[3]

To date, the service-augmenting/cost-efficiency dichotomy has largely served as a conceptual tool, supported by limited empirical findings. A more extensive test of the relative importance of these innovation characteristics is now possible through use of data originally collected to evaluate the Urban Technology System (UTS).[4]

The Urban Technology System was a program designed to increase the amount of innovation in medium-sized cities, populations from 50,000 to 500,000, through the use of resident technology transfer agents, back-up support for universities and private firms, and management support from Public Technology Incorporated (Newbold and Robinson, 1981). The program received primary sponsorship from the National Science Foundation. The data presented here cover the period 1974-1977, the "experimental" period of UTS.

A total of 52 cities participated in the evaluation, 27 of which were test sites; each test site had a technology agent employed in it throughout the experimental period. These cities were randomly selected from the geographic regions of the country, and exhibited different demographic and financial characteristics. During the evaluation of UTS, control sites were selected that matched the test sites with respect to demographic and financial factors.

Data are reported here from 35 of the 52 cities involved in the UTS evaluation. The data were collected by interviewing department heads within each of these cities regarding innovations their departments had adopted during the period 1974-1977. Data collection was begun in 1978 and was not completed until January 1982.

This lag between the experimental period and the data collection presents obvious problems in the reliability of the data base. One might expect that the major innovations would be remembered, while innovations with lesser impacts upon the city or upon the department in which they are adopted might not be recalled. Due to this, the assumption is made that any bias created by incomplete memory reporting will affect both cost efficient and service augmenting innovation recollection equally, with the bias favoring major innovations of either type as opposed to innovations with lesser impact.

Innovations were defined as a new technique, equipment upgrade, new capital acquisition, new service or significantly altered service, or a new method of service provision that was initiated in a city for the first time. Using this approach, each city is viewed as an autonomous innovator, and items that are new to a city are counted as innovations regardless of the fact that other cities may have been using the innovations for years.

The relative frequency of service-augmenting and cost-efficient innovations is presented in Table 7.1. The data are not arranged on a city-by-city basis; rather, they are categorized by functional area. Out of 1664 innovations recorded, 807 are classified as the service-augmenting type.

There are considerale differences between functional areas in the shares of service-augmenting and cost-saving innovation, ranging from a high of 75 percent for service-augmenting innovations to a low of 5 percent for service-augmenting and cost-efficient innovations in decreasing percentages. This distribution suggests that different functional areas react differently to the same general conditions affecting their cities. It adds support to the view that productivity and innovation are largely a duty of functional departments rather than city governments as such.

CONCLUSION

Theoretical propositions assume a timeless dimensionality; empirical findings are more often circumscribed by terminal points. This chapter has described an overlay between the two. It has first described the theoretical differences that exist between the concepts of innovation (or innovative behavior) and of productivity change (measured implicitly in terms of an unchanged quality of output) in public sector organizations. It then presented evidence to suggest that for a sample of cities in the mid-1970s there was a systemically induced bifurcation between the adoption of innovations and reductions in the cost of providing (qualitatively) unchanged levels of municipal services. It did not suggest that the service-augmenting innovations necessarily failed to meet broader, benefit-cost criteria concerning the efficiency of public expenditures for innovative techniques.

Walker and Chaiken (1982: 161) have recently written that the deteriorating fiscal conditions of state and local governments since

TABLE 7.1   Frequency of Service-Augmenting and Cost-Efficient
Innovations, 35 Cities

Functional Area	Total	Service-Augmenting		Cost-Efficient	
		n	%	n	%
Buildings and facilities	50	4	.06	46	.92
Courts	30	10	.33	20	.67
Data processing	68	9	.13	59	.87
Emergency medical service*	2	2	1.00	0	0
Finance	100	5	.05	95	.95
Fire	152	102	.67	50	.33
Health	83	62	.75	21	.25
Housing	45	36	.80	9	.20
Human services	17	8	.47	9	.53
Libraries	110	81	.74	29	.26
Licenses	11	2	.18	9	.82
Parks and recreation	143	84	.95	59	.41
Personnel	78	14	.18	64	.82
Planning	56	32	.57	24	.43
Police	242	160	.66	82	.34
Power and water	66	30	.46	36	.54
Purchasing	50	7	.14	43	.86
Traffic engineering	61	41	.66	20	.34
Transportation	37	22	.59	15	.41
Fleet maintenance	61	5	.08	56	.92
Road construction	9	5	.56	4	.44
Sewage treatment	19	10	.53	9	.47
Street maintenance	83	49	.59	34	.41
Trash collection	37	13	.35	24	.65
General services	52	13	.25	39	.75
Total	1664	807	.48	857	.52

*The low number of innovations reported for emergency medical service reflects the
fact that many cities combine this with fire service provision (Johnston, 1982).

the mid-1970s "will cause the innovative process in the public sector
to fall on hard times." We agree with this assessment. Thus the data
presented above suggesting the prevalence of service-enhancing innovations are likely to be quite time bound. Empirically closer connections between innovative behavior and cost-reducing innovations
may emerge in the 1980s as well as an association between the adoption of innovations and conventional measures of productivity improvements. The conceptual differences between innovation and
productivity will remain. It is hoped that they will be more clearly
identified in future work.

TABLE 7.2   Frequency Distribution of Service-Augmenting Innovations by Functional Area, 35 Cities*

Functional Area	Percentage of Service-Augmenting Innovations
Building and facilities	1-10
Data processing	
Finance	
Licenses	
Personnel	
Purchasing	
Fleet maintenance	
General services	21-40
Courts	
Trash collection	
Human services	41-60
Power and water	
Parks and recreation	
Planning	
Sewage treatment	
Transportation	
Road construction	
Street maintenance	
Fire	61-80
Police	
Traffic engineering	
Health	
Human services	
Libraries	

*Excludes emergency medical services (Johnston, 1982).

NOTES

1. A similar set of problems is found in Getz's (1980) study of public libraries. There, too, considerable effort is made to estimate the costs and benefits of libraries, and to describe and explain differential rates of innovation adoption. Still, no direct connection is made between the estimates of the efficiency of library services and adoption patterns:

A wide array of innovations is sweeping the public library industry. Most parts of the operation of a public library system may be changed by adopting innovations. . . . These innovations seem to be diffused rapidly across the large public library systems surveyed. While this study has not attempted to document the cost-saving potential of these innovations, substantial benefits are presumed to exist [Getz, 1980: 140-141].

2. The service-augmenting/cost-efficiency dichotomy for public sector innovations is by no means the only type of classification for such innovations, nor is the dichotomy itself necessarily always rigorously defined. An innovation may decrease unit costs of service provision (cost efficiency) while also increasing service quality (service augmentation). Thus there is some overlap between the classifications for certain types of innovations. One might also categorize public sector innovations in other ways; innovations resulting from other government agency mandates, internal agency productivity-enhancing innovations, innovations aimed at new service provision only, and innovations designed to increase staff morale are all examples.

The dichotomy is also not intended to be invidious. Increased efficiency is only one social welfare criterion. Provision (albeit via efficient methods of production) of a level and range of collective goods that accord with an aggregate set of individual utility functions is another.

3. There are other reasons to explain why an adopter might choose a service-augmenting innovation. Innovation may serve to enhance the peer-group ranking of an individual innovator since successful innovations require careful planning, technological knowledge or managerial skills, and resource management to enable funding of an innovation. Within professional communities, innovativeness is often seen as a positive attribute.

4. Description of the procedures used to collect the data are contained in CONSAD Research Corporation (1980).

REFERENCES

AHLBRANT, R., Jr. (1973) "Efficiency in the provision of fire services." Public Choice 10: 1-15.

BINGHAM, R. D. and T. P. McNAUGHT (1975) The Adoption of Innovation by Local Government. Milwaukee, WI: Marquette University.

CONSAD Research Corporation (1980) Evaluation of the Experimental Phase of the Urban Technology System: Detailed Case Studies of Selected UTS Innovations. NSF Contract ISP 78-27101. Division of Inter-governmental Science and Public Technology, CONSAD.

COULTER, P., L. MacGILLIVREY, and E. VICKERY (1976) "Municipal fire protection performance in urban areas: enviromental and organizational influences on effectiveness and productivity measures," pp. 231-260 in E. Ostrom (ed.) The Delivery of Urban Services. Beverly Hills, CA: Sage.

CZAMANSKI, D. (1975) The Cost of Preventive Services. Lexington, MA: D. C. Heath.

DENISON, E. (1979) Accounting for Slower Economic Growth. Washington, DC: Brookings Institution.

EVELAND, J. D., E. ROGERS, and C. KLEPPER (1977) "The innovation process in public organizations." University of Michigan.

FELLER, I. (1981) "Public sector innovation as 'conspicuous production.'" Policy Analysis 7: 1-20.

—— (1980) "Managerial response to technological innovation in public sector organization." Management Science 26: 1021-1030.

—— and D. MENZEL (1978) "The adoption of technological innovations by municipal governments." Urban Affaris Quarterly 13: 469-490.

—— and L. A. KOZAK (1976) Diffusion of Innovations in Municapal Governments. University Park: Center for the Study of Science Policy, Institute for Research on Human Resources, Pennsylvania State University.

FROHMAN, A. (1973) "Fighting fires: only the truck is new." Technology Review (May): 36-41.

GETZ, M. (1980) Public Libraries. Baltimore: Johns Hopkins University Press.

—— (1979) The Economics of the Urban Fire Department. Baltimore: Johns Hopkins University Press.

GREINER, J. H., J. P. HATRY, M. P. KOSS, A. P. MILLER, and J. P. WOODWARD (1981) Productivity and Motivation: A Review of State and Local Government Incentives. Washington, DC: Urban Institute Press.

GREYTAK, D., D. PHARES, and E. MORLEY (1976) Municipal Output and Performance in New York City Lexington, MA: D. C. Heath.

HATRY, H. and D. M. FISK (1971) Improving Productivity and Productivity Measurement in Local Governments. Washington, DC: Urban Institute.

HAYES, F. O. R. and J. E. RASMUSSEN [eds.] (1972) Centers for Innovation in the Cities and States. San Francisco: San Francisco Press.

HIRSCH, W. (1965) "Cost functions of an urban government service: refuse collection." Review of Economics and Statistics 47: 87-92.

JOHNSTON, M. I. (1982) "The cost efficiency-service augmenting innovation dichotomy: an empirical test." Prepared for the meeting of the Midwestern Political Science Association, Milwaukee, Wisconsin.

KENDRICK, J. (1977) Understanding Productivity. Baltimore: Johns Hopkins University Press.

LAMBRIGHT, W. H. (1979) Technology Transfer to Cities. Boulder, CO: Westview.

—— A. TEICH, and J. CARROLL (1977) Adoption and Utilization of Urban Technology: A Decision-Making Study, Analysis and Conclusions. New York: Syracuse Research Corporation.

McKEAN, R. (1972) "Property rights within government, and devices to increase governmental efficiency." Southern Journal of Economics 39: 177-180.

MECHLING, J. E. (1974) "A successful innovation: manpower scheduling." Journal of Urban Analysis 2: 259-313.

MERCER, J. and R. PHILIPS (1981) Public Technology: Key to Improved Government Productivity. New York: Amacon.

National Science Foundation (1983) The Process of Technological Innovation: Reviewing the Literature. Washington, DC : Division of Industrial Science and Technological Innovation, National Science Foundation.

NEWBOLD, P. and A. ROBINSON (1981) "The use of technology agents to promote innovative practices in urban service delivery." Prepared for the Third Annual Conference of the Association for Public Policy Analysis and Management, Washington, D.C.

NISKANEN, W. (1971) Bureaucracy and Representative Government. Chicago: Aldine.

OSTROM, E. (1975) "The need for multiple indicators in measuring the output of public agencies," in F. Scioli, Jr., and T. Cook (eds.) Methodologies for Analyzing Public Policy. Lexington, MA: D. C. Heath.

PERRY, P. and K. KRAEMER (1979) Technological Innovation in American Local Governments: The Case of Computing. New York: Pergamon.

ROESSNER, J. D. (1977) "Incentives to innovate in public and private organizations." Administration & Society 9: 341-353.

ROSS, J. and J. BURKHEAD (1974) Productivity in the Local Government Sector. Lexington, MA: D. C. Heath.

SAVAS, E. S. (1982) Privatizing the Public Sector. Chatham, NJ: Chatham House.

———— (1977) The Organization and Efficiency of Solid Waste Collection. Lexington, MA: D. C. Heath.

SPANN, R. M. (1977) "Rates of productivity change and the growth of state and local governmental expenditures," pp. 100-129 in T. Borcherding (ed.) Budgets and Bureaucrats. Durham, NC: Duke University Press.

SZANTON, P. (1978) "Urban public services? Ten case studies," pp. 117-142 in R. Nelson and D. Yates (eds.) Innovation and Implementation in Public Organizations. Lexington, MA: D. C. Heath.

Urban Institute (1970) The Struggle to Bring Technology to Cities. Washington, DC: Author.

WALKER, W. D. and J. M. CHAIKEN (1982) "The effects of fiscal contraction on innovations in the public sector." Policy Sciences 15: 141-165.

WOOLSTON, S. (1981) "Local government technology transfer — overview of recent research and federal programs," pp. 43-46 in S. Doctors (ed.) Technology Transfer to State and Local Government. Cambridge, MA: Oelgeschlager, Gunn & Hain.

YIN, R., K. HEALD, and M. VOGEL (1977) Tinkering with the System. Lexington, MA: D. C. Heath.

YIN, R., S. QUICK, P. BATEMAN, and E. MARKS (1978) Changing Urban Bueaucracies: How New Practices Become Routinized (R-2277-NSF; report to the National Science Foundation). Santa Monica, CA: Rand Corporation.

PART IV

PRODUCING MORE
PRODUCTIVE ORGANIZATIONS

8

PRIVATE SECTOR MONOPOLIES:
THE CASE OF CABLE
TELEVISION FRANCHISES

ELI M. NOAM

Columbia University

For many years, the economic discussion of the relation between
market structure and productivity has been characterized by two
points of view. On the one side are what may be termed the "competitive structuralists," that is, those who believe that noncompetitive
market structure has a direct and negative impact on performance, be
it through monopolistic and oligopolistic misallocations ("y inefficiencies") or through simple operational inefficiencies where
competitive pressures are weak ("x inefficiencies"). A different view
is taken by some institutionalist and political economists, in particular
by followers of Joseph Schumpeter. They, too, argue that market
structure makes a difference, but they see large or oligopolistic firms
as a main agent for innovation.

> What we have got to accept is that [the large firm] has come to be the
> most powerful engine of [economic] progress. . . . In this respect,

Author's Note: *This chapter is the first step in research on cable television, supported
by the National Science Foundation under Grant IS T-82-09485. Support by the Columbia Business School is also acknowledged. The author is grateful to Zvi Griliches,
Betsy Jaeger, Florence Ling, Mark Nadel, and Menachem Petrushka. Special thanks
go to Nadine Strossen.*

perfect competition is not only impossible but inferior, and has no
title to being set upon a model of ideal efficiency [Schumpeter, 1950:
106].

In this view, productivity improvements usually require internal
rearrangement of the production process, new management
techniques, capital outlays, and labor reallocation and training.
These tasks may well be most effectively undertaken by enterprises
that benefit from economies of scale, have large resources at their
disposal, and can hedge risks through diversification.

The empirical evidence for a relation between market structure
and productivity is ambiguous. Early research was contradictory (for
example, see Stigler, 1956; Phillips, 1956; Weiss, 1963; Allen, 1969). A
good number of studies have pursued this question, primarily through
investigations of patent grants and R&D expenditures of firms of
different sizes, or of their adoption of new production techniques.[1]

Typically, such studies are highly aggregated on the industry level,
and are estimated across different industries, comparing concentration indices with dependent variables such as productivity; such
procedure is usually chosen because it is difficult to find different
concentration ratios for the same industry. Yet industries vary widely,
and their comparison is problematic. For example, an important role
in productivity change is played by the presence of basic knowledge
ready for application, referred to as "technological opportunity"
(Phillips, 1971), which varies from industry to industry. One way to
escape the problem of comparison is to use the same industry across
different countries; but this only raises new problems.

This study, on the other hand, proposes to proceed by concentrating on one industry, and in one country only. It proceeds in a very
different fashion from the research mentioned above, in that it looks at
the rate of productivity increase within an industry that is, interestingly enough, characterized by thousands of local monopolies. Furthermore, a large number of new entries occur, making it possible to
determine the trend of state-of-the-art technology.

The results of the investigation can yield potentially interesting
conclusions; first, they shed light on the cable television industry
itself — an industry of much public policy importance — and, second,
they illuminate the relation of productivity and monopoly in general.

Methodologically, the objective of this chapter is to find and
measure the rate of technical progress in the operations of already
existing — and locally monopolistic — cable television companies,
and to contrast this *internal* rate of innovation with the *external* rate of

change in the "state-of-the-art" or "best-practice" technology. Technical progress is described, in the way used by economists, as those shifts in the production function over time that are unexplained by changes in factor inputs (Solow, 1957). These shifts, reflecting the productivity increase of firms over time, are decomposed in this chapter into three components:

(a) the effects of the "vintage" of technology, that is, of the age of the technology;
(b) the effects of maturity in operation, that is, of "learning by doing";[2] and
(c) the effect of economies of scale.

In including these three factors the study goes beyond other writings that do not distinguish among them, specifically not between vintage and maturity. This is a methodological contribution of this chapter. Empirically, it adds to the analysis of an industry whose importance — and list of unsettled regulatory questions — is growing, yet whose production characteristics have received only scant statistical attention (Babe, 1975; Owen, 1982). In providing some empirical evidence, this study can rely on data for nearly 5000 U.S. cable television systems.

BACKGROUND TO THE
PRODUCTIVITY ISSUE IN CABLE TELEVISION

While the substantial communications potential of cable television is well known, it is less recognized that the locally monopolistic industry structure of the medium may lead to its suboptimal development. This danger has been commented upon for the issue of product diversity, which may be lessened by the operator's gatekeeper control over programming (Sloan Commission, 1971; Cabinet Committee on Cable Communications, 1974). Far less attention has been given to the issues of productivity and innovation. The rapid development of cable television technology has been far from uniform in its diffusion.

A pattern is emerging in cable television service across the United States. Large companies that own cable systems, eager to win franchises in unwired cities, are quite willing to spend hundreds of millions of dollars to build modern systems. At the same time, they give much lower priority to rebuilding their older systems in areas where there are no competitive reasons to offer the more lavish services. . . .

> In Queens, for example, Teleprompter . . . is proposing 107 chan-
> nels. . . . In Manhattan, by contrast, Teleprompter offers . . . only
> 26 channels.

> The rates in the new systems, also born in a competitive atmos-
> phere, are far lower than those in New York. The same ATC that
> charges $11.75 a month in Manhattan for 26 channels is proposing a
> rate of $3.75 a month for 50 channels in Denver [New York Times,
> November 8, 1982: B-1, 29].

The root causes for such discrepancy may be sought in the structure of the industry. The cable television industry consists of a series
of parallel local monopolies, each de facto based on the award of a
local operating franchise. In a monopolistic situation, profit maximization does not necessarily lead to adoption of a "best-practice"
technology, even if such would be economically feasible under competitive conditions. For example, the upgrading of channel capacity
by the use of more sophisticated converters and the like may not be
undertaken, because it would primarily *divert* viewers from already-
existing program channels rather than *generate* new viewers; therefore, a monopolist in the supply of cable program channels normally
has incentives to supply less than the competitive capacity.[3] Within
each franchise area, the licensed company is, for all practical purposes, in control over the technical innovation of the transmission
system. While it is true that the cable operator is bound by the terms
of a local franchise contract, and has an incentive not to lose the
franchise for lack of innovation, such loss has not occurred outside a
handful of tiny localities:

> Where cities have tried to spur competition during re-franchising by
> inviting competitive bidding, they have been unable to inspire even
> a nibble of interest from any companies other than the incumbent
> operator. City officials contend that operators are reluctant to enter
> an already franchised area for fear that the same will happen to them
> on what they consider their turf. Operators accuse cities of using
> competitive bidding only as a ploy to get better service from an
> incumbent [Stoller, 1982: 36].[4]

In many instances city officials are uninformed about the available
technology set:

> If you start the refranchising process by asking officials what they
> want that they don't already have, you'll probably find that most of
> them don't have the slightest idea what is available. . . . So far, there

has been a lot of talk about rebuilds, but not a lot done [Tony Hoffman, a security analyst at A. G. Becker, as quoted in Rothbard, 1982: 22].

The more general question that such observations raise is the extent to which available innovation is adopted in a locally monopolistic setting. Because of its present institutional peculiarities, cable television provides an unusual opportunity to observe and contrast both the competitive and the monopolistic adoption of innovation within the same industry. Cable system operators usually pass through an intensely competitive phase at the beginning of their operation, when they vie with other companies in attempting to gain the local franchise. The normal franchising procedures call for applicant firms to present the merits of their systems; by the nature of the intensive bidding process that ensues, companies compete in the technology that is offered as well as in its cost-effectiveness, since the proposed rates are part of the bid.[5] After a franchise has been awarded, however, there is little competitive pressure for the operating company to upgrade a system according to the subsequent technological development.[6] This is not to say that there are no improvements; but they will be motivated by considerations other than the presence of intraindustry competition. Therefore, there is no reason to assume that established cable systems will necessarily keep up their internal improvements with the external rate of change in the industry.

Empirically, there are special advantages of analyzing the cable television industry:

(a) It consists of several thousand firms, all essentially operating in a local one-plant production mode, and all reporting data according to a uniform system.
(b) Each year brings the entry of hundreds of new systems, an unusual opportunity to observe the trend of new vintages.
(c) The technology is nearly entirely nonproprietary to the operators, and is generally available to all operating companies. Virtually no vertical integration into the manufacture of capital equipment exists.

THE MODEL

Three different causes for shifts in productivity are normally left unseparated: first, the internal improvements in operations, which is

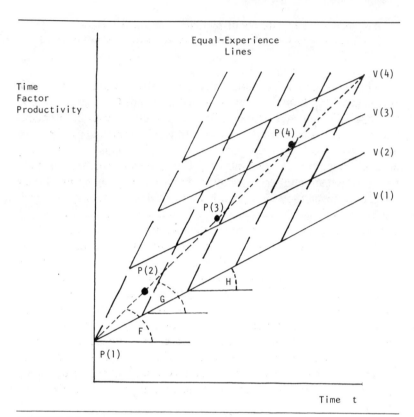

FIGURE 8.1

here termed the "maturity effect" of a system; second, the technical
progress external to the system, termed the "vintage effect"; and
third, the economies of scale that may result from expansion. To
illlustrate the first two factors: In Figure 8.1, time is mapped on the
abscissa, together with that period's output relative to inputs (total
factor productivity). Observations made at time t(1), t(2), and so on
then show points such as P(1), P(2) and so on, and an apparent
productivity trend F. However, the underlying reality may in fact be
more complex; internal productivity improvements of firms may increase at the rate of the slopes of the lines V(1), where each line
corresponds to the maturity trend of a given vintage of technology. At
the same time, technical progress raises each year's vintage productivity from V(i) to V(i+1). Hence the trend line F is in fact a

combination of the two rates of technical progress, that of movement along a function and that of a shift of the function itself. The slopes G of the lines connecting the "equal-maturity" points of different vintages reflect the rate of external technical progress, while the slopes H are the trend of the experience gains for a given vintage.

To this analysis one must add the factor of scale economy. To the extent that cable operations grow as time passes, they reap potentially existing economies of scale (Noam, 1983a, 1983b), apart from the effects of any technical progress.

Past research on the productivity of other industries has allowed for scale economies (Dhrymes and Kurz, 1964; Christensen and Green, 1976; Denny et al., 1982; Nadiri and Schankerman, 1981; Gollop and Roberts, 1981). But they do not distinguish between the vintage[7] and maturity[8] rats of productivity increase.

We now formalize the model, using a multiproduct setting. Consider the production of m outputs using n inputs. The cost function, uniquely corresponding to the production function under the assumption of duality theory, is at each time t

$$C(t) = f[P(l_t) \ldots P(n_t); \ Q(l_t) \ldots Q(m_t); \ V(s); \ M(t); \ K] \qquad [1]$$

where $C(t)$ is total costs of production; $P(i_t)$ is the prices for the factors of production i, given exogenously; $Q(j_t)$ is the output quantities for the different products of a multiproduct firm; $V(i)$ is the vintage of the plant; and $M(t)$ is the plant's maturity at the time t; and K is other factors that may affect cost of production. The partial logarithmic derivatives of cost with respect to input prices, output quantities, vintage, and maturity are the partical elasticities E with respect to these variables. The total change in cost of equation 3 can then be expressd as composed of the contributions of price and quantity changes and of vintage and maturity effects.

Furthermore, a cost-minimizing behavior by the firm is assumed. Using Shepard's lemma, the cost-price elasticities are then equal to the share of each input factor in total cost, that is,

$$S_i \equiv \frac{P_i X_i}{C} = \frac{\partial \ell n C}{\partial \ell n P_i} = E_{CP_i} \qquad [2]$$

where X_i is the quantity of input i, P_i is the price, and C is total costs. The estimation of these cost-share equations jointly with the cost function increases the degrees of freedom and the statistical weight of an empirical estimation.

For the purposes of estimation, let the cost function f be given by the translog cost function, a second-order logarithmic approximation to an arbitrary twice-differentiable transformation surface (Griliches and Ringstad, 1971; Christensen et al., 1973). The general translog function imposes no restrictions on production such as homogeneity, homotheticity, or unitary elasticities of substitution, and is hence covenient for the testing for the existence of these properties.[9]

A major problem with the application of a multiproduct specification of a cost function is that if even one of the products has the value zero, the observation's value becomes meaningless. For that reason, it is necessary to specify an alternative funcational form that is well behaved. As pointed out be Caves et al. (1980), the use of the log metric for outputs in the generalized translog function is unnecessary for a homogeneity of degree one in factor prices, a condition that is usually imposed. Instead, one can substitute the Box-Cox metric

$$g_i(Q_q) = \frac{Q_q^w - 1}{w} \qquad [3]$$

which is defined for zero values, and which approaches the standard natural logarithm $\ln Q$ as $w \to 0$. Using this expression, we can define the "hybrid" multiproduct translog cost function.

$$\ln C(P_i, Q_q, M, V, K_k) = a_0 + \sum_i a_i \ln P_i + \sum_q a_q \frac{Q_q^w - 1}{w} + a_v \ln V \qquad [4]$$

$$+ a_m \ln M + \sum_k a_k \ln K_k + \frac{1}{2} \sum_i \sum_j a_{ij} \ln P_i \ln P_j$$

$$+ \frac{1}{2} \sum_q \sum_p a_{qp} \frac{Q_q^w - 1}{w} \frac{Q_p^w - 1}{w} + \frac{1}{2} a_{vv}(\ln V)^2 + \frac{1}{2} a_{mm}(\ln M)^2$$

$$+ \frac{1}{2} \sum_k \sum_\ell a_{k\ell} \ln K_k \ln K_\ell + \sum_i \sum_q a_{qi} \ln P_i \frac{Q_q^w - 1}{w} + \sum_i a_{iv} \ln P_i \ln V$$

$$+ \sum_i a_{im} \ell nP_i \ell nM + \sum_i \sum_k a_{ik} \ell nP_i \ell nK_k + \sum_q a_{qm} \frac{Q_q^w - 1}{w} \ell nM$$

$$+ \sum_q \sum_k a_{qk} \frac{Q_q^w - 1}{w} \ell nK_k + a_{vm} \ell nV \ell nM + \sum_k a_{vk} \ell nV \ell nK_k$$

$$+ \sum_{mk} a_{mk} \ell nM \ell nK$$

The partial elasticities of total cost are then the logarithmic partial derivatives,

$$E_{CPi} = a_i + \sum_j a_{ij} \ell nP_j + \sum_q a_{iq} \frac{Q_q^w - 1}{w} + a_{im} \ell nM \qquad [5]$$

$$+ a_{iv} \ell nV + \sum_k a_{ik} \ell nK$$

$$E_{CQq} = Q_q^w \ a_q + \sum_p a_{qp} \frac{Q_p^w - 1}{w} + \sum_i a_{iq} \ell nP_i + a_{qm} \ell nM \qquad [6]$$

$$+ a_{qv} \ell nV + \sum_k a_{qk} \ell nK$$

$$E_{CM} = a_m + a_{mm} \ell nM + \sum_i a_{im} \ell nP_i + \sum_q a_{qm} \frac{Q_q^w - 1}{w} + a_{vm} \ell nV \qquad [7]$$

$$+ \sum_k a_{mk} \ell nK$$

$$E_{CV} = a_v + a_{vv} \ell nV + \sum_i a_{iv} \ell nP_i + \sum_q a_{qv} \frac{Q_q^w - 1}{w} + a_{mv} \ell nM \qquad [8]$$

$$+ \sum_k a_{vk} \ell nK$$

$$E_{CKk} = a_k + a_{kk}\ell nK + \sum_i a_{ik}\ell nP_i + \sum_q a_{qk} \frac{Q_q^w - 1}{w} + a_{mk}\ell nM \qquad [9]$$

$$+ a_{vk}\ell nV$$

Several parametric restrictions must be put on the cost function. The cost shares must add to unity, which implies that $\sum E_{CPi} = 1$; hence the cost function must be linearly homogeneous in factor prices at all values of factor prices, output, vintage, and maturity. That is,

$$\sum_i a_i = 1; \quad \sum_i a_{ij} = \sum_i a_{iq} = \sum_i a_{im} = \sum_i a_{iv} = \sum_i a_{ik} = 0 \qquad [10]$$

Furthermore, the cross partial derivatives of the translog cost function must be equal, by its second order approximation property, that is, the symmetry condition exists

$$a_{ij} = a_{ji} \quad \text{and} \quad a_{qp} = a_{pq}, \quad \text{where } i \neq j, \, p \neq q \qquad [11]$$

The cost function is homothetic if and only if it can be written as a separable function of factor prices and outputs (Shephard, 1970). The optimal factor share combination is then independent of output, that is, the expasnsion path is linear. From equation 5, it then must be

$$a_{iq} = 0 \qquad [12]$$

which imposes $n - 1$ independent restriction, where n is the number of inputs i. Furthermore, the function is homogeneous at the sample mean if overall cost elasticity with respect to output is constant, that is, if the conditions hold.[10]

$$a_{qp} = a_{iq} = a_{qm} = a_{qv} = a_{qk} = w = 0 \qquad [13]$$

Economies of scale must be evaluated along output rather than along input-mix, since the relative composition of inputs may change over the range of output. Only when the cost function is homothetic will the two be identical (Hanoch, 1975). The implication is that scale economies are better described by the relation of cost to changes in output rather than by that of outputs to changes in inputs, which makes a cost function an advantageous specification.

Following Frisch (1965), the cost elasticity with respect to output E is the reciprocal of scale elasticity E. For the multiproduct case, local overall scale economies, as shown by Fuss and Waverman (1982), are

$$E_s = \frac{1}{\sum\limits_q E_{CQq}} \qquad [14]$$

Product-specific economies of scale are, using the definition in Baumol et al. (1972),

$$E_{sq} = \frac{IC_q}{Q_q \dfrac{\partial C}{\partial Q_q}} \qquad [15]$$

where IC are the incremental costs of producing product q. This incremental cost is described by

$$IC_q = C(Q_1, \ldots Q_N) - C(Q_1, \ldots Q_{q-1}, 0, Q_{q+1} \ldots Q_N) \qquad [16]$$

This elasticity can be written as

$$E_{sq} = \frac{IC_q}{C} / E_{CQq} \qquad [17]$$

For the hybrid translog function, sample mean values are $P = Q = M = V = K = 1$; thus the cost functions simplify to

$$C(Q \ldots Q_N) = \exp(a_0) \qquad [18]$$

$$C(Q \ldots Q_{q-1}, 0, Q_{q+1} \ldots Q_N) = \exp\left(a_0 - \frac{a_q}{w} + \frac{a_{qq}}{2w^2} \right) \qquad [19]$$

so that equation 19[11] for the product-specific economies of scale becomes

$$E_{sq} = \frac{\exp(a_0) - \exp\left(a_0 - \dfrac{a_q}{w} + \dfrac{a_{qq}}{2w^2}\right)}{\exp(a_0) \cdot a_q}$$ [20]

The form of estimation that is used to determine this multiequation system is Zellner's (1962) iterative method for seemingly unrelated regressions. This technique is a form of generalized least squares, shown to yield maximum likelihood estimates that are invariant to which of the cost-share equations is omitted (Barten, 1969). In estimating such a system, it is generally assumed that disturbances in each of the share equation and the cost equation are additive, and that they have a joint normal distribution. These assumptions are made here too.[12]

DATA

The empirical estimation of this study is based on an unusually good body of data for several thousand cable television systems, all producing essentially the same service,[13] operating and accounting in a single-plant mode, supplying their local market only, and reporting data according to the fairly detailed categories of a mandatory federal form.[14]

The data cover virtually all 5000 U.S. cable systems, and are composed of four disparate and extensive files for each of the years 1976-1981 for technical and programming, financial, local community, and employment information.[15] The financial data include both balance sheet and income information.[16]

All variables are standardized around the sample mean in order to overcome the problem of arbitrary scaling that can become an issue in translog function.[17] Furthermore, the nonnormalized variables and a nonnormalized alternative definition of labor (total hours) are used to test for the robustness of the results of scaling.

LABOR INPUTS

The factor quantity is the number of full-time employees (with part-timers added at half value). Its cost is the average salary of employees.

CAPITAL INPUTS

Accounting data for different classes of assets are reported to the FCC in book value form. Although the great bulk of assets in the cable television industry have been acquired within the past decade, thus limiting the extent of inflationary distortion, it was considered prudent to revalue these assets. To do so, the study took advantage of a highly detailed engineering study, commissioned by the federal government, on the cost and pattern of investment in the construction of cable systems. In that report, the required investment flow in a medium-sized cable system over a period of ten years was calculated. (Weinberg, 1972: 128). We assume that (a) this distribution of investment over the first ten years is proportionally the same for all systems; (b) investment in the eleventh and further years is identical to that of the tenth year; and (c) the cost of acquiring capital assets required in a cable television system increases at the rate of a weighted index of communications and utilities equipment.

For each observation, we know the first year of operation and the aggregate historical value of capital assets. It is then possible to allocate capital investments to the different years and different types of investment, and to inflate their value to the prices of the observation year.[19] The input price P_k of this capital stock K is determined by its opportunity cost in a competitive environment, consisting of potential returns r on equity E and payments for debt D, with an allowance for the deductibility of interest expenses (tax rate = w).

$$P_k = r_E \cdot \frac{E}{k} + r_D (1 - w) \frac{D}{k} \qquad [21]$$

The required return on equity is determined according to the risk premium ρ required above the return on risk-free investments, R_F; that is, $r_E = R_F + \rho$. Ibbotson and Sinquefield (1979) found ρ for the Standard & Poor 5000 to be 8.8 for the period 1926-1977. Hence, using the capital asset pricing model (Sharpe, 1964; Lintner, 1965), an estimate of ρ for a specific firm is 8.8 times β, where β is the measure of nondiversifiable (systematic) risk. The average β for cable companies is listed by Moody's (1981) and can be used to calculate the risk premium over the treasury bill rate.

For r_D, the return on long-term debt, the following method was employed: for each observation it was determined, using several financial measures, what its hypothetical bond rating would have been, based on a company's financial characteristics. These "shadow" bond ratings for each observation were then applied to the actual average interest rates existing in the observation years for different bond ratings (Moody's, 1981). This procedure is novel but is based on previous study in the finance literature of bond ratings and their relation to financial ratios.[20]

Tax-free w is defined as the corporate income tax rate (federal and average net state). Debt is defined as long-term liabilities.

PROGRAMMING INPUTS

The third production factor of the model is the input of programming. A cable system that carries no communications messages would be of no interest to subscribers. Therefore, cable operators supply programs in addition to providing the communication wire. These programs are not produced or generated by the operators; with trivial exceptions,[21] programming is supplied by broadcasters and program networks.[22] Program costs are both direct and indirect. Direct costs are the outlays for program services, for example, to pay-TV networks and to suppliers such as Cable News Network (CNN), which charge operators according to the number of their subscribers plus the cost of program importation and its equipment. Direct costs, however, are only part of the total programming; indirect costs that must also be considered are the forgone earning from advertising. For example, CNN is able to sell some of its air time to advertisers. This time is in effect a compensation in kind by the cable operator to CNN for the supply of the program. Similarly, local broadcasters are carried by cable for free, and the programming cost of these "must-carry" channels to cable operators, too, is that of forgone earnings, largely in advertising revenues.

Direct costs are reported to the FCC and are available. Included are also such capital costs as those of origination studios and signal importation equipment and cost to carriers. The indirect cost of forgone advertising revenue is defined as the potential minus the actual advertising revenue obtained by cable operators. Actual figures are reported to the FCC; potential revenues are estimated by reference to the average advertising revenue in television broadcasting per household and viewing time.[23] The unit price of programming inputs is their total divided by the number of program hours and channels.

It is one of the convenient properties of cable television that is uses very little in inputs beyond those of capital, labor, and programming. It does not use raw materials or intermediate inputs to speak of, apart from programming. Even its energy requirements are quite small, in the order of .7 percent of total expenses, if capital expenses are included (Weinberg, 1972: Tables C-1, C-2). Office supplies, telephone, postage, insurance, and so on add another 1.8 percent of costs that include capital inputs. For consistent treatment of inputs and outputs, this small residual input is added to the inputs K, L, and P; since one cannot determine for what the residual input is a substitute, we prorate it to K, L, and P.

OUTPUTS

Costs and revenues in cable television are nearly entirely for subscription rather than actual use. Pay-per-view billing systems are exceedingly rare, and in their absence there are only negligible marginal costs to the operator for a subscriber's actual viewing of the channels. Hence the numbers of actual and potential subscribers — as opposed to their viewing — are measures of the operator's outputs.

Cable television operators' major outputs are then of the following dimensions: (a) basic service subscriptions; (b) pay-TV service subscriptions; and (c) the number of *potential* subscribers that are reached. The latter is reflected by the number of "homes passed." The larger this number, the more subscribers can potentially be enrolled.

VINTAGE

Vintage is defined according to the year in which the cable operator commenced transmission, expressed by that year divided by the sample mean. Most cable systems, particularly those of medium or large size, have started operation in the past 15 years.

MATURITY

To estimate the maturity effect, that is, the productivity gains due to operational experience — holding equal for vintage and scale economies — for each observation maturity is defined as the time lapsed since the commencement of operations. For each observation, there are therefore one vintage value and a series of maturity observations.

TECHNICAL VARIABLES

Two other variables are introduced in order to adjust for differences in the cable systems that may affect costs of production and ability to attract subscriptions. First, the density of population has a role in determining cost. The further houses are from each other physically, the more capital and labor inputs must go into reaching each.[24] To allow for density variations, we define D as the length of cable trunk lines per household passed. The resultant ratio is used as a proxy for density.

A second variable is the number of video channels offered by a cable operator. Clearly, the more channels offered, the more inputs required. At the same time, one would expect subscription outputs to be affected positively, *ceteris paribus*, since the cable service is more varied and hence probably more attractive to potential subscribers.

RESULTS

The three-stage estimation of the model yields statistically strong results; system R^2 is .9610. Most of the parameter estimates have very high t values and are significant at the .01 level, particularly the first-order terms and their squares.

We first look at the economies of scale in the system. Using equation 14, we find an overall elasticity of scale of $E = 1.0728$. This means that cost increase is proportionally less than that of output, and that the relative cost decrease is in the range of 7 percent for each doubling of output.

We next look at the effects of maturity in operation on cost. Here we find at the sample mean a coefficient of $-.2827$; that is, cost decreases fairly pronouncedly with experience in operation — holding everything else equal. Cable systems seem to reduce costs as they mature, gain experience, and absorb innovations.

However, these internal productivity increases are considerably smaller than those due to the *external* changes in technology. Isolating the vintage effect, we find a coefficient of $-.9223$, indicating a very substantial cost reduction that accompanies the introduction of new vintages of cable technology.

A look at the control variables is interesting, too. Here we can observe the coefficient for density to have a value of $a(D) = .0897$,

TABLE 8.1   Regression Coefficients of Cable Television Cost Function

Variable	Parameter Estimate	t Ratio
a(0)	−0.3531	(16.5549)
a(P1)	0.2944	(19.2708)
a(P2)	0.3937	(33.6621)
a(P3)	−0.3118	(5.8929)
a(Qa)	0.2587	(4.6172)
a(Qb)	0.0228	(4.3273)
a(Qc)	0.6506	(32.3799)
a(D)	0.0897	(2.0221)
a(E)	0.0978	(3.5970)
a(V)	−0.9223	(4.0401)
a(M)	−0.2827	(4.3183)
a(P1) (P1)	0.0305	(3.7581)
a(P1) (P2)	0.1916	(9.0650)
a(P1) (P3)	−0.2527	(12.3445)
a(P1) (Qa)	0.3394	(7.6900)
a(P1) (Qb)	−0.1049	(2.3791)
a(P1) (Qc)	0.0617	(4.4189)
a(P1) (D)	0.1841	(4.3476)
a(P1) (E)	−0.2295	(5.1174)
a(P1) (V)	1.9556	(4.0270)
a(P1) (M)	0.2229	(3.1701)
a(P2) (P2)	0.3241	(20.8342)
a(P2) (P3)	−0.8400	(26.2213)
a(P2) (Qa)	−0.0776	(1.5564)
a(P2) (Qb)	0.4071	(7.7252)
a(P2) (Qc)	0.5099	(22.7455)
a(P2) (D)	−0.1828	(3.1995)
a(P2) (E)	−0.9596	(13.9032)
a(P2) (V)	−5.2167	(8.3702)
a(P2) (M)	−0.6017	(6.5762)
a(P3) (P3)	0.5464	(25.8846)
a(P3) (Qa)	−0.2618	(4.8682)
a(P3) (Qb)	−0.3021	(5.5893)
a(P3) (Qc)	−0.5717	(21.1098)
a(P3) (D)	−0.0012	(0.0196)
a(P3) (E)	1.1891	(15.7176)
a(P3) (V)	3.2611	(5.1043)
a(P3) (M)	0.3787	(4.3185)
a(Qa) (Qa)	−0.0909	(2.1082)
a(Qa) (Qb)	0.3126	(3.8775)
a(Qa) (Qc)	0.0532	(1.4516)
a(Qa) (D)	−0.2617	(3.3656)
a(Qa) (E)	−0.9160	(6.3550)
a(Qa) (V)	−0.4586	(0.3587)

(continued)

TABLE 8.1 Continued

Variable	Parameter Estimate	t Ratio
a(Qa) (M)	−0.0822	(0.4751)
a(Qb) (Qb)	−0.0634	(1.3644)
a(Qb) (Qc)	0.1121	(3.1282)
a(Qb) (D)	0.1813	(2.0675)
a(Qb) (E)	0.2354	(1.6430)
a(Qb) (V)	0.6078	(0.4725)
a(Qb) (M)	0.0738	(0.4187)
a(Qc) (Qc)	0.2070	(21.9804)
a(Qc) (D)	0.0749	(1.8272)
a(Qc) (E)	−0.6012	(12.3100)
a(Qc) (V)	−2.0652	(4.7361)
a(Qc) (M)	−0.2051	(3.3710)
a(DD)	−0.0951	(1.8131)
a(DE)	0.0115	(0.0900)
a(DV)	−7.0066	(5.2132)
a(DM)	−1.0726	(4.7507)
a(EE)	0.8912	(9.1418)
a(EV)	−1.9036	(1.1501)
a(EM)	0.1087	(0.4030)
a(VV)	0.1658	(5.4133)
a(VM)	1.5182	(4.7460)
a(MM)	0.5853	(3.7343)
R^2	.9610	

with a good statistical significance. That is, costs are declining with density, which is an expected result, though its magnitude is not particularly great. Furthermore, cost savings decline with density and there are diminishing economies to density. This would conform to the observation that in highly dense inner-city franchise areas costs increase again.

The number of channels, on the other hand, is associated with increasing cost; this, too, is as intuitively expected. Here cost increases rise with channels, implying increasing marginal cost of channel capacity.

What do these results suggest? They show productivity increases — defined as reductions in production cost that are not due to changes in input cost — resulting from economies of scale, vintage, and maturity. This, of course, is not surprising. However, the relative contribution of these factors to production cost reduction is very interesting. The effect of economies of scale is relatively small. Operating experience, that is, "internal" innovation, on the other hand, has a much larger effect. And by far the largest contribution is made by the "external" development of the technology, as expressed by the contribution of new vintages to cost reduction.

Some differential between internal and external contributions to cost reduction, of course, could be expected. Adapting an existing technology is likely to be more costly and slower than starting with a brand new technology. But when the rates of cost decrease are as far apart as we find them to be, it is a strong indicator that more than these usual adjustment issues are at hand. Clearly, if cable systems were to compete head on, a cost differential as large as we observe would all but assure that the older systems would be driven off the market, unless they can *maintain* a vast difference in scale, and unless they have been operating for a very substantial time.

Other than in those unusual circumstances, then, a competitive situation would not permit a firm with the slower "internal" rate of cost reduction to survive entry in the face of the rapid change in technology. But, of course, they *do* survive in the real world. One reason is that no head-on competition exists, outside of a very few instances of "overbuilds," because existing operators are not contested by competitive entry and are instead protected by legal barriers such as de facto franchise monopolies.

The existence of such a productivity trend differential therefore raises a challenge to public policy. It suggests, first, the need for a reduction of legal entry barriers as a way of removing a protection to inefficiency. Sluggish operators should be subject to challenge by new entrants with more advanced technology, so that they would gain incentives to innovate.

When such a contesting of an existing market does not materialize as a reality or reasonable possibility, regulatory policies may be called for to reduce the differential in productivity trends. Instruments of such a policy could be regulatory oversight, franchise contracts that have built-in innovation requirements, and refranchising conditions requiring upgrading.

Clearly, these changes are likely to be painful to the cable television industry. It is likely to point to its record of internal innovation. It is also likely to demonstrate the major capital requirements that must be part of such an upgrading, and argue that cable firms would then have to be permitted to abandon the redistributory aspects of their operations, such as universal service, public and government access channels, and undifferentiated subscription rates. However, these arguments disregard the fact that substantial capital investments are made today in new systems, which tend to be under at least as many redistributive requirements as old systems, and that these new systems are still low-cost producers relative to older systems.

For some time now, concern has been growing whether the communication revolution, of which cable television is an important part, would lead to the emergence of a class of "information poor," who would not be able to afford the new offerings (and lose some of the previously "free" ones), either for reasons of low income or because they live in remote or low-density areas. We can now add the concern of service differentials between newer and older systems. The former may have a great diversity of program types and program sources, spread over many dozens of channels, as well as interactive services such as videotex, home banking, home shopping, and burglar alarms. The older systems, at the same time, may have not much more than a dozen of one-way channels. Perversely, those communities that welcomed cable television first are likely to find themselves neglected in terms of system innovation, while those that took a long time to permit cable can enjoy the benefits of advanced systems. Of course, this scenario is painted in somewhat stark colors; but it points to a real danger.

The present study, through its statistical estimation of cost-reducing productivity increases, thus points to the need to reduce the gap between internal and external innovation through policies that lower entry barriers and encourage competition or through some regulatory mechanism. The aim of this chapter was to demonstrate the problem. The analysis of optimal public policy responses ought to be a subject for further work.

NOTES

1. Excellent reviews of the literature may be found in Nelson (1981), Kamien and Schwartz (1975), Scherer (1980), Mansfield (1968), Norris and Vaizey (1973), Weiss (1971), Johnston (1966), and Vernon (1972). A recent survey of empirical evidence is presented by Scherer (1984).

2. Maturity may include the internal adoption of innovation, and is a more descriptive term than "experience," which may assume a static technology.

3. This would hold true even when access onto cable is leased to outside program syndicators under a system of common carriage, unless regulation forces requirements for an upgrading of capacity, or unless perfect price discrimination for access is possible.

4. Cable operators usually have been astute in the refranchising. The major trade publication of the industry quotes good advice to its members: "Do it while it is

quiet. . . . Start your negotiations while the public eye is focused on other issues" (Rothbard, 1982).

5. It is of course possible that bids are nonoptimal in response to excessive local requirements. In most new franchising, however, bids are above the minimum requirements.

6. This may change some years from now as direct satellite broadcasting (DBS), multipoint distribution systems (MDS), subscription television (STV), and satellite master antenna systems (SMATV) become established. Cable operators, however, do not appear to be affected at present by potential competition. In an industry survey, 78 percent of operators responded in the negative to a question asking whether they thought that DBS would have an inhibiting effect on their growth (Multichannel News, April 26, 1982: 46).

7. In another line of inquiry, that of "vintage" capital models, capital has been held to embody technical progress, and has been disaggregated according to its age. Those models, very different from the present analysis, go back to the "embodied capital" hypothesis (Abramovitz, 1952; Solow, 1960; Salter, 1966; Solow et al., 1966; Dhrymes and Kurz, 1964). Another approach has been to measure inputs in quality-adjusted units (Denison, 1978; Griliches and Jorgenson, 1967).

8. Starting with Arrow (1962), research considered experience processes or "learning by doing" (Kaldor, 1962; Alchian, 1963; Rapping, 1965; Flaherty, 1981; Duchatelet, 1977, Boston Consulting Group, 1968).

9. Furthermore, as Diewert (1974) has demonstrated, a Divisia index of total factor productivity that is based on a translog function is exact rather than approximate.

10. This imposition of $w = 0$ leads to a general multiproduct cost function, and this is reasonable. For the concept of homogeneity to be meaningful, all output quantities must be able to vary, and none can be restriced to zero, obviating the need for the transform (3).

11. Without the hybrid specification, an equation of the type of equation 19 could not be expressed numerically in translog form.

12. The parameter w is found by minimizing the residual sum of $\sigma^2(w)$ (Madalla, 1977: 315).

13. Reporting is done according to local operations; national cable companies (multiple systems operators, or MSOs) must therefore report their different operations separately.

14. These reports are likely to be fairly accurate due to cable companies' vulnerability to FCC charges of misreporting in a period in which they are actively seeking new franchises.

15. FCC, Cable Bureau, Physical System File; Community File; and Equal Employment Opportunity File.

16. To assure confidentially, financial data had been aggregated in the publicly available FCC documents; particularly detailed subaggregations — for each state according to seven size categories, and with many such categories of financial information — had been made available to the author specially.

17. On the statistical aspects of this scaling, which is widespread in translog estimations, see Denny and Fuss (1977).

18. All input prices are assumed to be independent of production level. Futhermore, input prices are not controlled by cable operators. For programming, some market power will exist in the future if cable should become a dominant medium. As an advertising outlet, cable television has no particular market power.

19. The formula employed is as follows: current value = book value × T, where T is the adjustment factor.

20. Such models have existed since 1966 (see Horrigan, 1966), and have been refined by Pogue and Saldofsky (1969), Pinchas and Mingo (1973, 1975), and Altman and Katz (1976). The model used here is taken from the Kaplan and Urwitz survey (1979: Table 6, Model 5), which determines bond rating with a fairly high explanatory power ($R^2 = .79$). The financial variables used in that model are as follows: (a) cash flow before tax/interest charges; (b) long-term debt/net worth; (c) net income/total assets; (d) total assets; (e) subordination of debt. Bond ratings ranging from AAA (model values ≥ 9) to C (≤ 1) can then be obtained for each observation point by substitution of the appropriate financial values. Bond rates are those reported by Moody's Investor Services (1981). For low ratings, no interest rates are reported by the services. For the lowest rating (C), the values estimated by an investment banker specializing in cable television were used (4 percent above prime); for the next higher ratings, interest rates were reduced proportionally until the reported ratings were reached.

21. These are usually restricted to a studio for a low-budget public-access channel, or an automated news/weather display.

22. It would be faulty to view the quantity of programs themselves as the outputs of a cable operator rather than as inputs. Neither are they produced by operators, as mentioned, nor are they sold on a quantity basis. Under the currently existing subscription-based system of revenue generation (as opposed to the embryonic pay-per-view system), programs serve as an incentive to buy subscriptions, not as the product itself.

23. This calculated by dividing total TV advertising billing (McCann-Erickson, as reported in Television Factbook, Inc., 1980: 76a) by a number of TV households (Arbitron, as reported in Television Factbook, Inc., 1980: 104a) and by viewing time. Nielsen figures for average weekly viewing of TV households is 42.6 hours; of cable households, 51.7 hours (Nielsen Cable Status Report, May 1981). TV advertising revenues per houshold viewing hours is found at close to 5.5 cents.

24. On the other hand, in dense inner-city operations, costs may go up, too, because cable must be buried underground. For the year of observation, however, only few inner-city franchises existed.

REFERENCES

ABRAMOVITZ, M. (1952) " Economics of growth," pp. 132-178 in B. Haley (ed.) A Survey of Contemporary Economics, Vol. 2 Homewood, IL: Irwin.

ALCHIAN, A. A. (1963) "Reliability of progress curves in the air frame production." Econometrica 31: 679-693.

ALLEN, B. R. (1969) "Concentration and economic progress: note." American Economic Review 59: 600-604.

ALTMAN, E. and S. KATZ (1976) "Statistical bond rating classification using financial and accounting data," in M. Schiff and G. Sorter (eds.) Proceedings of the Conference on Topical Research in Accounting. New York: New York University School of Business.

ARROW, K. (1962) "The economic implications of learning by doing." Review of Economic Studies (June).

BABE, R. E. (1975) Cable Television and Telecommunications in Canada. East Lansing: Michigan State University Graduate School of Business Administration.

BARTEN, A. P. (1969) "Maximum likelihood estimation of a complete system of demand equations." European Economic Review 1: 7-73.

BAUMOL, W. J., J. C. PANZAR, and R. WILLIG (1982) Contestable Markets and the Theory of Industrial Structure. New York: Harcourt Brace Jovanovich.

Boston Consulting Group (1968) Perspectives on Experience. Boston: Author.

Cabinet Committee on Cable Communications, Office of Telecommunications Policy (1974) Cable Report to the President. Washington, DC: Government Printing Office.

CAVES, D. W., L. R. CHRISTENSEN, and M. W. TRETHEWAY (1980) "Flexible cost functions for multiproduct firms." Review of Economics and Statistics 62: 477-481.

CHRISTENSEN, L. R. and W. H. GREEN (1976) "Economics of scale in U. S. electric power generation." Journal of Political Economy 84: 655-676.

CHRISTENSEN, L. R., D. JORGENSEN, and L. LAU (1973) "Transcendental logarithmic production frontiers." Review of Economic Statistics 55: 28-45.

DENISON, E. G. (1978) "Effects of selected changes in the institutional and human environment upon output per unit of input." Survey of Current Business 58: 21-44.

DENNY, M. and M. FUSS (1977) "The use of approximation analysis to test for separability and the existence of consistent aggregates." American Economic Review (June): 492-497.

———— and L. WAVERMAN (1981) "The measurement and interpretation of total factor productivity in regulated industries, with an application to Canadian telecommunications," in T. Cowing and R. Stevenson (eds.) Productivity Measurement in Regulated Industries. New York: Academic.

DHRYMES, P. J. and M. KURZ (1964) "Technology and scale in electricity generation." Econometrica 32: 287-315.

DIEWERT, W. E. (1976) "Exact and superlative index numbers." Journal of Econometrics 4: 115-145.

———— (1974) "Application of duality theory," pp. 106-171 in M. D. Intriligator and D. A. Kendrick (eds.) Frontiers of Quantitative Economics, Vol. 2. New York: Elsevier.

DUCHATELET, M. (1977) "Learning by doing and imperfect competition." Stanford, CA: Stanford University Press.

FLAHERTY, M. T. (1981) "Industry structure and cost reducing investment." Econometrica 49.

FRISCH, R. (1965) Theory of Production. Dordrecht, Netherlands: Raidel.

FUSS, M. and L. WAVERMAN (1982) "Multi-product multi-input cost functions for a regulated utility: the case of telecommunications in Canada," in G. Fromm (ed.) Studies in Public Regulation. Cambridge: MIT Press.

GOLLOP, F. M. and M. J. ROBERTS (1981) "The sources of economic growth in the U.S. electric power industry," in T. Cowing and R. Stevenson (eds.) Productivity Measurement in Regulated Industries. New York: Academic.

GREER, D. F. and S. A. RHOADES (1976) "Concentration and productivity changes in the long and short run." Southern Economic Journal 43: 1031-1044.

GRILICHES, Z. and D. JORGENSEN (1967) "The explanation of productivity change." Review of Economic Studies (July).

GRILICHES, Z and V. RINGSTAD (1971) Economies of Scale and the Form of the Production Function: An Econometric Study of Norwegian Manufacturing Establishment Data. Amsterdam: North-Holland.

HANOCH, G. (1975) "The elasticity of scale and the scope of average costs." American Economic Review 65: 492-497.

HORRIGAN, J. O. (1966) "The determination of long-term credit standing with financial ratios." Journal of Accounting Research 4 (supplement): 44-62.

IBBOTSON, R. G. and R. A. SINQUEFIELD (1979) Stocks, Bonds, Bills, and Inflation: The Past (1926-1976) and the Future (1977-2000). Charlottesville, VA: Financial Analysis Research Foundation.

JOHNSTON, R. E. (1966) "Technical progress and innovation." Oxford Economics Papers 18: 158-176.

KALDOR, N. (1962) "Comment on Professor Arrow's paper 'The economic implications of learning by doing.' " Review of Economic Studies (June).

KAMIEN, M. I. and N. L. SCHWARTZ (1975) "Market structure and innovation: a survey." Journal of Economic Literature 13: 1-37.

KAPLAN, R. S. and G. URWITZ (1979) "Statistical models of bond ratings: a methodological inquiry." Journal of Business 52: 231-261.

LINTER, J. (1965) "Security prices, risk, and maximal gains from diversification." Journal of Finance 20: 587-616.

MADDALA, G. S. (1977) Econometrics. New York: McGraw-Hill.

MANSFIELD, E. (1968) Industrial Research and Technological Innovation: An Econometric Analysis. New York: Norton (for the Cowles Foundation for Research in Economics at Yale University).

Moody's Investor Services (1981) Moody's Bond Survey. Chicago: Author.

NADIRI, M. I. and M. A. SCHANKERMAN (1981) "The structure of production, technological change, and the rate of growth of total factor productivity in the U.S. Bell system," in T. Cowing and R. Stevenson (eds.) Productivity Measurement in Regulated Industries. New York: Academic.

NELSON, R. R. (1981) "Research on productivity growth and productivity differences: dead ends and new departures." Journal of Economic Literature 19: 1029.

NOAM, E. M. (1983a) "Economics of scale in cable television: a multi-product analysis." Working Paper Series, Research Program in Telecommunications and Information Policy, Columbia University.

——— (1983b) "Private sector monopolies and productivity: the case of cable T. V. franchises." Working Paper Series, Research Program in Telecommunications and Information Policy, Columbia University.

NORRIS, K. and J. VAIZEY (1973) The Economics of Research and Technology. London: Allen & Unwin.

OWEN, B. M. and P. K. GREENHALGH (1982) " Competitive policy considerations in cable television franchising." Draft, Economists, Inc., Washington, D.C.

PHILLIPS, A. (1971) Technology and Market Structure: A Study of the Aircraft Industry. Lexington, MA: D. C. Heath.

——— (1956) "Concentration, scale, and technological change in selected manufacturing industries, 1899-1939." Journal of Industrial Economics 4: 189.

PINCHAS, G. E. and K. E. MINGO (1975) "A note on the role of subordination in determining bond ratings." Journal of Finance 30: 201-206.

—— (1973) "A multivariate analysis of industrial bond ratings." Journal of Finance 28: 1-18.

POGUE, T. F. and R. M. SALDOFSKY (1969) "What's in a bond rating?" Journal of Financial and Quantitative Analysis 4: 201-228.

RAPPING, L. (1965) "Learning and World War II production function." Review of Economic Statistics (February).

ROTHBARD, G. (1982) "When renewal means rebuild: What if you do everything right and the city says it's not good enough?" Cablevision (June 28): 21ff.

SALTER, W.E.G. (1966) Productivity and Technical Change. Cambridge: Cambridge University Press.

SCHERER, R. M. (1984) "Technological change in the modern corporation," in B. Bock et al., The Modern Corporation: Size and Impacts. New York: Columbia University Press.

—— (1980) Industrial Market Structure and Economic Performance. Chicago: Rand McNally.

SCHUMPETER, J. (1950) Capitalism, Socialism, and Democracy, New York: Harper & Row.

SHARPE, W. F. (1964) "Capital asset prices: a theory of market equilibrium under conditions of risk." Journal of Finance 19: 425-442.

SHEPHARD, R. W. (1970) Theory of Cost and Production Functions. Princeton, NJ: Princeton University Press.

Sloan Commission (1971) On the Cable: The Television of Abundance. New York: McGraw-Hill.

SOLOW, R. M. (1960) "Investment and technical progress," in K. Arrow et al. (eds.) Mathematical Methods in the Social Sciences. Stanford, CA: Stanford University Press.

—— (1957) "Technical change and the aggregate production function." Review of Economic Statistics 39: 312-320.

—— J. TOBIN, C. E. VON WEIZÄCKER, and M. YAARI (1966) "Neoclassical growth with fixed factor propositions." Review of Economic Studies 33: 79-115.

STIGLER, G.J. (1956) "Industrial organization and economic progress," in L. D. White (ed.) The State of the Social Sciences. Chicago: University of Chicago Press.

STOLLER, D. (1982) "The war between cable and the cities." Channels (April/May).

Television Factbook, Inc. (1980) Television Factbook. Washington, DC: Author.

VERNON, J. M. (1972) Market Structure and Industrial Performance. Boston: Allyn & Bacon.

WEINBERG, G. (1972) Cost Analysis of CATV Components (PB 211-012). Washington, DC: National Technical Information Service, U.S. Department of Commerce.

WEISS, L. W. (1971) "Quantitative studies of industrial organization," in M. D. Intriligator (ed.) Frontiers of Quantitative Economics. Amsterdam: North-Holland.

—— (1963) "Average concentration ratios and industrial performance." Journal of Industrial Economics 11: 250.

ZELLNER, A. (1962) "An efficient method of estimating seemingly unrelated regression and tests for aggregation bias." Journal of the American Statistical Association 57: 348-368.

9

PUBLIC SECTOR MONOPOLIES

JEFFREY D. STRAUSSMAN
ALEXANDER ROSENBERG

Syracuse University

Imagine a public official proclaiming that he is *against* productivity improvement. Or perhaps that productivity is all rubbish (a view difficult to maintain even when the service in question is sanitation)? In this age of "cutting government back to size," productivity improvement is embraced by all as one effort, albeit a modest one, to improve the performance of the public sector. More bang for fewer bucks, you might say. It is clearly nonpartisian, and it seems to have appeal at all levels of government.

At the risk of raining on everyone's parade, we wish to raise a pessimistic note concerning the prospects for genuine productivity improvements in the public sector. In so doing we do not challange the claims by some that real gains have been made. Perhaps more garbage has been picked up for the same cost in some jurisdictions. Or the number of arrests for a given law enforcement budget have really increased. Rather, we wish to make an argument that some of the *inherent* features of nonmarket production present fundamental obstacles to productivity improvements in the public sector. At the same time, we argue that the obstacles may be overcome *if* marketlike mechanisms are adapted to the public sector.

Authors' Note: *This chapter appears, in a slightly different version, under the title,* "*Maximization, Markets and the Measurement of Productivity in the Public Sector,"in* New Directions in Public Administration, *Barry Bozeman and Jeffrey D. Straussman, eds. (Monterey, CA: Brooks/Cole Publishing Company, 1984).*

The normative view that productivity improvement is desirable has a set of descriptive presuppositions. It is necessary, we believe, to first present these descriptive presuppositions and determine whether they are now satisfied, or even satisfiable, in a public sector setting. Unless this is accomplished we cannot sensibly proceed to questions concerning the possiblity or the desirability of specific efforts to improve productivity. At present productivity discussions have it backwards. That is, the desirability of productivity improvement is asserted (again, who would deny that it is a nice thing), and then we construct mechanisms to obtain productivity gains that rest on very shaky assumptions about economic and organizational behavior. This is not merely an abstraction. When productivity arrangements between public managment and public unions break down, the source of the breakdown may rest in these shaky assumptions rather than "bad faith" on the part of either side. Our effort, then, is simply to get the descriptive horse before the normative cart.

A NECESSARY CONDITION FOR PRODUCTIVITY IMPROVEMENT

The quest for productivity gains must presume that we can at least improve public sector "output" — here defined as clean streets, safe streets, educated children, and so on. Productivity further means that these outputs *should* be maximized; that is, cleanliness, public safety, and education are worthwhile objectives to try to reach. But simply saying that clean streets are better than dirty streets, or that a mean reading score for, say, sixth graders of 6.2 is better than 5.6 is not enough. If we believe that productivity gains can in fact be achieved we are implicitly making a crucial descriptive assumption. We are assuming that economic agents — civil servants in particular — do actually try to maximize some outputs such as utility, income, or a bundle of household commodities. For example, the teacher, while perhaps valuing education, really wants to maximize such things as personal income, prestige, leisure,and job satisfaction. Given the supposition that civil servants are already motivated to maximize something, the objective is to channel the *personal* goals of civil servants toward politically determined objectives — clean streets, public safety, or quality education. *This is where the normative dimension of productivity joins with the descriptive one.* For instance, pronouncements that we should improve performance in public education in itself provide no guarantee that teachers will actually try to mold their actions to achieve this goal unless we can make the attainment of their personal goals (income, prestige, and so on) contingent on the achievement of the politically determined objective. This is not to say that teachers do not "value" quality education. Nor are we suggesting that some, perhaps many, teachers have quality education as their primary objective. Rather, we are simple assuming that teachers most likely have personal objectives that are more important to them — provide them with more utility, if you will. (Those who doubt these assertions might simply reflect on the likely success of a productivity scheme that asks public employees to work harder, better, or longer for the "good of the community" without any divisible benefits.)

If we can make the political objective and the personal objectives of civil servants *by-products* of one another we have a greater likelihood that productivity gains will be realized. Logically this means that individual utility maximization by the civil servant is a *necessary condition* for the argument that productivity in the public sector can be improved. If we were discussing conditions of economic competition, we could end our argument here, for in the competitive model the assumption that economic agents are utility maximizers is both necessary and sufficient for improvements in productivity. Nonmarket approaches to productivity must obviously search elsewhere for theoretical guidance.

The literature on the "economics of bureaucracy" is appropriate here. Specifically, the factual assertion that civil servants try to maximize private goals — income and nonincome perquisites of public office — has been argued persuasively by others (Niskanen, 1971; Stockish, 1976; Wolf, 1979). The empirical dimensions of what is the effort to expand the agency budget, according to Niskanen (1971: 38), essentially is an aggregation of the bureaucrat's utility functions. However, budget expansion, in turn, can affect productivity *adversely* since such expansion may drive up agency budgets above their optimal level. According to Wolf (1979: 117), budget maximization strategies can "boost agency *supply* curves above technically feasible ones, resulting in redundant total costs, higher unit costs, and lower levels of real nonmarket output than the socially efficient ones." The rationale for budget expansion lies not in the predisposition of individual bureaucrats to maximize budgets per se, but rather in the demand and supply characteristics of public sector products. The lack of a market "test," the difficulty of measuring output, the unique relationship between agencies and their legislative overseers are well known to observers of the public sector. They create the environment for what Wolf has called "nonmarket failure" — the gap between objectives and actual implementation.

The problems of measuring productivity and, more important, stimulating productivity improvements are associated with these characteristics identified by Wolf. For example, the fact that bureaucrats do not necessarily maximize some unambiguous objective such as clean streets lies not in any deficiency of the bureaucrat. Rather, it lies in the absence of a clear consensus on what "clean streets" means. Nor is there agreement on the components of the production process (and the interrelationship among the components) that will achieve the objective. Given that bureaucrats are self-interested utility maximizers, their utility maximization may be unrelated or perhaps even inversely related to productivity. For example, Sterne et al. (1972) found that the ill-defined objective of "serving the elderly in need" through a lunch program was displaced by budget maximization, attained by feeding a high number of elderly regardless of need. In an important respect, productivity may have actually declined. Similarly, Staaf (1977) showed that educational personnel most clearly attempt to maximize salary schedules rather than any other output.

From the vantage point of neoclassical economic theory, markets would be an improvement as a way to organize economic activities. A market approach to public sector activities requires the assumption that all agents are rational, all maximize something in common. The trouble with this assumption is its great theoretical distance from data that can be collected and the ease with which it can be defended from falsifications. For purpose of illustration, let as assume that public agencies attempt to maximize their next budgetary allocation. On this factual finding can hinge schemes for improving their productivity, for we may make the next budgetary allocation contingent on some level of output of a mandated product (potholes filled, streets cleaned, cases covered), so that the maximization of the latter will be a by-product of the attempt to maximize the budget.

Linking the two outputs may of course not, by itself, increase productivity. This is the sense in which the descriptive assumption of maximization is normally at best a necessary condition for the desired aim of increasing productivity. But it is an important nontrivial necessary condition for the latter. If there is no actual maximization, there is nothing on which we can base economic and organizational changes that will affect the desired maximization. If it turns out that bureaucrats maximize things that cannot be linked to political objectives, then there is simply no hope of making the outputs joint by-products, and so increasing productivity of the political objective. For example, if an air-traffic controller maximizes hours of on-the-job sleep, there is no way of improving his or her productivity in the provision of air safety. And, again, if there is nothing that he or she can be determined to maximize (pay, prestige, vacation time, or the like), there is no way of improving his or her productivity.

THE "NONISSUE" OF PRODUCTIVITY IN A PERFECTLY COMPETITIVE ENVIRONMENT

Maximization of a personal product is a necessary condition for maximization of a politically determined product, but not in and of itself a sufficient one, for it may be practically or theoretically impossible to link them. These impossibilities surface in the difficulties surrounding the operationalization and employment of productivity measures that are essential to the determination of whether we have linked personal and political objectives. And this is where the market approach derives its greatest strength, for *it obviates the construction and application of such measures by supervisory political agents.*

Consider the daunting problem of efficiency versus effectiveness. Productivity consists not only of minimizing cost per unit of output to meet the need for which it is ostensibly produced. If we measure productivity by cost per unit output alone, without adding a dimension to our measure reflecting its quality, our measure of productivity will produce artifactual readings of performance. For example, suppose we measure social service by numbers of cases processed per week. The result of introducing this measure is that using it to increase caseworkers' income, or budget, or other benefits, may be simply to increase the number of cases "processed" while so decreasing quality of service as to make for what would be universally counted as a decline in productivity. Much of the work in public sector productivity theory focuses on measures that will not have this effect. But the obstacle that any successful measure must surmount is very great. The only measure that *cannot be corrupted* is one that is so inextricably linked to political objectives that the only practicable way civil servants can increase their personal utility is by actually increasing productivity of the political objective itself. The measure must be constructed with ingenuity that is greater than the ingenuity of the civil servants whose activities are being measured!

The necessary prerequisites to productivity gains in the public sector are cumbersome. This cumbersomeness does not arise in the perfectly competitive model of an economy on which the market approach to productivity is founded. In the perfectly competitive world of neoclassical micro-economics there is no problem of productivity, because all economic agents and institutions always maximize the productivity of their inputs of land, capital, and labor. Where agents are numerous and rational, commodities divisible and infinitely substitutable, market entry and exit unrestricted, prices inelastic and returns to scale nonexistent, all factors of production are used at their highest level of productivity. The perfectly competitive market effectively assimilates issues of efficiency and effectiveness in production, since the demand for a firm's goods reflects buyers' assessments of the goods in terms of price and quality. A low-quality good must fetch a lower price, and so provide a smaller return than a high-quality good. If firms can maximize their profits at the lower price, then of course the productivity of their factors has not declined, but has remained at its optimum level.

By diminishing quality a firm has simply entered the market for another good altogether. In the neoclassical model the market provides an *information* network that producers use to fine-tune their mix of factors in order to provide for consumer wants at the prices they are willing to pay. In a purely competitive market we may be sure that the marginal productivity of every input or factor with respect to every output will be equal to its price. In such a market the entrepreneur is provided with unambiguous signals when his or her productivity departs from the optimum: sales fall, receipts fall, or both. Of course, if the entrepreneur is perfectly rational and fully informed about production techniques and market prices this will never happen, and the problem of productivity simply does not arise within the compass of the perfectly competitive model.

In the unreal world of perfect competition between rational agents, productivity and utility are both maximized as by-products of one another, not only by each individual agent, but by the economy as a whole, up to the constraints of Pareto optimality. The proof that perfect competition generates a market-clearing equilibrium that is Pareto optimal both in production and consumption is of course of the chief theoretical ornaments of contemporary economic theory. Long before this result was rigorously proved, the presumption of Adam Smith's beneficent hidden hand was already providing motivation for making the real world as much like the world of perfect competition as it could be. Market-oriented approaches to public sector activities are a recent variant on this thrust. The thrust is of course parried by citing the deviation of the real world from the competitive model, and the even greater divergence of the public sector from the economics of the market. Moreover, it is ironic that while our problems of measuring productivity derive from differences between the public sector and the perfect market, in a perfect market there is no need for the sort of measures of productivity we seek.

The welfare economic rationale for market mechanisms either within the public sector or between the sorts of firms that actually exist and compete so imperfectly has of course evaporated. Where agents are not rational, where there are indivisibilities, returns to scale, incomplete information, there is no certainty of Pareto optimas; indeed there is every sign of the lack of equilibria necessary to such desired states.

What rationale then remains for the market approach in the real world of public and private endeavors? In fact, these considerations do not deprive market approaches of much of their attractiveness at all, for the appeal of these approaches does not rest on their welfare-economic aspects but on the strength of the market as an informational distribution system and as a force constraining the personally efficient use of the distributed information. Thus a market of buyers and sellers will be sensitive to information about changes in prices (and changes in the supplies and demands they reflect) even when the sellers and buyers compete imperfectly. All that is required is that they be at least intermittently rational and that they compete at all. For example, a pure monopolist in the supply of records and a pure monopolist in the supply of books may compete in the market for leisure products. As a means of decentralizing or disaggregating the needs and wants of the members of a society, the price system is unrivaled. By contrast with central planning, a price mechanism is simply far superior means of communicating to producers how much of what to produce.

The price mechanism, then, is not defended on normative grounds. Rather, it is merely an effective way to provide individuals with information to aid decision making. And if productivity is of concern to economic agents, the price mechanism will be primary in the construction of indicators to monitor its improvement. Public sector producers lack this critical informational tool. The governmental environment in which most agencies operate separates the production of goods and services from information about the quality and quantity of their output. The electoral, legislative, and bureaucratic channels through which information relevant to optimal output is now channeled are long, noisy, misdirected, and subject to breakdowns. Market approaches in the public sector are nothing but the attempt to circumvent this poor information system in favor of one we anteced-ently know to be superior. This approach assumes that, like other rational agents, bureaucrats are maximizers of private outputs, and the non-optimum levels of productivity characteristic of the present arrangements in the public sector reflect less-than-optimal ways of harnessing bureaucrats' optimizing strategies to the needs and wants of the society. It holds further that optimal ways of harnessing their strategies cannot be determined centrally, but must be left to the production unit with the most direct source of information about the demands for its products. Thus attempts to introduce marketlike reforms in the public sector can be defended as a way of improving the bases of decision making, reforms that are necessary if productivity gains are to be detected.

MARKETLIKE APPROACHES
IN THE PUBLIC SECTOR

It may be useful, at this point, to summarize some key points. We have argued, in essence, that attempts to improve productivity in the public sector must direct individual-maximizing behavior toward politically determined outcomes. but unless the two are by-products of one another, there is no reason to assume that what civil servants maximize will actually improve productivity. In particular, it is im-probable that the maximization of some *intermediate* factor output — specified through collective bargaining negotiation, for example — will (a) necessarily produce desired final output and/or (b) be sus-tained by the maximizing agents (for example, civil servants). To put it another way, "second best" solutions that surrogate the market are unlikely to resolve the problems surmounted by the market because they do not tap the best source of relevant market information and do not link it inextricably to agents' utilities or private production func-tion.

Consider two simple case illustrations of the above point. In the city of Flint, Michigan, a productivity "bargain" was struck between the city and the union representing waste collectors. The city wished to curb waste-collection cost primarily by cutting the amount of overtime pay. The union, in turn, wanted to increase the collectors' income. A productivity scheme was designed so that workers presumably had an incentive to reduce overtime pay since a pool of savings would be shared by the city and the workers — after adjusting for quantity (tonnage collected) and a quality (complaints) dimension (Greiner et al., 1977: 500). Workers were supposed to maximize the following: a "productivity coefficient," which consisted of an overtime-reduction factor; a quality factor; a route-completion factor; and tonnage collected. The maximization of these variables would increase the productivity bonus, which, presumably, is what workers "really" wanted, instead of, say, overtime hours of work.

A similar case of productivity bargaining occurred between the city of Orange, California, and the association representing the police. The agreement called for across-the-board wage increases that were tied to a reduction in the reported number of four "repressible" crimes: rape, robbery, burglary, and auto theft (Greiner et al., 1977: 64). While the experiment was tried for one year and then discontinued, researchers form the Urban Institute concluded that, on balance, the experiment *was* successful.

From the perspective of our argument both cases are problematical. Consider the implicit assumptions behind both. Workers were asked to maximize something in both cases. But what is in fact put forth to be maximized is neither (a) what the workers ultimately wish to maximize (they want to maximize income but must maximize other variables to reach their real objective) nor (b) what the respective city governments wish to maximize — clean streets in the former case and public safety in the latter. It is an empirical question as to whether lower cost per ton of garbage is related to clean streets, or the reduction in reported crime is positively related to public safety. A great deal of literature has been written on the problems of measuring intermediate outputs and the distinction between outputs and the objectives (or consequences) of public programs (see Ross and Burkhead, 1974; Levy et al., 1974). Suffice it to say that a productivity bargain that commits workers to maximize an intermediate output may have dysfunctional effects. Consider the Orange, California, case again. According to the Urban Institute report. "The department's response to the incentive program was to focus primarily on the prevention of burglaries, which historically had comprised about 80 percent of the four incentive crimes reported to police" (Greiner et al., 1977: 63). From the standpoint of the productivity argument this discussion seems rational. But as Thurow (1970) has shown, the allocation of a law enforcement budget to achieve a given level of efficiency will create equity effects both for potential victims *and* potential perpetrators of crime (both of which should enter into a quality dimension of productivity). Thus it is quite conceivable that the probability of being raped may increase if a decision is made to allocate law enforcement resources to maximize the reduction in burglaries. (This is simply one example of what Campbell [1979: 84] calls the "obtrusive and unintended effects" of quantitative indicators.) Consequently, even if law enforcement personnel did indeed maximize the production of an intermediate good, it is by no means certain that the politically determined objective (such as public safety) will inevitably be improved or increased.

Consider a perhaps even more fundamental problem. In both cases it is assumed that the intermediate outputs maximized and the politically determined objectives will be by-products of one another. But a simple point shows that this is not automatically so. Once a "productivity frontier" is reached workers have no incentive to maximize intermediate outputs. Consider the example of Orange, California, once again. According to the Urban Institute report, "After reducing the city's already low rate of incentive crimes enough to earn the maximum possible wage increases, police in Orange apparently felt that further reduction would be difficult, if not impossible. Indeed, most employees . . . felt that they had reached the point of diminishing returns and that if they continued with such a plan, they would, in effect, be competing against themselves (that is, against their own good record)" (Greiner et al., 1977: 66). What this implies is that, at some point, workers may have no incentive to continue to maximize a negotiated indicator if the given indicator no longer is related to wage increases, utility, or the like. When this occurs, the variable that was previously maximized is neither sufficient nor necessary for the improvement of productivity in the public sector.

Where does this leave us? To restate an earlier point, the difficulty of improving productivity in the public sector is, to a great extent, *informational.* The problem of public sector productivity is not, as some would suggest, measurement, but rather the kinds of organizational arrangements that would allow maximizing agents — civil servants — to pursue their interests in ways that will lead to improved politically determined outcomes. This, pure and simple, is the rationale for some of the market-based reforms that are receiving increased attention in public administration. This current attention comes from two basic sources. The marketlike reforms discussed below have some appeal because they seem to be "reasonable" responses to growing fiscal scarcity — especially at the local level. Second, the reforms have conservative appeal in the current political climate because they seem to encourage "limited government." Our arguments are based on neither perspective. To reiterate: The justification for marketlike reforms in the public sector rests solely on the argument that they should improve the bases of decision making and thereby enhance productivity. The last part of this chapter sketches out some of these market-based reforms and notes some special problems of implementation.

CONTRACTING

Governments, particularly at the local level, have for some time contracted with private firms, nonprofit organizations, and other jurisdictions for a range of services. The rationale for contracting is straightforward, and the expected benefits include the following:

- cost savings
- choice of contractor(s)
- expertise of contractor(s)
- public management flexibility offered by the contracting method of service provision

The growing interest in contracting is related to the deterioration of the fiscal condition of many local governments. But this assumes only that contracting will be less costly than the direct (monopolistic) provision of services by local government agencies.

Whether contracting will actually improve public sector productivity is an empirical question. Still, we may make some inferences about the necessary conditions for potential productivity gains. First, the contractor must seek to maximize a private goal, such as income or budget. Second, the local government must have some options available (choice) so that the availability of the contract (for the contractor) is by no means certain. Third, the local government must be able to act on these options. For example, a local government that contracts for a service must be able to choose among alternative bids or supply the service itself as an alternative to contracting. Under these conditions demand and price factors make it possible to join maximizing behavior by the contractors with politically determined objectives. And under these conditions productivity gains may be realized. The fact that, in practice, many contract arrangements fall short of the above expectations means that factors intervene (often referred to as "political influence") to nullify the supply and demand factors.

USER FEES

Approximately 15 to 20 percent of locally raised revenue comes from user fees. The rationale for user fees is straightforward. First, fees presumably improve "allocative efficiency" since community residents could articulate their preferences for local public goods and services more accurately than through the voting mechanism. As one proponent of a greater reliance on user fees put it, "If the government sets a price on the product — thereby opening up a market through which consumers can register their vote for or against, by either paying the price or not consuming the product — the price could guide the city in the production of its services" (Mushkin et al., 1979: 126). Second, from the standpoint of bureaucratic performance, user fees are intuitively appealing since they avoid the bilateral relationship between agency and legislature. That is, the legislature no longer is faced with an all-or-nothing appropriation decision. On the contrary, the production of both quality and quantity of local government services becomes price sensitive — assuming that the local government agency does not enjoy a monopoly of the good or service that is nonsubstitutable. Under the conditions outlined above the prospects for productivity improvement seem reasonably straightforward. However, the personal objectives of the civil servant are usually conspicuously absent from user fee mechanisms; consequently, a user fee approach is not in itself sufficient to ensure improvements in productivity.

PUBLIC SECTOR - PRIVATE SECTOR COMPETITION

Although there are analogous services provided in both the public and private sectors, consumers of public goods and services rarely have the opportunity to choose between the two. But if citizens could exercise such choice, the competition or even the threat of competition would make public producers (that is, local government agencies) more efficient.

There are very few examples of this situation. A survey by the Urban Institute noted that in Witchita,Kansas, and St. Paul, Minnesota, private and public refuse haulers compete with each other. While public collection is slightly more expensive, the cost difference between public collection and private collection is trivial (Fisk et al., 1978: 14-17). In contrast, a study by E. S. Savas (1974: 478-479) found that private refuse collection in Bellerose, Long Island, comparable to collection in an adjacent area in the New York City, was about one-third of the cost of municipal collection in New York City. While admittedly sketchy, these examples suggest that public-private competition may reduce the cost of provision by a public monopoly.

Creating a competitive environment is necessary but not sufficient. The information concerning efficiency must enter the public budgeting process so that public agencies are held accountable for cost containment or cost reduction. The legislature must use the cost information when making appropriations. While obvious, this requirement has not been easily accepted given the routines of the typical budget process. An additonal element is being introduced into budgetary decision making. But the history of budget reform suggests that information about efficiency does not automatically permeate budget routines (Straussman, 1979).

COMPETITIVE BUREAUS

The concept of competitive bureaus flies in the face of orthodox public administration theory, which views "coordination" and "centralization" as superior to organizational fragmentation. Yet there is little evidence to support this conventional wisdom.

Critics from the public choice school have seriously questioned this traditional view of bureaucracy. Specifically, coordination and centralization merely promote the monopoly position of bureaus. But why should competition between or among bureaus reduce this tendency? A bureau faced with competition from other bureaus will find that the elasticity of demand for its services may increase when citizen-consumers realize that there are alternatives available. For any single bureau providing the given good or service, the level of demand should decline. Two conclusions follow. First, bureaus faced with this situation will have an incentive to search for more efficient ways to produce their goods and services. Second, the legislature should be able to use the information to make appropriations that more accurately reflect the "true" costs of producing public goods and services.

Aside from obvious problems of political feasibility, there are three potential caveats that ought to be mentioned with regard to competitive bureaus. While bureaus often provide similar services, they usually do not provide identical ones. It is assumed that there is an elasticity of demand for like services among public bureaus. But bureaus try to reduce this possibility by stressing the uniqueness of their output. The empirical question is whether citizen consumers perceive that the services of bureaus are indeed similar. For instance, would public assistance recipients who are declared employable recognize that job placement services are available from both a unit in a typical social services department (generally at the county level) and a state employment office? The consumer — in this case the recipient of public assistance — needs to recognize that the services available are similar. Next, the bureaus, in turn, must acknowledge that the consumers will act as if choice is available to initiate a quasi-competitive environments. But while this would be sufficient in the private sector, it is not in the public sector. As in the case of the previous option — private sector-public sector competition — the legislature needs to see benefits in the competitive situation and incorporate such information into appropriations decisions. How else would gains from competition in the public sector be realized? As with the previous option, the funding arrangements for specific goods and services do not often provide the necessary fiscal atmosphere that encourages economizing. Returning to the example of job placement alternatives, federal funding of state employment agencies may remove part of the superficial competitive characteristics that seem to be present merely because both agencies provide similar services. But the similarities end once funding sources are considered. The legislature (as well as the respective agencies) may not have the required incentives to take advantage of competitive bureaus as a quasi-market option.

CONCLUSION

We close this discussion and review with some reiteration and qualification. Our argument for the implementation of market mechanisms has been resolutely nonideological and at least partially nontheoretical. Much of the resistance to such mechanisms stems from the perception that they reflect politically controversial perspectives and practically irrelevant theoretical possibilities. However, we have not suggested that the decentralization fostered in a price system is good in itself, or that it is a logically sufficient condition for a Pareto optimal result in the public or private sector. Rather, exposing public service and its producers to a demand curve, to prices they do not themselves set,provides them with the best available information about how to increase productivity and provides them with a strong motive to act on this information.

Some qualifications to our proposal must be kept in mind. Universally and invariably the hopes of reformers overreach the actual improvements attained. Indeed, improvements are often overwhelmed by unintended consequences of the reform originally unknown to the reformer. We can have no assurance that market-inspired forms would be different. Moreover, market-based options by themselves offer no guarantee that the obtained informational advantages of the market will actually be utilized. In particular, the implementation problems of market-based reforms must themselves be linked to — made a natural by-product of — the output maximized by political decision makers, especially legislators who appropriate public funds. Implementation presents a series of obstacles, some of which have been hinted at in our brief discussion of the four marketlike mechanisms. Yet implementation logically follows an understanding of the conceptual problems that make productivity difficult to achieve in the public sector. This prior state—the stage of conceptual clarification — has yet to be reached. Perhaps we have moved in the right direction.

REFERENCES

CAMPBELL, D. T. (1979) "Assessing the impact of planned social change." Evaluation and Program Planning 2: 67-90.

FISK D., H. KIESLING, and T. MULLER (1978) Private Provision of Public Service: An Overview. Washington, DC: Urban Institute.

GREINER, J. et al. (1977) Monetary Incentive and Work Standards in Five Cities: Impacts and Implications for Management and Labor. Washington, DC: Urban Institute.

LEVY, F., A. MELTSNER, and A. WILDAVSKY (1974) Urban Outcomes. Berkeley: University of California Press.

MUSHKIN, S. et al. (1979) "The tax revolt: an opportunity to make positive changes in local government," in S. Mushkin (ed.) Proposition 13 and Its Consequences for Public Management. Cambridge, MA: Abt.

NISKANEN, W. (1971) Bureaucracy and Representative Government. Chicago: Aldine.

ROSS, J. and J. BURKHEAD (1974) Productivity in the Local Public Sector. Lexington, MA: D. C. Heath.

SAVAS, E. S. (1974) "Municipal monopolies versus competition in delivering urban services," in W. Hawley and D. Rogers (eds.) Improving the Quality of Urban Management. Beverly Hills, CA: Sage.

SCHICK, A. (1966) "The road to PPB: the stages of budget reform." Public Administration Review 26: 243-258.

STAAF, R. J. (1977) "The growth of the educational bureaucracy: do teachers make a difference?" in T. Borcherding (ed.) Budgets and Bureaucrats. Durham, NC: Duke University Press.

STERNE, R., A. RABUSHKA, and H. SCOTT (1972) "Serving the elderly: and illustration of the Niskanen Effect." Public Choice 13: 81-90.

STOCKFISH, J. A. (1976) Analysis of Bureaucratic Behavior: The Ill-Defined Production Process. Santa Monica, CA: Rand Corporation.

STRAUSSMAN, J. D. (1979) "A typology of budgetary environments: notes on the prospects for reform." Administration & Society 11: 216-226.

THUROW, L. (1970) "Equity versus efficiency in law enforcement." Public Policy 18: 451-462.

WOLF, C. (1979) "A theory of nonmarket failure: framework for implementation analysis." Journal of Law and Economics 22: 107-139.

10

PRODUCTIVITY IMPROVEMENT, MANAGEMENT SCIENCE, AND POLICY EVALUATION

STUART S. NAGEL
University of Illinois

American public policy development may have reached a critical point in entering the 1980s. For the past twenty years, public policy has emphasized equity rather than efficiency. Thus public policy has emphasized issues relating to minorities, women, poverty, and so on. Since 1980, however, there has been an increased emphasis in American government on productivity or effeciency, although possibly more in terms of rhetoric than performance. In this context, productivity improvement refers to achieving more benefits from given costs achieving a desired benefit level with lower costs, or, better yet, achieving more benefits with lower costs. From 1960 to 1980, the emphasis aimed at a more equitable division of the national pie. Now there is an increasing emphasis on trying to make the pie bigger.

That emphasis on increased productivity is also appearing in other places, such as West Germany, Japan, and Scandinavia, although not necessarily with a loss of equity. The new emphasis is thus not confined to the United States or to a conservative administration. Unlike previous periods of productivity emphasis (such as 1920-1960 or 1870-1900), the post-1980 period emphasizes the role of public policy in actively stimulating private sector productivity, especially through tax policy, rather than relying on marketplace forces, which were so important in those earlier periods. In the late 1800s, for example, the key incentives for technological innovation were to increase sales and reduce expenses. In the late 1900s, the key incentives are more likely to include tax breaks and government subsidies. The new concern for productivity could mean new opportunities for policy evaluation to aid in achieving more efficient government and a more efficient private sector by way of governmental incentives. The increased governmental role challenges goverment, business, and the academic world to work together to increase societal benefits and decrease societal costs.[1]

The chapter attempts to clarify ways in which policy evaluation methods can contribute to productivity improvement. Policy evaluation methods can be defined as a set of skills associated with deciding which of various alternative public policies will maximize or increase benefits with constant costs, minimize or decrease costs with constant benefits, or maximize benefits minus costs in achieving a given set of goals. Both the benefits and the costs can be either monetary or nonmonetary in nature. Policy evaluation may also be concerned with problems of equity that relate to how the benefits or the costs are distributed among various groups. Maximizing benefits minus costs tends to be the overall criterion, since it tends to maximize the favorable change in society's net worth (or its assets minus its liabilities), as a result of adopting one policy rather than another. The assets and liabilities can also be either monetary or nonmonetary.

The above definition represents a management science or operations research perspective on policy evaluation, as contrasted to philosophical analysis of goals, a political science analysis of process, or a sociology-psychology emphasis on determining the effects of policies through variations on the pretest-posttest, experimental-control model. Management science is thus the connecting link in this analysis between productivity improvement and policy evaluation.

Productivity improvement is usually thought of as the result of better technology and better worker motivation. These elements may be important for increasing benefits minus costs, or output minus input. Yet one can argue that with labor-saving technology we can be more productive with even less motivated workers, and that there is usually more room for improvement in technology than there is in motivation. This chapter argues that one can often be more productive with constant technology and motivation if better choices are made between alternative policies or decisions, and that a management science perspective on policy evaluation can aid in making such decisions. Better policy evaluation or decision making can also help in choosing among alternative technologies and among alternative methods for improving worker motivation.

A systematic analysis of the leading books in the field of policy evaluation reveals that although they contain many chapters arranged in a variety of ways, the methods presented tend to fall into five basic categories: *benefit-cost analysis* (optimum choice among discrete alternatives without probabilities); *decision theory* (optimum choice with contingent probabilities); *optimum-level analysis* (finding an optimum policy where doing too much or too little is undesirable); *allocation theory* (optimum-mix analysis); and *time-optimization models* (optimum choice, level, or mix applied to time minimization).[2]

This chapter is organized in terms of these five categories. Each section briefly describes the methodology and presents a concrete example of where policy evaluation can enable governmental decison makers to arrive at decisions that are likely to produce greater benefits minus costs than will alternative decisions. The examples vary in subject matter, but one can reason by analogy from them to still other subject matters. The chapter thus combines a conceptual scheme for organizing policy evaluation methods along with concrete illustrative examples that demonstrate the value of systematic policy evaluation for improving the productivity of government policies, including policies designed to stimulate the private sector to be more productive.

BEING MORE PRODUCTIVE
WITH DISCRETE ALTERNATIVES

" Discrete alternatives," in this context, means alternatives that each represent a lump-sum project, in the sense that one can meaningfully adopt only one unit of the project, not multiple units and not fractions of units. These situations are analogous to buying ties in a clothing store: One would not buy three of the same tie for oneself, and one would not buy half a tie.

Table 10.1 provides benefit and cost data for set of five projects in order to illustrate what is involved in such situations. The object is to allocate scarce resources among one or more of those projects in order to make the most productive use of those resources. Each project indicates the benefits at given costs, the net benefits or profitability, and the benefit/cost ratio or efficiency measure. Table 10.1 could

TABLE 10.1   Data for Illustrating Productive Decision Making When
Faced with Discrete Alternatives

Project	Benefits $	Rank	Costs $	Rank	Benefits=Costs $	Rank	Benefits/Costs $	Rank
D	4.20	5	3.00	2	1.20	5	1.40	4
E	13.50	1	10.00	5	3.50	1	1.35	5
F	3.50	4	2.00	1	1.50	4	1.75	1
G	9.00	2	6.00	3	3.00	2	1.50	3
H	6.40	3	4.00	2	2.40	3	1.60	2
Totals	36.60		25.00		11.60		7.60	
Averages	7.32		5.00		2.32		1.52	

NOTES: If the projects are mutually exclusive. Project E is the best buy, provided
that one can afford the $10 cost. If the projects are not mutually exclusive,
all the projects should be bought provided that one can afford $25 total
cost. If the projects are not mutually exclusive and one has only $10 avail-
able, the best or most profitable combination is G and H, even though they
are individually not the most profitable, efficient, effective, or least expensive. By "best" is meant maximizing benefits minus costs within the constraints that relate to the nature of the projects, the available budget, and
whether the situation is mutually exclusive or allows combinations.

represent, for example, a set of alternative dams within a river seg-
ment. At any given place in the river, it is meaningless to build two
duplicative dams, one behind the other or one on top of the other,
since one dam does all the good that can be done. Likewise, it is
meaningless to build half a dam, since the water can flow over half a
dam as easily as it can no dam. Alternative dams are thus not only
lump-sum projects, but are also mutually exclusive.

For a start, in using Table 10.1, we can compare Project E or Dam
E, which has the highest net benefits, with Project F or Dam F, which
has the highest efficiency. One basic principle in policy evaluation is
to prefer high net benefits over high efficiency. By doing so, we will be
better off after that choice is made, assuming other things remain
constant. To be more specific, if we invest $10 in Project E, at the end
of the relevant time period, we will have the equivalent of $10 in
principal and $3.50 in interest, for total assets of $13.50. If, however,
we invest $2 in Project F, at the end of the time period we will have $2
in principal, $1.50 in interest, and $8 in idle funds, for total assets of
only $11.50 The $8 in idle funds may or may not be able to find an
alternative investment opportunity that pays interest at a rate higher
than the .75 of Project F or the .35 of Project E. An alternative

perspective is the following: If we buy Project E we will have $13.50 in benefits, whereas if we buy Project F we will have $3.50 in benefits plus $8 in unspent funds, for a total of only $11.50. In other words, we come out behind by going with the more efficient Project F than by going with the more profitable Project E, regardless of whether we view the situations from the perspective of an investor or of a consumer. Thus if the projects were mutually exclusive, Project E would be the best buy, provided that we could afford it.

The situation becomes a bit more complicated, but more interesting, if the projects are *not* considered mutually exclusive, so that we can buy more than one project. An example of a set of five nonmutually exclusive lump-sum projects might be five different ways of notifying or reminding released defendants to appear in court. The projects could include (1) sending defendants postcards a few days before their trials, (2) phoning them within that time period, (3) going to their homes, (4) having them report to a court officer within that time period, or (5) putting a general notice in the newspaper emphasizing that people who fail to appear for their court dates get arrested. It would not be meaningful to send each defendant three postcards simultaneously, or to send each half a postcard. Nor would it be meaningful to go to their homes twice in that time, or to go only halfway to their homes. Deliberately notifying only some of the defendants might be considered unconstitutional treatment. The data in Table 10.1 could apply to those five notification projects, rather than to five alternative dams. The benefits would be the dollars saved by not having to rearrest no-shows, as contrasted to the flood damage avoided. If we had an unlimited budget (that is, a budget of $25 or more) that is capable of buying all the projects, then we would buy all of them since they are all profitable. This assumes that there are no unusual interaction effects among the five projects, such that buying all five somehow would cause more no-shows than buying a combination of fewer than all five.

Suppose we have only $10 available to spend for those five notification projects. Which ones are the best to buy or invest in? One might think we should use the $10 to buy the first most profitable project, then the second, and so on, until we exhaust our $10. That, however, would be fallacious reasoning, because we would then spend all our $10 on Project E for a profit of only $3.50 By distributing our $10 among other less profitable projects, we could make more total profit. For example, we could buy projects F, H, and D. They would collectively cost us only $9, leaving $1 left over. Buying those three would include the first and second most efficient projects. More important, the sum of the net benefits for those three projects adds to $5.10, which is substantially more than the $3.50 we would get by spending our $10 on the single most profitable project. In other words, what is most profitable to do with mutually exclusive lump-sum projects may not be most profitable when the projects are not mutually exclusive.

Although buying F, H, and D with our $10 makes more sense than just buying E, it is still not the most profitable way to allocate our $10, although it may be a highly efficient way, since it yields $5.10 for an investment of only $9. It has the defect, though, of allowing $1 that otherwise might be profitably spent to remain idle. We could use our whole $10 to buy projects G and H. At first glance, that looks irrational, because those projects individually do not score best on benefits, costs, net benefits, or efficiency. At second glance, however, one can see that the G and H combination will produce a total profit of $5.40, which is higher than that produced by any other combination of $10 worth of projects, including F, H, and D. More specifically, the G and H combination gives us, at the end of the time period, total assets of $15.40, which consists of $10 in principal and $5.40 in interest. The F, H, and D combination, on the other hand, gives us at the end of the time period total assets of only $15.10, which consists of $9 in principal, $5.10 in interest, and $1 in idle funds.

The general rules one might derive from this analysis are, first, if a government agency is interested in maximizing the good that it does, it should spend its whole budget or as much of that budget as possible. Second, the budget should be spent for each of the projects in the order of their efficiency. These two rules together should lead to an optimum allocation of scarce resources among the lump-sum projects that are often present in governmental decision making. If a governmental agency is not interested in maximizing the good that it does, but rather is more interested in minimizing its expenditures while achieving a minimum amount of benefits, then it should apply a slightly different set of rules. Suppose the minimum benefit level is $5. Then, the least expensive way of achieving at least $5 in benefits would be to purchase projects F, H, and D. Those three projects are arrived at by choosing the projects in the order of their efficiency, which means project F first, followed by project H. That, however, generates only $3.90 in benefits for $6 in costs. The next project in order of efficiency is Project G. Buying it, however, would overshoot the $5 mark by $1.90 and would double the costs. We therefore turn to

Project D, which is the fourth most efficient project. Buying that project will exceed the $5 minimum by only 10¢ and will incur only an additional $3 in costs. Thus we are still rank ordering the projects in order of efficiency, but we do not seek to spend the whole budget — rather, we are spending as little as possible to meet the minimum benefit level.

One might object to the difficulty of mesuring both benefits and costs in the same units, especially monetary units. With varying degrees of effort, however, one can usually assign a monetary value to controlling floods, getting the average defendant to show up for a trial date, or obtaining other public sector benefits. The human mind implicitly makes such calculations in deciding whether benefits are worth the costs. Thus quantifying benefits in terms of cost units is only a matter of making that kind of thinking more explicit. A common alternative is to talk in terms of maximizing benefits subject to a maximum cost constraint, or sometimes minimizing costs subject to a minimum benefit constraint, rather than maximizing benefits minus costs. Those alternatives may sometimes be satisfactory, but they are not as desirable, as is indicated by their inapplicability to deciding between projects E and F if the benefits for those two projects were not both measured in dollars. In other words, 3.5 F units for $2 could be worth more or less than 13.5 E units for $10, but $3.50 is clearly worth less for $2 than $13.50 is for $10. This assumes that F units and E units are different outputs, such as highway miles built and students trained. The analysis based on Table 10.1 also assumes that the five projects include all the alternative investments available. The desirability of maximizing benefits minus costs applies to both business firms and government agencies, although business firms may generally find it easier to measure benefits and costs in dollars as a common unit.[3]

BEING MORE PRODUCTIVE
WITH CONTINGENT PROBABILITIES

"Contingent probabilities" in this context means probabilities that events will occur and influence the benefits or the costs that alternative projects or decisions produce. Thus if a project produces $10 in benefits, but only if an event occurs that has a .60 probability of occurring, then that project has expected benefits of only $6, which equals the $10 discounted by the .60 probability that the contingent event will occur.

Figure 10.1 provides data for a project in which contingent probabilities are important. The project is one of determining whether a federal agency should or should not gather certain expensive data. There are basically two alternatives. One either gathers the data or one does not gather the data. We could, however, make things more complicated by talking in terms of gathering multiple quantities or percentages of data, and thus have many cells in our figure. Such an extension can logically be made after clarifying the simpler choice between two alternatives. Likewise, there are basically two outcome possibilities. Either the data gets used in a certain way or it does not get used. Again, we could later complicate things by talking in terms of multiple uses and multiple tables.

With two alternative decisions and two alternative occurrences, there are four possible outcomes. Two are clearly undesirable or costly, namely, to gather the data and not have them used (cell C_g) and not to gather the data when they would have been used if they had been gathered (cell n). Two outcomes are clearly desirable or beneficial, namely, to gather data that subsequently get used (cell B_g) and not to gather data that would not have been used if they had been gathered (cell B_n). Of the two undesirable outcomes, it is normally worse not to gather data that would have been used, although sometimes the other undesirable outcome may be worse. If cell C_n is considered the worse of the two costs, then for convenience we can anchor it at a value of -100. For the sake of consistency, we could then also anchor cell B_g at $+100$ as the better of the two beneficial outcomes. Now all we have to do is determine how many times worse a cell C_n outcome is than a cell C_g outcome. If failing to gather needed data in a given situation would be 10 times as bad or as costly as gathering the data and not having them used, then the value of cell C_g on our -100 to $+100$ scale would be -10. Likewise, for the sake of consistency, the value of cell B_n would be $+10$. In this context, many people would find it simpler to work with the benefit/cost ratio of 100/10, or 10/1. Likewise, instead of talking in terms of a scale of 0 to 100, or 1 to 10, one could insert dollar amounts (or other units) into the cells for the benefits and the costs.

Now, with that information for our hypothetical situation, we can determine the expected values of gathering or not gathering the data. The expected value of gathering the data equals $(+100)(P) + (-10)$, where P is the probability that the data will be used. In other words, the expected value of gathering the data equals the benefits and the costs of the gathering, discounted by the probabilities of the benefits

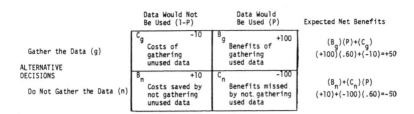

	Data Would Not Be Used (1-P)	Data Would Be Used (P)	Expected Net Benefits
ALTERNATIVE DECISIONS Gather the Data (g)	C_g -10 Costs of gathering unused data	B_g +100 Benefits of gathering used data	$(B_g)(P)+(C_g)$ $(+100)(.60)+(-10)=+50$
Do Not Gather the Data (n)	B_n +10 Costs saved by not gathering unused data	C_n -100 Benefits missed by not gathering used data	$(B_n)+(C_n)(P)$ $(+10)+(-100)(.60)=-50$

NOTE: P = probability of use; B = benefits; C = costs; g = gathering the data; n = not gathering the data.

RULES FOR APPLYING THE FIGURE: (1) Determine the alternative decisions (that is, what are the data to be gathered or not gathered). One can have multiple rows. (2) Determine the alternative occurrences (that is, what is the potential use that will occur or not occur). One can have multiple tables. (3) Determine the ratio of the costs of gathering the data to the benefits of gathering the data, but ignore the positive and negative signs. (4) If P is greater than that ratio, gather the data. If less, don't gather the data.

ALTERNATIVES TO RULES 3 AND 4: (3) Determine the probability that the data will be used. (4) If the cost/benefit ratio is greater than that probability, gather the data. If less, don't gather the data.

FIGURE 10.1 Data for Illustrating Productive Decision Making When Faced with Contingent Probabilities

and costs occurring. Likewise, the expected value of not gathering the data equals $(+10) + (-100)$ (P), which equals the benefits and the costs of not gathering, discounted by their respective probabilities. Note that the cost of gathering the data is not discounted by any probability, since we must bear that cost when the data are gathered regardless of whether they are used. Likewise, we save that cost when we do not gather the data, regardless of whether the data would have been used. We could take into consideration an amount for embarrassment cost, which would have to be discounted by $1 - P$ since it is only incurred if the data are not used.

Logically, what we want to do now is determine how high P has to be before the expected value of gathering the data will exceed the expected value of not gathering the data. To do that, all we have to do is set those two expected values equal to each other and solve for P. Doing so will give us the threshold probability above which we should gather the data and below which we should not gather the data. One can show algebraically that the threshold value of P (or P*) equals C_g/B_g, ignoring the plus and minus signs. That means the threshold probability with this data is 10/100, or .10. In other words, if there is better than a .10 probability that the data will be used, then we should gather it. Otherwise, it's not worth the trouble.

The above analysis can be applied without requiring the users to be capable of translating costs or benefits into dollars, satisfaction units, or any kind of absolute units. All the users have to do is determine which of the two undesirable outcomes is the more undesirable, and the rough ratio of the undesirability of the more undesirable outcome to the less undesirable outcome, taking the facts of the specific situation into consideration. The users can then apply the simple formulas of C_g/B_g or the cost/benefit ratio to determine the threshold probability. They should then ask whether the actual perceived probability in this specific situation is greater or less than the threshold probability. If greater, gather the data; if less, don't. If the cost of gathering the data is greater than the benefits even before the benefits are discounted by the probability of their occurring, then of course one would not want to gather the data no matter how high the probability that the data will be used.

The same type of analysis could be used to determine what the cost/benefit ratio has to be in order to justify gathering the data. Suppose we know that the data have a .60 probability of being used. We have previously determined that the threshold probability is equal to the cost/benefit ratio. Therefore, if P equals .60, then the cost/benefit ratio has to be less than .60 to justify gathering the data. If the cost/benefit ratio is greater than .60 and there is only a .60 probability of the data being used, then the data should not be gathered.

This same simple analysis can be applied to a variety of governmental problems where adopting or not adopting a policy or decision is related to the occurrence of an event that has a roughly known probability of occurring, or at least where one knows a rough cost/benefit ratio of adopting or not adoping a decision. By following the simple rules developed above, governmental decision makers can make more productive decisions that will provide more benefits minus costs than would the alternative decisions.[4]

BEING MORE PRODUCTIVE
WITH MIDDLING POSITIONS

These situations involve policies that produce benefits at first, but then the benefits reach a peak and start to fall off. The object in such situations is to find the point on a policy continuum where the benefits are maximized. These situations may also involve policies that reduce costs at first, but then the costs reach a bottom and start to rise. The object in such situations is to find the point on a policy continuum where the costs are minimized.

Figure 10.2 provides data for a policy problem in which doing either too much or too little is undesirable. The policy problem is one of finding an optimum percentage of defendants to hold in jail prior to trial in order to minimize the sum of the holding costs and releasing costs. An alternative way of stating the problem would be to maximize the sum of the holding benefits (that is, the releasing costs avoided) and the releasing benefits (that is, the holding costs avoided). One could also say the problem is one of maximizing the holding benefits minus the holding costs or one of maximizing the releasing benefits minus the releasing costs.

In 1969, questionnaires were mailed to judges, prosecuters, defense attorneys, and bail project directors from numerous cities, although here we only use the data from the 23 cities that provided complete information for all the basic variables. The 7 basic variables for each city were as follows:

(1) JC: Jail costs (in dollars) per day per inmate. This figure was multiplied by 30 to put it on a per month basis.

(2) LJ: Average length of time spent in jail before trial (in months) for those defendants who are held in jail pending trial.

(3) A: Number of individual defendants arraigned in 1968, that is, brought before a magistrate or judge to determine whether the individual should be held or released before trial.

(4) %H: Percentage of arraigned individuals held pending trial.

(5) %RF: Percentage of arraigned individuals who were released, but who failed to show up in court for trials.

(6) %RC: Percentage of arraigned individuals who were released, but who were arrested for committing another crime while released.

(7) %HG: Percentage of persons held in jail before trial who were found guilty.

From these basic variables, three sets of transformed costs can be calculated, with regard to holding, releasing, and total cost. There are three *holding* costs, calculated on a per defendant basis for each city, as follows:

$\#H$ = Number held   = $\%H \cdot A$

(1) THC_1 = total jail cost   = $\#H \cdot LJ \cdot \$JC$ per day $\cdot$ 30 days

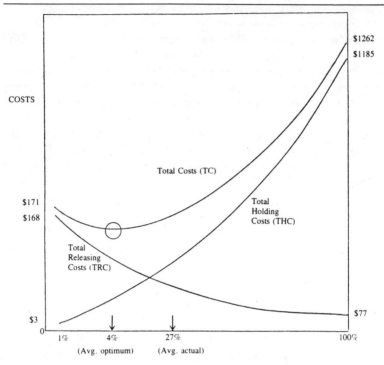

NOTE: Percentage of defendants held before trial (%H). Formulas: THC = $1185 (%H)$^{1.31}$; TRC = $77 (%H)$^{-.17}$; TC = THC + TRC.

FIGURE 10.2   Data for Illustrating Productive Decision Making When Doing Too Much or Too Little Is Undesirable

(2) THC_2 = total GNP cost   = $\#H \cdot LJ \cdot$ \$360 per month

(3) THC_3 = total bitterness cost   = $\#H \cdot LJ \cdot$ \$300 per month $\cdot$
                                                                              $(1.00 - \%H_G)$

There are two *releasing* costs, calculated as follows:

                 $\#R$ = Number released   = $A - \#H$

(1) TRC_1 = total rearrest cost   = $\#R \cdot$ \$200 $\cdot \%R_F$

(2) TRC_2 = total crime-committing cost   = $\#R \cdot$ \$1000 $\cdot \%R_C$

Total costs are then calculated from the following simple formulas:

                 THC = total holding costs   = $THC_1 + THC_2 + THC_3$

                 TRC = total releasing costs   = $TRC_1 + TRC_2$

                 TC = total costs   = THC + TRC

Constants rather than variables in the above costs include $360 a month as the average lost gross national product when a defendant was kept in jail for 30 days pending trial. That figure is based on an assumption of $2.00 per hour in 1969 wages at 40 hours a week and 4.5 weeks a month. In calculating bitterness costs, it is assumed that bitterness is generated mainly among those detained defendants who are *not* subsequently found guilty (that is, the complement of $\%H_g$). The bitterness costs for these defendants are figured at approximately $300 per month. This means that if these defendants were paid $300 a month, they would generally feel compensated for their bitterness. The figure is not equal to lost wages, on the assumption that these defendants recognize that legitimate, nondeliberate mistakes can be made in the criminal justice process. It is assumed that it would cost approximately $200 to rearrest a defendant who fails to show up for trial. It is further assumed, in the absence of any better information, that the average released defendant who commits a crime while released costs the victims and society approximately $1000. The effects of changing these tentative figures on the optimum percentage to hold can be determined as part of a sensitivity analysis designed to determine how the changes affect the optimum percentage to hold.

For each of the 23 cities, we can plot a point showing the percentage held ($\%H$) and the total holding costs. If we draw a smooth curve through those 23 points that minimizes the sum of the distances squared from the points to the line, we get a positive convex curve such as that shown in Figure 10.2. The equation for that curve is THC $= 1185(\%H)^{1.31}$. This means that if $\%H$ becomes 100 percent (or 1.00 when expressed as a decimal), then the total holding costs equal $1185 per defendant. The 1.31 means that as $\%H$ goes up 1 percent, the holding costs go up at a faster rate of 1.31 percent. At the left end of the graph, if $\%H$ becomes 1 percent, or .01, then the total holding costs per defendant equal $3, although for simplicity here we ignore the fixed holding costs that remain constant regardless of how low the percentage held becomes. Similarly, for each of the 23 cities, we can plot a point showing the percentage held and the total releasing costs. If we draw a least-squares curve through those 23 points, we get a negative convex curve such as that shown in Figure 10.2. The equation for that curve is TRC $= 77(\%H)^{-.17}$.

Since total costs are the sum of holding costs and releasing costs, we can show an asymmetrical valley-shaped total cost curve by adding the distance from the horizontal axis up to the THC curve and the distance from the horizontal axis up to the TRC curve in order to create the TC, or total cost, curve. The equation for that curve is TC $= 1185(\%H)^{1.31} + 77(\%H)^{-.17}$, since TC = THC + TRC. Figure 10.2

is not drawn exactly to scale in order to enlarge the area where the total cost curve reaches its bottom point. Also, if the percentage held were allowed to go to 0 percent rather than 1 percent on the figure, then at that point TRC and TC would equal infinity. At 1 percent, THC = $3, TRC = $168, and TC = $171, as determined by a hand-held calculator that can raise numbers to decimal powers.

The total cost curve goes up as %H decreases from 4 percent to 0 percent, and the total cost curve goes up again as %H increases from 4 percent to 100 percent. This is so because from 4 percent to 0 percent the TRC curve is rising faster than the slowing THC curve is falling; after 4 percent, the THC curve is rising faster than the slowing TRC curve is falling. At 4 percent, the slope of the TRC curve is the same as the slope of the TCH curve. The easiest way to determine where the total cost curve bottoms out is to insert a set of decimals into the above equation that shows total cost as a function of percentage held, then simply calculate what the total cost would be for each decimal with a calculator. Doing so would reveal that total cost bottoms out between 0 percent and 10 percent. Inserting each percentage between those two percentages reveals that 4 percent is the bottom point.

What we have done here is analogous to what a rational business firm producing one product is supposed to do when it decides on the optimum level of goods to produce in order to maximize its total profits. In the absence of this kind of analysis the decisions or policies reached may not be so profitable or productive. This is especially likely to be the case if the individual decision makers are not seeking to maximize societal benefits minus societal costs, as in this situation, where individual judges may not feel so bothered by the societal holding costs, but may be quite sensitive to the embarrassment that comes from releasing a defendant who fails to appear or who commits a crime after being released. In other words, their individual benefit-cost analysis may not necessarily be consistent with a societal benefit-cost analysis, and they may thus be slighting societal productivity.[5]

BEING MORE PRODUCTIVE
WHEN ALLOCATING SCARCE RESOURCES

"Continuum alternatives" in this context refers to alternatives capable of being adopted in multiple units or fractions of units. These situations are analogous to a city buying police, courts, and corrections to fight crime. If we have $1,000,000 to spend, we can think of each of those three purchases as ranging from $0 up to $1,000,000, with any possible combination of expenditures for those three items that totals more than or equal to $0 or less than or equal to $1,000,000.

Figure 10.3 provides data to illustrate what is involved in such situations. In 1970 the Auerbach management consulting firm was asked to develop teams of attorneys and other persons to evaluate the approximately 200 Office of Economic Opportunity legal sevice programs across the country. Each program was evaluated on 113 different dimensions. The 114th dimension referred to the overall satisfaction of the evaluators. That dimension was scored on a scale from 1 to 12, with 1 being as bad as possible, 12 being as good as possible, and 7 being acceptable. A key controversy in providing legal services to the poor has been how to allocate time, effort, and money between routine case handling and law reform work. Law reform mainly involves taking appeals designed to establish new precedents with regard to enforcing the legal rights of the poor. The percentage of the budget devoted to law reform was determined for each legal service program, with the complement of that percentage being devoted to routine case handling. Those percentages were then translated into dollars per client, and a statistical analysis was made to determine the relation between satisfaction and expenditures for law reform and case handling.

The average legal service agency spent $68.34 per client, of which $6.16 went to law reform and $62.18 went to case handling. The average agency also received a satisfaction score of only 6.51, just below the acceptable level. We can plot on a three-dimensional surface a dot for each legal service agency showing its satisfaction score, its law reform expenditures per client, and its case-handling expenditures per client. We can then fit a line or a plane to those dots in order to minimize the squared distances from the dots to the line. Doing so produces results like those shown in Figure 10.3. The top left of the figure shows that as law reform expenditures increase, satisfaction also increases. When there is an increase of $1 for law reform per client in the average legal services agency, satisfaction scores go up .34 of a satisfaction unit. On the other hand, there is virtually no relation between an increase in case-handling dollars and an increase in satisfaction. The top right of the figures shows that as case-handling expenditures increase by $1, satisfaction goes down by .03 of a unit, which amounts to almost no change.

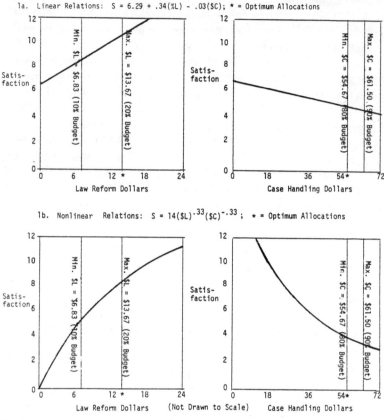

1a.   Linear Relations: S = 6.29 + .34(%L) - .03($C);   * = Optimum Allocations

1b.   Nonlinear   Relations: S = 14($L)$^{.33}$($C)$^{-.33}$;   * = Optimum Allocations

NOTE: S = satisfaction score of each legal services agency as determined by a team of evaluators; $L = dollars allocated to law reform activities, as determined by multiplying the total agency budget by the percentage spent on law reform and dividing by the number of clients; $C = dollars allocated to routine case-handling activities, as determined by multiplying the total agency budget by the percentage spent on case handling and dividing by the number of clients.

FIGURE 10.3   Data for Illustrating Productive Decision Making When Faced with Continuum Alternatives

Given this information, how would one logically allocate the $68 budget of the average legal services agency between those two activities? If there were no minimum or maximum constraints on law reform or case handling, one would allocate the whole $68 to law reform since it has a consistently higher marginal rate of return than case handling in producing additional satisfaction per incremental dollar. The Office of Economic Opportunity in Washington, D.C., however, has issued evaluation guidelines that imply that legal service agencies should spend no more than about 20 percent of their budget on law reform, and no less than 10 percent. That means expenditures for case handling should be no more than 90 percent of an agency budget and no less than 80 percent. If these constraints are imposed upon the two graphs in the upper part of Figure 10.3, one can readily see that the optimum allocation to law reform dollars would be 20 percent of the $68 budget, and the optimum allocation to case-handling dollars would be 80 percent of the $68 budget. In other words, when one assumes linear relations between policy inputs and goals for different activities, one should allocate all the budget to whatever activity has the best slope or marginal rate of return up to whatever maximum constraint needs to be recognized, and then switch to the next to the best activity, and so on. Before making those allocations, however, one should give each activity whatever the minimum constraints provide for.

The lower part of Figure 10.3 involves a more realistic fitting of curves to data. It recognizes that as one increases policy inputs, satisfaction may increase, but probably at a diminishing rate of increase (rather than a constant rate), as is shown in the lower left. Likewise, the lower-right part of the figure recognizes that as one increases an input that lowers satisfaction, the decrease is also likely to occur at a diminishing or plateauing rate, rather than a constant rate. The numerical parameters for the nonlinear equation can be obtained through the same kind of statistical analysis used to obtain the numerical parameters for the linear equation, except one instructs the computer to arrive at a best-fitting curve rather than a straight line. In this context, recognizing those diminishing returns does not affect the optimum allocation. This is so because case handling has a slightly negative marginal rate of return (MRR), and law reform has a postive MRR. Thus one would want to give the maximum possible to law reform and the minimum possible to case handling, regardless of whether the relations are linear or nonlinear.

If, however, case handling would have produced a positive-shaped curve such as that in the lower-left corner, but not rising so high, then the optimum allocation might have involved giving less than the maximum to law reform and more than the minimum to case handling. If we give the maximum to law reform, we may be wasting some of our money as we approach that maximum where the law reform curve gets relatively flat, relative to the beginning part of the case-handling curve or the part just above the case-handling mini-mum. Although the law reform curve may be steeper at any given dollar figure than the case-handling curve, the law reform curve may not be steeper at its maximum constraint than the case-handling curve is at its minimum constraint. Under those circumstances, the op-timum allocation would involve first giving each activity its minimum allocation, which is $6.83 for law reform and $54.67 for case handling, or a total of $61.50. The remaining $6.84 should then be allocated to the two activities in proportion to their elasticity coefficients. That means that when the relation among satisfaction, law reform, and case handling is $S = a (\$L)^b(\$C)^B$, then law reform should receive $b/(b+B)$ part of $6.84, and case handling should receive the com-plementary $B/(b+B)$ part of $6.84. One can prove algebraically that with both those nonlinear relations being positive (that is, having postive exponents), then the optimum allocation involves allocating in proportion to those exponents after satisfying the minimum and maximum constraints.

Although the optimum allocation methods when faced with con-tinuum alternatives are fairly simple to apply, the actual allocations may be quite different in the absence of such policy evaluation analysis. For example, among the legal services agencies, the average allocation of the agencies in the survey was $6.16 to law reform and $62.18 to case handling. If those two figures are inserted into the linear equation shown at the top of Figure 10.3, then the predicted satisfac-tion score is only 6.51. If, on the other hand, the optimum allocations of $13.67 and $54.67 were used, the predicted satisfaction score would be 9.27, which is a substantial improvement at no additional total cost. Likwise, with the nonlinear equation, the optimum allocation pro-duces substantially more satisfaction than the actual allocation. The actual allocations were less productive of evaluator satisfaction, possibly because legal services attorneys found it easier to do routine case handling than law reform, and because they may have mista-kenly thought that the conservative evaluators would downgrade them if they did more law reform work. The evaluators, however, were generally prominent lawyers who recognized that law reform requires more technical skill than routine case handling, even if they did not agree with the results of the law reform cases that were won.[6]

BEING MORE PRODUCTIVE
WHEN SAVING TIME

Time-optimization models are decision-making systems designed to minimize time consumption. Time-optimization models often involve variations on optimum choice, risk, level, or mix analysis, but applied to situations in which the goal is to minimize time. Some time-optimization models are peculiar to a temporal subject matter, for example: (1) queueing theory, for predicting and reducing waiting time and backlogs from information concerning arrival and service rates; (2) optimum sequencing, for determining the order in which matters should be processed so as to minimize the average waiting time; and (3) critical-path analysis, for determining what paths, from start to finish are especially worth concentrating on with regard to delay-reduction efforts.

Optimum sequencing can provide a good example of how policy evaluation can improve productivity by providing the increased benefits of time saving with no substantial increase in monetary or non monetary costs. Figure 10.4 provides data to illustrate what is involved. Suppose a court or other government agency has 3 cases to process. The first case is predicted to take 20 days, the second to take 10 days, and the third to take 5 days. If the cases are handled on a traditional first-come, first-served basis, then Figure 10.4 shows that the first case will have zero waiting time, 20 days service time, and 20 days total time. The second case will spend 20 days waiting for the first case, 10 days being serviced, and thus 30 days total time. The third case will have to wait 30 days for the first 2, 5 days for its own servicing time, and 35 total days. The sum of the total times is 85, which means an average of 28 days per case.

On the other hand, we could reorder the cases at the end of each day or week so that the shorter cases are first. Then the new first case will have no waiting time, 5 days service time, and 5 days total time. The new second case will wait only 5 days for the first case, 10 days being serviced, and thus 15 total days. The third case will wait 15 days for the first 2, 20 days for itself, and 35 total days. The sum of these 3 total times is only 55 days, for an average of only 18 days. This means that by reordering the cases we drop from an average time of 28 days to only 18 days, or a saving of about one-third off the original average. No other arrangement of cases will save as much time as taking the shortest cases first, as indicated by the orders between order 1 and order 6 in Figure 10.4.

Alternative methods for saving case time tend to be quite expensive, such as hiring additional judges or other processing personnel. The time saved may not justify the extra expense. Optimum sequencing, however, costs only some record-keeping time. One useful kind of record keeping is to know the average processing time for various types of cases such as larceny or assault among criminal cases and

Order 1				Order 2				Order 3			
Case	T_w	+ T_s	= T	Case	T_w	+ T_s	= T	Case	T_w	+ T_s	= T
20	0	20	20	10	0	10	10	5	0	5	5
10	20	10	30	20	10	20	30	20	5	20	25
5	30	5	35	5	30	5	35	10	25	10	35
		SUM = 85				SUM = 75				SUM = 65	
		AVG. = 28				AVG. = 25				AVG. = 22	

Order 4				Order 5				Order 6				Days Saved
Case	T_w	+ T_s	= T	Case	T_w	+ T_s	= T	Case	T_w	+ T_s	= T	
20	0	20	20	10	0	10	10	5	0	5	5	30
5	20	5	25	5	10	5	15	10	5	10	15	15
10	25	10	35	20	15	20	35	20	15	20	35	-15
		SUM = 80				SUM = 60				SUM = 55		30
		AVG. = 27				AVG. = 20				AVG. = 18 (Optimum)		10

NOTE: T_w = waiting time; T_s = servicing time; T = total time.

FIGURE 10.4   Data for Illustrating Productive Decision Making When Faced with Arranging Cases in an Optimum Order

two-car collisions or auto-pedestrian matters among personal injury cases. More sophisticated prediction systems can be developed for predicting how much servicing time a case will need, but applying those statistical systems involves only checking a prediction table, after the table has been prepared.

Other methods for saving case time may create problems of unconstitutional or unfair procedure, such as seeking to accelerate the processing by abolishing jury trials, oral hearings, right to counsel. or other safeguards for proper procedure. Optimum sequencing creates no such legal problems as long as no case is allowed to exceed the maximum constraint provided for by constitutional or statutory interpretation. One can build into the system a provision that no case should be allowed to wait more than a certain number of days, unless the person bringing the case consents. Note, however, that although the average case has saved 10 days between order 1 and order 6, the 20-day case now takes 15 days more, whereas the 10-day case takes 15 days fewer, and the 5-day case takes 30 days fewer. That would be considered unfair if taking 35 days exceeded a maximum constraint. Otherwise, this is an example of one case losing a little in order to enable the other two cases to gain a lot for the overall good. One could even provide compensation to any case that loses some time as a result of being shifted from a first-come, first-served policy to a policy of shortest cases first. Foir example, if losing a day is worth $1, then the 20-day case could get a $15 deduction from its filing fee. On the other hand, one can argue that the 20-day case is already getting a gift of much more free processing time than the 10-day or 5-day case. The 20-day case should therefore be willing to wait a little longer in return for the extra processing service. If the other cases were required to pay $15 to the 20-day case in proportion to their days saved, the 5-day case would pay $10 and the 10-day case would pay $5. Each of the cases would still be better off, or at least no worse off, under the optimum-sequencing arrangement.

Variations on optimum sequencing can be developed when there is more than one judge or court, and when there is more than one processing stage through which the cases go. This method for evaluating alternative sequencing clearly illustrates that a good system for deciding among alternative ways of doing things can increase productivity just as much as, if not more than, improved technology (such as using word processing to write judges' opinions) or improved motivation of workers (such as judges who take shorter coffee breaks and lunch hours).[7]

CONCLUSIONS

This article frequently mentions maximizing benefits minus costs. What, however, are some of the benefits and costs of applying policy evaluation methods to government problems? First, such methods can enable one to arrive at decisions that are more productive or efficient in the sense of increasing societal benefits minus costs. A good example of that important benefit is the first example, which involves choosing a combination of lump-sum projects with a fixed budget where the best combination is not obvious unless one knows the relevant decision-science rules or policy-evaluation principles. The optimum-sequencing example just given also clearly shows that non obvious decision-making principles can increase productivity, although the principles may be obvious after they have been learned.

Second, such methods can generate insights to enable one to make recommendations for favorably influencing the decision making of others, including decisions that increase productivity. The data-gathering or paperwork problem is a good example of that. If we want to make data gathering more rational or benefit-cost effective, that analysis tells us we should concentrate on doing three things. We should try to increase the probability that the data will be used, possibly by increasing its visibility. We should try to decrease the costs of data gathering, possibly by providing for more automatic data-gathering routines. And we should try to increase the benefits of gathering data, possibly by providing more opportunities or ways in which data can serve as inputs into governmental decision making.

Third, such methods can facilitate predicting what decisions are likely to be reached by knowing how changes influence the decision makers. In the legal services example, we can predict that the behavior of legal service attorneys would probably shift to more emphasis on routine case handling, rather than law reform, if the evaluators were to consist of clients or other poor people rather than fellow lawyers. This is so because clients tend to emphasize having their own cases resolved, even if they are family matters that have no precedent value. Lawyers, on the other hand, admire the technical legal skills involved in establishing new precedents in arguing before appellate courts.

Fourth, such methods can provide a better understanding of why actual decisions differ from the alleged optimum decisions. One can then either attempt to adjust one's criteria as to what constitutes optimum decisions or attempt to change the actual decisions toward more optimally productive decisions. In the pretrial release example, for instance, the alleged optimum percentage of defendants to hold before a trial is only 4 percent, whereas the actual percentage of defendants held is about 27 percent. A partial explanation for the discrepancy may be that judges misperceive the fact that a high percentage of defendants are likely to appear for trial without committing a crime while released. Judges may need some educating concerning these facts and more detailed facts concerning the probability that different types of defendants will appear for trial. Another partial explanation may be that judges are not sufficiently sensitive to holding errors and are overly sensitive to releasing errors. Their sensitivity for holding errors could possibly be increased by publicizing that the high holders tend to have about the same appearance rates as the low holders, and yet the high holders are consuming taxpayers' resources with their excessive holding of defendants prior to trial.

In general, policy evaluation based on management science methods seems capable of improving decision-making processes so that decisions are more likely to be arrived at which will maximize or at least increase societal benefits minus costs. Those decision-making methods may be even more important than worker motivation or technological innovation in productivity improvement. Hard work means little if the wrong products are being produced in terms of societal benefits and costs. Likewise, the right policies are needed to maximize technological innovation, which is not so likely to occur without an appropriate public policy environment.

The costs of applying policy evaluation methods may include hard work in gathering and processing data, and hard thinking in deciding what data to gather and how to process them. Although many applications of policy evaluation methods are available, the field is still quite new. Given its low level of development, a small amount of effort may have a high marginal rate of return in improving public policy productivity. What may be needed especially are more government people who can understand and apply policy evaluation methods and thereby aid in achieving productivity improvement in the 1980s.

NOTES

1. On productivity improvement, see Thurow (1980), Schwartz and Choate (1980), Dogramaci (1981), and Nagel (1981b). One important indicator of the increased concern for productivity is the greatly increased number of books and articles on the subject of productivity in the late 1970s and early 1980s, as well as the increased use of the concept in political rhetoric by both Republicans and Democrats.

2. On policy evaluation methods in general, see White et al. (1980), Stokey and Zeckhauser (1978), Dunn (1981), Quade (1975), and Nagel (1981a).

3. On choosing among discrete alternatives, see Thompson (1981), Gohagan (1980), Black (1968), and Sassone and Schaffer (1978). For a method useful in dealing with nonmonetary benefits that does not require monetization, see the discussion of incremental analysis in Nagel (1983b). Incremental analysis in this context means handling nonmonetary benefits by converting the decisions into questions as to whether a given nonmonetary return is worth more or less than a given dollar cost, even though we do not know how many dollars the nonmonetary return is worth.

4. On making decisions under conditions of risk, see Mack (1971), Lee (1971), Holloway (1979), and Nagel and Neef (1979). For further details on handling missing information when making decisions under conditions of risk and uncertainty, see Nagel (1983c).

5. On making decisions where doing too much or too little is undesirable, see Brennan (1973), Shockley (1971), Starr and Miller (1962), and Nagel and Neef (1977).

6. On allocating scarce resources in general, see Kotler (1971), Lee (1976), McMillen (1970), and Himmelblau (1972). For a method useful in allocating resources that does not require determining the marginal rate of return of alternative

allocations, see Nagel (1983a: chap. 16). The method is called "percentaging analysis" and is related to what others call "multiattribute utility analysis" or "analytic heirarchy analysis." These approaches have in common the idea of scoring activities, places, or persons on multiple goals, and then aggregating the sources for each activity, place, or person in order to determine how much of the resources should be allocated to each.

7. On the applicability of decision sciences and policy evaluation to time minimization, see Bohigan (1971), Byrd (1975), Baker (1974), and Gross and Harris (1974).

REFERENCES

BAKER, K.(1974) Introduction to Sequencing and Scheduling. New York: John Wiley.

BLACK, G. (1968) The Application of Systems Analysis to Government Operations. New York: Praeger.

BOHIGAN, H. (1971) The Foundations and Mathematical Models of Operations Research with Extensions to theCriminal Justice System. Yonkers, NJ: Gazette.

BRENNAN, M. (1973) Preface to Econometrics: An Introduction to Quantitiative Methods in Economics. Cincinnati, OH: South-Western.

BYRD, J. (1975) Operations Research Models for Public Administration. Lexington, MA: D.C. Heath.

DOGRAMACI, A. (1981) Productivity Analysis: A Range of Perspectives. The Hague: Martinus Nijhoff.

DUNN, W. (1981) Public Policy Analysis: An Introduction. Englewood Cliffs, NJ: Prentice-Hall.

GOHAGAN, J. (1980) Quantitiative Analysis for Public Policy. Beverly Hills, CA: Sage.

GROSS, D. and C. HARRIS (1974) Fundamentals of Queueing Theory. New York: John Wiley.

HIMMELBLAU, D. (1972) Applied Non-Linear Programming. New York: McGraw-Hill.

HOLLOWAY, C. (1979) Decision Making Under Uncertainty: Models and Choices. Englewood Cliffs, NJ: Prentice-Hall.

KOTLER, P. (1971) Marketing Decision Making: A Model Building Approach. New York: Holt, Rinehart & Winston.

LEE, S. (1976) Linear Optimization in Management. Princeton, NJ: Petrocelli/ Charter.

LEE, W. (1971) Decision Theory and Human Behavior. New York: John Wiley.

MACK, R. (1971) Planning on Uncertainty: Decision Making in Business and Government Administration. New York: John Wiley.

McMILLEN, C., Jr. (1970) Mathematical Programming: An Introduction to the Design and Applications of Optimal Decision Machines. New York: John Wiley.

NAGEL, S. (1983a) Public Policy: Goals, Means, and Methods. New York: St. Martin's.

────── (1983b) "Nonmonetary variables and benefit-cost evaluation." Evaluation Review 7: 37-64.

──────(1983c) "Unknown variables in policy/program evaluation." Evaluation and Program Planning 6.

────── (1981a) Policy Evaluation: Making Optimum Decisions. New York: Praeger.

────── (1981b) The New Productivity. Camden, NJ: Rutgers Forum for Policy Research and Public Service.

────── and M. NEEF (1979) Decision Theory and the Legal Process. Lexington, MA: D. C. Heath.

────── (1977) Legal Policy Analysis: Finding an Optimum Level or Mix. Lexington, MA: D. C. Heath.

QUADE, E. (1975) Analysis for Public Decisions. New York: Elsevier.

SASSONE, P. and W. SCHAFFER (1978) Cost-Benefit Analysis: A Handbook. New York: Academic.

SCHWARTZ, G. and P. CHOATE (1980) Being Number One: Rebuilding the U.S. Economy. Lexington, MA: D. C. Heath.

SHOCKLEY, J. (1971) The Brief Calculus: With Applications in the Social Sciences. New York: Holt, Rinehart & Winston.

STARR, M. and D. MILLER (1962) Inventory Control: Theory and Practice. Englewood Cliffs, NJ: Prentice-Hall.

STOKEY, E. and R. ZECKHAUSER (1978) A Primer for Policy Analysis. New York: Norton.

THOMPSON, M. (1981) Benefit-Cost Analysis for Program Evaluation. Beverly Hills, CA: Sage.

THUROW, L. (1980) The Zero-Sum Society: Distribution and the Possibilities for Economic Change. New York: Penguin.

WHITE, M. et al. (1980) Managing Public Systems: Analytic Techniques for Public Administration. Belmont, CA: Duxbury.

11

A SYSTEMS APPROACH TO
ORGANIZATIONAL PRODUCTIVITY

RUPERT F. CHISHOLM

Pennsylvania State University, Capitol Campus

The decline of American productivity growth over the past twenty years is clear and threatens the future standard of living of Americans and our ability to compete in the international marketplace. Certainly, many factors contribute to the current situation and these "causes" exist at both the macro (for example, tax laws, societal values) and micro levels (the organization and specific organizational units). This chapter focuses on a system-oriented perspective to improve productivity and total organizational effectiveness called the "sociotechnical system" (STS) approach. Sociotechnical system theory has been used to improve the effectiveness of organizations in the United States and Western Europe. Increasingly, the approach is being applied to information-processing and service-oriented organizations. Experience and research suggest that the approach has great potential for improving organizational effectivness and the quality of employees' work lives.

The chapter includes four sections. The first section identifies several key environmental phenomena that are affecting late twentieth-century organizations to an increasing degree. The next section discusses the need for an expanded definition of organizational productivity. The third section, which is the heart of the chapter, covers the STS approach to organizational improvement. This section describes key STS concepts, analysis and design of a work system, implementing a new STS design, experiences with the sociotechnical approach, and practical implementation issues. The final section discusses the future of STS design and several public policy implications of applying STS theory.

ENVIRONMENTAL FORCES
IMPINGING ON ORGANIZATIONS

Open systems theory (see Katz and Kahn, 1978) posits that environmental factors have a pervasive impact on how organizations function. Therefore, an attempt to determine more appropriate forms of future organizations, ways of conceptualizing and measuring organization productivity, and possible ways of bringing about the planned change of organizations requires an understanding of the environmental context in which these organizations will operate. This section highlights several key features of the emerging environment of American organizations.

Several scholars (for example, Bell, 1976; Etzioni, 1979; Kerr, 1979) from various fields note that the American society and economy are undergoing a basic transformation from industrialism to postindustrialism. Tofler's (1980) *Third Wave* gives a popular description of this change process. Hallmarks of this transition include increased professionalism of the workplace, rising importance of theoretical knowledge, and a growing share of the economy devoted to providing services, as opposed to goods (Bell, 1976). Concurrently, a change in Americans' perceptions and expectations of work is occurring. The emergence of the term "quality of work life" (QWL) over the past ten years reflects this change. Trist (1976) discusses changes in values that accompany the emerging postindustrial era and feels that these value shifts will contribute to new organizational forms (such as redesigned workplaces and work roles). Yankelovich (1974) draws similar conclusions from U.S. surveys. He observes that new definitions of work began to emerge in the 1960s and will continue to develop in the present decade. For example, Americans are beginning to define success less in strict economic and occupational terms and are placing greater emphasis on the inherent meaning of work and the quality of their total lives. Campbell's (1981) conclusions based on repeated attitude surveys over the past thirty years support this interpretation. He asserts that we are entering an era of "psychological man" in which individuals have heightened expectations of a full life (including meaningful work, identification with community, and positive marital relationships). Results of a recent quality of employment survey (Staines and Quinn, 1979) also show that from 1969 to 1977 American workers experienced significant decreases in job satisfaction, life satisfaction, and intentions to remain in their present jobs. Changes between 1973 and 1977 exceeded those for the 1969-1973 period. Thus it appears that important changes in job attitudes and expectations are occurring. Organizations will experience continuing pressure for change to become congruent with these shifts in values and expectations.

Emery and Trist (1965) identify higher levels of interdependence among components of the environment, increased heterogeneity, and greater rapidity of change as contributors to the "turbulent fields" in which current organizations tend to operate. For example, there is a continuing intrusion of social, technological, political, and economic environments into organizations (Davis, 1979). The impact of EEO and OSHA regulations on organizations exemplifies this intrusion. The higher levels of interdependence, complexity, and uncertainty of turbulent environments pose conditions that are inhospitable to traditional bureaucratic structures. Therefore, new organizational forms that emphasize adaptability and cooperation are required to match the new environment (Davis, 1979).

Bell (1976) states that the utilization of theoretical knowledge is the driving force behind the postindustrial revolution. Automation and the use of high-speed computers to facilitate the rapid handling of information are closely related phenomena. Cummings and Srivastva (1977) note that new information-handling technologies require different principles of work design than older mechanized technologies. Information-handling technologies require work designs that foster the interdependence and human capicities to gather, analyze, and respond to different types of information quickly (Cummings and Srivastva, 1977). Unfortunately, while the new technologies require different work designs, traditional job design principles (such as job simplification, maximizing throughput, and efficient machine use) are most important to systems analysts and engineers who design jobs (Taylor, 1979). Thus, in an era of increasingly sophisticated information-processing technology, obsolete design criteria persist.

In brief, the rapidly emerging postindustrial environment places several pressures for change on organizations. Changing employee values and attitudes constitute one such force. The increasing interdependency, rapidity of change, and uncertainty of the environment also pose more turbulent conditions for organizations. These factors, combined with the central importance of information-processing technology, require new organizational forms that are more responsive to environmental demands and change.

TOWARD AN EXPANDED DEFINITION OF PRODUCTIVITY

Various definitions of organizational productivity exist. Tuttle (1983) identifies five different perspectives: economic, engineering, accounting, management, and psychological. The economic, engineering, and accounting definitions take a traditional view of productivity as a ratio(s) of some measurable output(s) to some measurable input(s). Specific input/output measures vary among these three approaches, but the basic notion of a ratio is common. On the other hand, American managers appear to have a much broader definition of organizational productivity that includes both measures of output (such as efficiency, effectiveness, and quality) and behavioral variables (such as absenteeism, turnover, and workplace disruption) (Katzell, et al., 1975). Industrial/organizational psychologists tend to focus on measures of workplace behavior (such as job satisfaction and work involvement) that often relate only indirectly to measures of output (Tuttle, 1983). This view supplements the productivity definitions that American managers hold.

At a minimum, productivity must be redefined as only one limited dimension of *total* organizational effectiveness. And organizational effectiveness must include the effects of the organization on all key constituencies over the long run. Employees constitute one key constituency of an organization and, as a result, the impacts of assuming work roles for extended periods of time must be considered. Growing evidence suggests that employees' work experiences do have unintended consequences that carry over to other spheres of their lives, with attendant social consequences. These impacts include mental and physical health (Kornhauser, 1965), alienation (Chisholm, 1978), and political participation (Elden, 1981). In brief, from a societal perspective, one key "output" of an organization is the quality of the employee (as a total person) who works, terminates, and/or retires from it. Therefore, a complete and valid definition of organizational effectiveness has to include measures of the often subtle impacts of employment on individuals over extended periods. This redefinition also implies a new view of the organization-employee relationship:

Employees are a resource of total society as well as of the particular organizations for which they happen to work at a given time (Trist, 1973). Hence organizations and society have a responsibility for developing, not depleting, these resources.

THE SOCIOTECHNICAL SYSTEMS APPROACH

The traditional view of organizations has emphasized carrying out the primary task of the system (producing certain products or providing a defined set of services). This view assumes that any attempt to improve the well-being of employees comes at the expense of organizational efficiency and productivity. However, another approach assumes that the potential exists for reaching both the objectives of organizational effectiveness and desirable human outcomes. Sociotechnical systems theory (Cummings and Srivastva, 1977; Hill, 1971; Trist et al., 1963) provides one avenue for reaching the dual goals of organizational effectiveness and high-quality work experiences for employees (QWL).

KEY CONCEPTS

Sociotechnical systems theory involves several key concepts and assumptions. One basic assumption of the theory has been alluded to above: Organizations and the subunits of organizations (such as departments) are open systems. This means that organizations depend on the environment for a continuous flow of critical *inputs* (information, supplies and equipment, new employees, financial resources). Without the timely importation of these critical inputs an organization ceases to exist. Organizations take these various inputs and *transform* them to outputs. The organization exports *outputs* (information, services, products, waste) back to the environment. Only by producing enough outputs that are positively valued in the environment can an organization attract new matter-energy and information inputs that activate a new input-transformation-output cycle. Thus the existence of organizations is problematical and over time depends on the delivery of useful services or the production of useful products. Figure 11.1 illustrates a sociotechnical system operating in an environment.

From a sociotech perspective, "technology" simply means all the knowledge, information, material resources, techniques, and procedures used to convert system inputs into outputs. Many public organizations use "soft" technology to provide services. For example, a

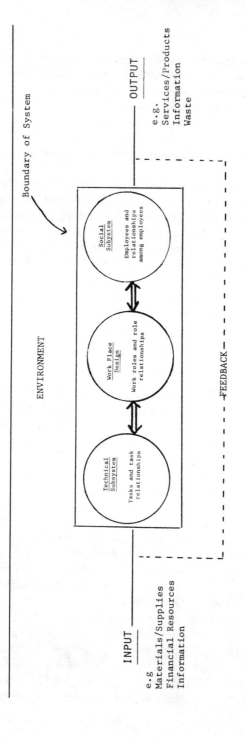

FIGURE 11.1 Open Sociotechnical System

mental health clinic uses various therapeutic techniques, knowledge of a client's family situation and individual characteristics, and a physical environment to improve client's psychological functioning. On the other hand, a city department of public works uses "hard" technology (asphalt, paving equipment, workers' knowledge and skills) to pave a street. Historically, the American economy has rested heavily on manufacturing industries that use hard technologies (for example, steel production, mining, agriculture). However, an increasing proportion of the economy is being devoted to services that result from applying soft technologies. Although the specific nature of technology varies from one work system to another, each sociotechnical system must have one core technology. The core technology is that used to carry out the transformation process that must be performed for the work system to survive (Cummings and Srivastva, 1977). More complex systems may contain several additional technologies that carry out other transformation processes. Thus a high school carries out counseling functions and sponsors athletic events and extracurricular activities that require special inputs and conversion processes. However, the core technology revolves around educating young people, the primary task (Miller and Rice, 1967) of the system.

The notion of joint optimization is another key sociotech concept. Figure 11.1 indicates that work systems consist of a technical subsystem that carries out the transformation processes necessary to convert inputs into outputs. In addition, work systems contain a social subsystem (employees and relationships among them) that controls the technical system. These two subsystems "behave" differently: The technical system tends to follow closed-system laws (such as engineering and Newtonian physics); the social system acts according to open-system principles of psychology, social psychology, and sociology. The social system is much less predictable and deterministic than the technical system. However, each subsystem places important constraints on the other. For example, the use of a particular microcomputer in a state department of transportation prescribes limits within which computer operators must be selected. Thus the technical subsystem has a potent impact on who becomes a member of the social subsystem. On the other hand, failure to give adequate attention to human factors and the interaction between human beings and machinery and equipment were the basic causes of the Three Mile Island nuclear accident (President's Commission, 1979). In this instance, nuclear operators' inability to respond as the situation required made it impossible for the highly sophisticated technical system to function within required limits. In short, the technical and social systems are independent (follow different behavioral principles) but correlative (affect each other significantly). Therefore, designing the best possible match between requirements of these two subsystems consitutes the most viable strategy to optimize functioning of the total work system. This principle of joint optimization is central to the theory of sociotechnical systems.

STS theory also rests on a set of assumptions about human beings and their behavior in the workplace. One assumption is that a high proportion of employees have the capacity and desire to contribute more on their jobs than ordinary organizational structures, processes, and workplace designs allow. Sociotech also assumes than unleashing deep employee motivation occurs by meeting human needs through carrying out task-relevant activities. For example, meeting employee needs for social support occurs by designing a set of interdependent work roles around the actual tasks of the STS: Support is not provided as effectively in isolation from task performance (for instance, creating support groups after working hours). A third assumption is that employees are not fixed entities, but that they are continuously becoming either more or less than they currently are (Allport, 1960). Thus the needs and expectations of employees are not static but change over time based upon workplace experiences. In short, one product of organizations is people (Herbst, 1975).

ANALYSIS

The effects of the sociotechnical system approach depend on the change *process* used in addition to the specific *content* of steps followed and information generated. Therefore, careful design of the analysis, design, and implementation processes based on in-depth understanding of the organizational context in which the work system functions is imperative. This initial design process is flexible, with built-in short feedback loops to assure that necessary adjustments are made based on information generated and experience; the STS design process does not produce a static, "blueprint" design.

STS analysis aims to determine how the system functions at the current time. The general analytical approach involves a summary scanning of the technical system, examining the technical system to identify key variance control needs, examining the social system to determine how key variance control needs and the psychological/ sociological needs of employees are met, and the impact of main environmental systems on STS functioning. Such a detailed analysis helps assure that a thorough understanding of interactions between the social and technical subsystems occurs. The process also generates an understanding of how the work system relates to its environment.

The traditional model for analyzing an STS involves six steps (Cummings and Srivastva, 1977):

(1) initial scanning
(2) identification of unit operations
(3) identification of key process variances
(4) analysis of the social system
(5) workers' role perceptions
(6) environmental analysis

A variance is a deviation from some standard or specification. Key variances are those that significantly affect the quality or quantity of production, social costs (such as stress), or operating costs (such as overtime). Technical system analysis focuses on (1) identifying variances that result from how technology is arranged or operated, (2) tracing how variances that occur in one part of the STS link to other parts of the system or organization, and (3) determining how variances are controlled and the requirements of variance control (Pasmore et al., 1980). A brief description of the traditional STS analytical model appears below. More detailed versions appear in Cummings and Srivastva (1977) and Hill (1971).

Initial scanning involves obtaining an overview of the technical system and the environment in which it operates. Specific topics covered during this step normally include the layout of the STS, existing structure and basic groupings of employees, main inputs and outputs of the system, and system goals (social and technical). Defining the boundary of the STS (that is, what activities and employees are inside as opposed to outside the system) is a key decision at this stage (Markus, 1983).

Step two, identifying unit operations, involves determining the major segments or stages required to transform inputs into outputs. Each unit operation is relatively self-contained and has a clear effect on transforming inputs (such as information) into outputs. Typical effects of unit operations include changing the state (for example, data analysis), location (for example, transmitting information from one location to another), or storage of an input. Normally, the inputs, transformations, and outputs of each unit operation are defined.

The third step involves identifying key process variances and the relationships among them. Concern focuses upon key variances that arise from inputs or the transformation process itself in normal operation. Constructing a matrix of variances helps identify localized clusters of variances and control problems that result from variances that carry through a series of unit operations. Figure 11.2 is a variance matrix of an Army data-processing center. This chart demonstrates the detailed analyses of variances that occur through normal system functioning. It also identifies relationships among key variances. For example, planning, programmer skill, and programmer stability are key variances that affect quality of teamwork.

Identifying the main characteristics of the existing social system occurs in step four. Reviewing the set of work roles, the content of each role, role flexibility, spatial and temporal relationships, and pay relationships are included in this analysis. Preparing a table of variance control is a crucial step. This table indicates the following information about each key variance: where it occurs; where observed; where controlled; by whom; tasks required to control variance; information required to control and the source of information. Typically, preparing the variance control table leads to several tentative hypotheses for STS redesign.

The next step involves determining employees' perceptions of their work roles, through interviews, questionnaires, or a combination of the two. Pasmore et al. (1980), Cummings and Srivastva (1977), and others describe questionnaires used to obtain information on the psychological requirements of employees' roles. Figure 11.3 lists sample questions from the Job Diagnostic Survey (Hackman and Oldham, 1980). In addition, information may be gathered on perceived rewards of the role, sacrifices, personal costs, and causes of dissatisfaction, and employee suggestions for changes in role. Standard survey instruments (such as the Survey of Organizations; Taylor and Bowers, 1972) may generate additional information about the social system. However, since each STS is unique in certain respects (Vaill, 1967), it is important that data-gathering techniques have sufficient flexibility to surface these unique features.

The final step involves analyzing how the environment affects STS functioning. Identifying key variances that directly affect the STS in organizational units that supply inputs, maintain, or accept outputs is required. For example, incorrect information from a supplying unit may constitute a key variance for a work system. If so, this

VARIANCES

	1	2	3	4	5	6	7	8	9	10	11	12	13	14	15	16	17	18	19	20	21	22	23
1. User Selection	1																						
2. User Contract	X	2																					
3. User Request	X	X	3																				
4. Interpretation of Work	(X)	X	X	4																			
5. Distribution to Teams			X	X	5																		
6. Planning of Work			X	(X)	X	6																	
7. Distribution to Programmer					X		7																
8. Program Flowchart								8															
9. Programmer Skill						X			9														
10. Computer Availability						X				10													
11. Programmer Stability					X	X	X		X		11												
12. Quality of Teamwork					X	(X)	X	X	(X)		(X)	12											
13. Workload					X	(X)	X			X	X		13										
14. Program Documentation							X	X	X		(X)		X	14									
15. Data Quality			X												15								
16. Program Quality	(X)			X			X	X	(X)	(X)	X	(X)(X)	X	(X)		16							
17. User Presentation													X	X	X	(X)	17						
18. Program Revision	X	X	X			X	X	X	X	X	X		X	X	X	18							
19. User Knowledgeability	X	X	X								X	X			(X)				19				
20. User Stability	X	X																		20			
21. System Release	X	X	X		X		(X)(X)		(X)	X	X	X	X	X	X		21						
22. Terminal Installation																						22	
23. Program Maintenance	X	X	X				(X)		X	(X)	X	X	X	X	(X)	X							

UNIT OPERATIONS	PROGRAM CONTRACTING	PLAN-NING	PROGRAM DEVELOPMENT	TEST	REVIEW	RELEASE

X = VARIANCE RELATIONSHIP
(X) = KEY VARIANCES

SOURCE: Pasmore et al. (1982b: p. 163). Reprinted by permission of Plenum Publishing Corp.

FIGURE 11.2 Variance Matrix

key variance must be identified and ways of relieving the adverse impact on the STS devised. Determining the impact of the total organization (such as developments plans and operating policies) on the work system also occurs during this stage.

Pasmore et al. (1978) note that the traditional analytical model is most applicable to systems that use "hard" technologies than trans-

SECTION TWO

Listed below are a number of statements which could be used to describe a job.

You are to indicate whether each statement is an *accurate* or an *inaccurate* description of the job you are rating.

Once again, please try to be as *objective* as you can in deciding how accurately each statement describes the job - regardless of your own *feelings* about that job.

Write a number in the blank beside each statement, based on the following scale:

How accurate is the statement in describing the job you are rating?

1	2	3	4	5	6	7
Very Inaccurate	Mostly Inaccurate	Slightly Inaccurate	Uncertain	Slightly Accurate	Mostly Accurate	Very Accurate

_____1. The job requires a person to use a number of complex or sophisticated skills.

_____2. The job requires a lot of cooperative work with other people.

_____3. The job is arranged so that a person does *not* have the chance to do an entire piece of work from beginning to end.

_____4. Just doing the work required by the job provides many chances for a person to figure out how well he or she is doing.

_____5. The job is quite simple and repetitive.

_____6. The job can be done adequately by a person working alone - without talking or checking with other people.

_____7. The supervisors and co-workers on this job almost *never* give a person any "feedback" about how well he or she is doing the work.

_____8. This job is one where a lot of other people can be affected by how well the work gets done.

_____9. The job denies a person any chance to use his or her personal initiative or discretion in carrying out the work.

_____10. Supervisors often let the person know how well they think he or she is performing the job.

_____11. The job provides a person with the chance to finish completely any work he or she starts.

_____12. The job itself provides very few clues about whether or not the person is performing well.

_____13. The job gives a person considerable opportunity for independence and freedom in how he or she does the work.

_____14. The job itself is *not* very significant or important in the broader scheme of things.

SOURCE: J. R. Hackman and Greg R. Oldham, *Work Redesign,* © 1980, Addison-Wesley, Reading, Massachusetts. Pgs. 300-301. Reprinted with permission.

FIGURE 11.3

form inputs into tangible matter-energy outputs. Hence an additional way of analyzing the technological subsystem of work units that use primarily "soft" technology to transform information, knowledge, and skills into services is needed. An approach has been developed to help analyze the technical component of soft technology work systems. This sociotask approach has been used in a recent field experiment in an Army data-processing center (Pasmore et al., 1980).

The sociotask approach treats each role in a work system as a unit operation and focuses on the basic tasks included within each role. Input tasks, transformation (processing) tasks, and output tasks are identified (see Figure 11.4). A detailed analysis of each task is conducted (for example, required/discretionary; sources of feedback). The next step involves developing a list of task problems (variances), analyzing how these are controlled, and stating possible recommendations for improved work system design. The sociotask approach provides a useful supplement to the traditional analytical model.

DESIGN

As noted earlier, hypotheses for redesign begin to emerge during the detailed analysis of the STS. These are summarized, new hypotheses developed, and all proposed changes tested against appropriate criteria (such as increased control of key variances and increased level of meeting employees' psychological needs). Applying the principle of joint optimization is crucial at this stage. Proposals for change become the basis for developing an action program.

Often, an improved overall work system design is possible by using employees' untapped capacities to plan, conduct, and evaluate the quality of their work as a means of controlling key variances. The main design principle is to place control of key variances in the transformation process and coordination required for control at the lowest possible level (Taylor, 1975). Properly designed role sets show greater stability and depend less on external supervision than traditional work groups. Therefore, in many cases, it is possible to establish a semiautonomous (or automonous) work group that carries out many of the traditional supervising functions (scheduling work, assigning work to employees, monitoring the quantity and quality of work). Of course, designing more responsibility for internal coordination and control into work group members' roles requires a redefinition of the supervisor or manager's role and other roles that interact with an autonomous work group. Providing support and training to employees in the redesigned roles is crucial.

IMPLEMENTATION

Several aspects of the implementation process are unique to the STS approach. These unique features include continuous employee

ROLE: KEY PUNCH OPERATOR

TASK DESCRIPTION	REQUIRED (R) OR DISCRETIONARY (D)	INDEPENDENT (I) OR COOPERATIVE (C)	ACTIVITIES PERFORMED INFORMATION NEEDED TECHNOLOGY USED	SOURCES OF FEEDBACK CONCERNING PERFORMANCE
INPUTS				
1) Receiving key punching data and instructions	R	C	When ready to start a job the operator asks her supervisor for a data list and instructions for key-punching.	The main sources of feedback for this activity is the supervisor. Occasionally, customers who submit the data for keypunching complain that instructions were not followed; this information may be relayed through the supervisor to the operator.
2) Obtaining blank cards for keypunching	R	I	Operator goes to storage cabinet for cards	Task itself
PROCESSING				
3) Operate keypunch machine to transfer data from code sheets to computer cards	R	I	Keypunch machine operation requires limited operator training	Other operators (through next stage of verification). Occasionally receive feedback from supervisor regarding performance (speed and quality).
4) Keeping area clean	D	I	Picking up cards, disposing of waste	Supervisor, task itself
OUTPUTS				
5) Return completed data deck to supervisor for delivery to customer	R	I	Cards banded and identified by customer name	Supervisor

PROBLEMS IN TASK PERFORMANCE	WHO IDENTIFIES PROBLEM	WHO SOLVES PROBLEM	WHAT INFORMATION IS USED IN PROBLEM SOLVING	RECOMMENDATIONS FOR CHANGE
1) Instructions not followed	Customer	Keypunch operator/ Supervisor	Customer instructions	Have keypunch operator deal directly with customer instead of going through supervisor.
2) Cards not available	Keypunch operator	Supervisor	Order forms	Assign operators responsibility for ordering cards
3) a) mistakes made b) card jams c) machine breakdown d) uneven workload	a) other operators b) keypunch operator c) keypunch operator d) keypunch operator	a) other operator b) keypunch operator c) maintenance personnel d) supervisor	a) verification machine b) knowledge of how to clean machine c) technical knowledge d) knowledge of task assignments	a) have operators verify own cards b) look into card quality c) increase preventive maintenance; train operators to fix common problems; have spare keypunches available. d) form operators into teams and assign work on team basis.
4) Not done often enough	Supervisor	Operator	Customer Complaints	Increase encouragement of area cleanliness; assign cleanliness as team responsibility
5) Work not completed on time	Customer/Supervisor	Supervisor/Operator	Customer Complaints	Have operator return feedback to customer directly

SOURCE: Pasmore et al. (1980: 59). Reprinted by permission.

FIGURE 11.4 Example of Problem Assessment

participation in the change process, use of minimum design specifications, and creating a sanctioned experiment.

Creating a small action group containing several operating employee members is one means of structuring in real employee involvement. This group conducts the STS analysis, develops recommendations for redesign, and oversees the implementation of the new system design. Although higher management approval of recommended changes is needed, the action group actually manages the process of developing a more effective work system. Membership in the action group contributes greatly to meaningful employee involvement in the design process. One basic aim of the design process is to build into the STS the ongoing capacity to redesign itself as changes occur in the work system or environment (Cummings and Srivastva, 1977). In-depth involvement of action group members helps structure in this capacity and provides useful learning about the design process.

Using minimum design specifications fits with designing into the STS the self-renewing capacity noted above. Since work groups and other social systems pass through successive stages of development rather than are designed to a final state (Herbst, 1966), it is necessary to provide the work group with the resources required to achieve system objectives and maintain dynamic equilibrium at each developmental stage. Assuring that the work group has reasonable clarity about STS objectives and the necessary knowledge, skills, and material resources plus the ability to request additional resources as required is sufficient. It is unnecessary (and impossible), to attempt to prescribe in detail the precise characteristics of the fully operating STS.

Establishing the design of an STS as a sanctioned experiment involves several things. To begin with, there is a need to establish a norm of social learning through the STS experiment (Trist, 1973). Therefore, employees must receive guarantees regarding basic conditions of employment; no job loss, no reduction in pay, and the lifting of pressures for normal production during early stages of the experiment. These guarantees are required to "free up" employees to look for improved ways of designing and operating the work system. Because of the lag involved as the social system passes from one developmental stage to the next, it is desirable to think in terms of different levels of protection against pressures for normal production at various times during the development process. Trist (1973) identifies three general levels of protection: (1) conceptual (complete protection against normal pressures to deliver services or produce products; emphasis is placed on learning new role requirements, how to mesh with other roles, and other aspects of the new STS); (2) experimental (substantial protection to allow employees to experiment with using newly acquired knowledge and skills); (3) operational (limited protection to enable employees to experience working in the new STS under fairly realistic operating conditions). Again, the basic goal of the implementation process is to develop the STS as a learning system that has the capacity to redesign itself as new conditions come into being.

EXPERIENCES WITH STS DESIGN

The STS approach has been applied in many different types of organizations in a variety of cultural settings (a British coal mine, an Indian textile mill, an American hospital, a Swedish auto plant, and a Norwegian ship design). The Norwegian industrial democracy program (Gustavsen and Hunnius, 1981) represents the most comprehensive attempt to apply sociotech theory. This program, begun in the mid-1960s, aims to strengthen workplace democracy and improve the social psychological work environment throughout the Norwegian economy. Experience to date has been primarily in manufacturing organizations that use various "hard" technologies to produce tangible products. However, the approach is being applied increasingly to white-collar work systems.

Several reviews of STS studies have appeared in the literature during the past decade (for example, see Friedlander and Brown, 1974; Taylor, 1979; Srivastva et al., 1975; Walton, 1979). In general, these reviews indicate that the results of STS applications are quite positive. For example, Srivastva et al. (1975) report the following percentages of studies with positive results on various outcome variables: productivity, 93 percent; costs, 88 percent; withdrawal (absenteeism, turnover), 73 percent; employee attitudes, 70 percent. A review by Pasmore et al. (1982b) covers 134 recent North American studies. The results of this comprehensive review are instructive.

Table 11.1 summarizes results of the Pasmore et al. (1982b) review. Data in the first column indicate that, in general, the STS approach has not been applied comprehensively to the design of work systems. Instead, a few features have been used much more frequently than others. Using autonomous work groups (including self-direction and rotation among work group roles) was the only feature applied in a

TABLE 11.1 The Use and Effectiveness of Commonly Discussed Features of Sociotechnical System Design in 134 Work Restructuring Experiments

Feature	Percentage of Studies Using This Feature (N = 134)	Measures of Success (percentages)							
		Productivity	Cost	Absenteeism	Turnover	Attitudes	Safety	Grievances	Quality
Autonomous work groups	53	89	85	86	81	100	100	0	100
Skill development	40	91	95	100	100	94	100	100	100
Action group	22	100	90	80	78	93	100	100	100
Reward system	21	95	80	100	91	95	100	0	100
Self-inspection	16	90	90	89	86	100	80	50	92
Technological change	16	60	100	75	100	92	100	100	100
Team approach	16	80	80	75	100	100	0	100	100
Facilitative leadership	14	100	100	78	100	100	80	66	100
Operators perform maintenance	12	88	88	100	83	100	100	0	100
Minimal critical specification	9	100	100	100	100	100	100	100	100
Feedback on performance	9	100	100	100	100	100	100	100	100
Customer interface	9	100	100	75	67	100	0	100	100
Self-supply	8	80	80	100	67	100	100	0	100
Managerial information for operators	7	67	83	100	100	100	100	0	100
Selection of peers	6	100	100	100	100	100	100	0	100
Status equalization	4	100	100	100	100	100	100	0	100
Pay for learning	4	100	100	100	75	100	100	0	100
Peer review	3	100	100	100	100	100	100	0	100

SOURCE: Adapted from Pasmore et al. (1982b: 1192), by permission of Plenum Publishing Corp.

*Number of successful attempts divided by number of total attempts using this feature and reporting results on this dimension (for example, 89 percent of studies using autonomous work groups and reporting productivity data were successful).

majority of the cases (53 percent). Technical skill development (40 percent), forming an action group to guide the change process (22 percent), and changing the pay system to make it congruent with the STS philosophy (for example, paying employees on a group basis) were the features applied most frequently. Self-inspection of work quality, changes in the technical system, and use of teams other than autonomous work groups (traditional direct supervision and no job rotation) tied for fifth place in frequency of use (16 percent each).

Data in Table 11.1 also indicate relationships between STS features and organizational outcomes. In interpreting the data the tendency to emphasize positive results and downplay negative findings in published studies should be borne in mind. Increased productivity occurred in 89 percent of the cases in which autonomous work groups were used and that reported productivity changes. Skill development has a "success ratio" of 91 percent for productivity. Beyond these two features, only the use of an action group and changes in the reward system to make it more consistent with STS approach were used in more than 20 percent of the studies. Improved productivity occurred in virtually all projects that included these two features. Surprisingly, the lowest success ratio (60 percent) takes place for increased productivity in the comparatively few projects that changed technology to be more consistent with the desired social system. Examining the pervasiveness of design feature/outcome relationships also is important. Overall, autonomous work groups and skill development appear to affect virtually all of the outcome variables measured (productivity, cost, attitudes, and so on). Success ratios indicate that other design features also relate positively to a high proportion of the outcome variables. Thus, while broad use of STS design features did not occur in the vast majority of cases, each feature appeared successful when it was applied (Pasmore et al., 1982b).

The data in the first column raise an important theoretical/ practical issue. Since the STS approach is systemic, failure to apply key features of sociotech in a broad, intergrated fashion should reduce the positive outcomes derived from many of these experiments. Of course, it is impossible to know what outcomes would have occurred in the situation reported if key STS features had been applied more broadly. However, broad applications seem to lead to higher success on outcome measures. Thus, in general, it appears that the more comprehensive use of the basic STS features the better (Pasmore et al., 1982b).

IMPLEMENTATION ISSUES

Experience in applying sociotech indicates that an organization must satisfy several requirements to enhance the likelihood of success. These requirements include support from higher organizational levels, the need for extensive employee training, special attention to redefining supervisory roles, and a realistic assessment of potential costs and benefits.

An STS experiment requires the active leadership of the largest directly implicated system. For instance, if the focal system is a department, the top management of the entire organization must provide strong, active support to make the experiment successful. Support must be based on agreeing with the basic direction of change and the underlying philosophy. Active involvement in establishing conditions that provide an environment that supports the STS experiment is required. Briefly stated, key managers outside the immediately involved work system must believe that the experiment is worthwhile and must be willing to provide ideas, psychic energy, and resources to support the experiment as the change process unfolds.

The STS approach is a "deep" intervention that attempts to redesign key organizational variables and relationships among them. The depth of the intervention requires considerable training of employees directly involved. Typical training topics include the theory and key concepts of sociotech, role requirements of the new work system, objectives of the STS, interpersonal skills training, and technical skills training. In addtion to formal courses, creating conditions that enable employees to learn from workplace experiences is crucial. Experiential learning may be fostered by building in processes that encourage employees to analyze their day-to-day experiences and to use these as a basis for recommending ways of improving work unit functioning. Sponsors must recognize that STS experiments involve considerable lag (that is, the social subsystem takes a relatively long time to develop the capacity to manage the new work system effectively), which requires extensive training and strong organizational support.

Planned organizational change efforts frequently fail to pay sufficient attention to redesigning the supervisor's or manager's role. Because of interdependence, basic changes in employees' work roles require complementary changes in the work system manager/ supervisor's role. Establishing semiautonomous work groups, the most frequently applied STS technique, requires a reorientation of a supervisor's attention to external relations management. For instance, a supervisor of a semiautonomous work group spends the major part of his or her time assuring that employees have the necessary materials, information, and other resources required to carry out work-unit functions. The supervisor also provides necessary training, and psychological support, and attempts to lessen irritating restrictions from the environment. Internal regulation, how employees organize themselves and plan to perform the work, is performed by work team members. Substantial training, coaching, and support is required to have supervisors acquire understanding of the new work role and to develop the capacity to carry out the new role requirements.

STS projects involve significant costs for organizations. Typical costs include temporary declines in work output, training costs, management and consultant salaries, and increased wages or salaries to employees (Chisholm, 1983). Perhaps even more important are several comparatively "hidden" costs, such as the risk of failure for both the organization and certain employees (notably the managers and supervisors who sponsor and support projects). "Failure" may result in an organizational unit that functions less effectively than before the intervention and jeopardizes management/supervisor careers. The decision of whether or not to attempt an STS effort must be approached realistically, with awareness of the tangible and hidden costs involved and with a balanced view of the investment of time, energy, and other resources likely to be required for potentially successful implementation. An experimental frame of mind that is willing to accept failure (or partial failure) as well as unqualified success also seems necessary. Walton (1979) comments that workplace innovations fall along a broad spectrum of effectiveness and usually are neither spectacular "successes" nor dismal "failures."

THE FUTURE OF STS DESIGN

In the past, positive outcomes of STS applications have resulted mainly from improved adaptation of the socal subsystem to technological requirements. Relatively few experiments have involved changed technological processes. In the future, more attention must be paid to the selection of appropriate technology (Schnumacher, 1973) that best fits the total circumstances: long- and short-term impacts on the social and physical outcomes of those affected both directly and indirectly (Trist, 1981). While technologies have pervasive impacts on the operating policies and practices of organizations, the pervasiveness of impacts varies greatly from one technology to another. Choosing a technology is a complex management decision process based on premises, ideology, organizational strategy, and awareness of technological alternatives (Skinner, 1979).

In many future cases, overall effectiveness of organizations may be enhanced by working backward from employees' social/psychological requirements to choose a technology that provides a better basic fit with these needs. Fortunately, computers, microprocessors, and other rapid information handling devices constitute the lead technology of the postindustrial era (Emery, 1978). This type of technology has the potential to improve employee QWL substantially. However, this potential will be realized only if new criteria are used to select, design, and mesh the technology with human requirements.

> To be successful, however, this process takes more than a new ideology, a firm policy, good intentions, new objective functions, and design criteria that are heavily weighted toward a good work environment. Also necessary are several other management skills that are still rare: an ability to anticipate the effect of a technology on working environment and the skills to design EPTs (equipment and process technologies) which produce favorable working environments without sacrificing conventional objectives of cost, delivery, and quality [Skinner, 1979: 223-224].

Sociotech provides a useful way of determining technological impacts on the working environment and of reaching the dual objectives of improved organizational effectiveness and enhanced QWL.

This chapter has focused on applying STS design to primary work systems. However, it would be a mistake to conclude that the approach is limited to this level of system. Several successful STS change efforts have involved an entire work location (plant) (for example, see Walton, 1972; Poza and Markus, 1980). Hill (1971) describes the application of sociotech to an entire industrial organization with multiple locations. "A distinctively American innovation above the level of the single organization has been the appearance of soci-technical projects on a community-wide basis and in a framework of economic and social development" (Trist, 1981: 55). The Jamestown (New York) Area Management Committee exemplifies this phenomenon. Trist (1981) also perceives a need to use the sociotech approach to develop industry-level institutions that foster interorganizational collaboration based on participative democratic principles. The Norwegian industrial democracy program (Gustavsen and Hunnius, 1981) has focused on developing the economy of a small nation. Ziegenfuss (1983) has used a sociotech approach for a comparative study of two organizations' models of mental health care, a first application to the mental health field. Thus the STS approach appears to have considerable potential for improving organizations or organzational components at several levels of analysis and in both the private and public sectors.

Success in improving organizational effectiveness and QWL requires the cooperative efforts of several parties (management, employees, unions, government officials, behavioral scientists). Given this, what role should federal and state governments play in the future? Possible options fall under two types of strategies: pressure and facilitation. Pressure strategies include legislating standards for QWL, regulating change processes within organizations, and passing legislation that penalizes organizations with low QWL. Facilitation strategies include funding demonstration projects, disseminating information, and funding research (Beer annd Driscoll, 1977). Using the sociotech approach to develop communitywide and industry level institutions and processes that foster interorganizational collaboration is especially appropriate for a democratic society in the emerging postindustrial environment.

REFERENCES

Allport, G. W. (1960) "The open system in personality theory." Journal of Abnormal and Social Psychology 61: 301-311.
BEER, M. and J. W. DRISCOLL (1977) "Strategies for change," in J. R. Hackman and J. L. Suttle (eds.) Improving Life at Work. Santa Monica, CA: Goodyear.
BELL, D. (1976) The Coming of Post-Industrial Society: A Venture in Social Forecasting. New York: Basic Books.
CAMPBELL, A. (1981) The Sense of Well-Being in America. New York: McGraw-Hill.

CHISHOLM, R. F. (1983) "Quality of working life: critical issue for the 80's" Public Productivity Review 7: 10-25.

—— (1978) "The web of work for technical and managerial employees." Journal of Vocational Behavior 13: 101-112.

CUMMINGS, T. G. and S. SRIVASTVA (1977) Management of Work. Kent OH: Kent State University Press.

DAVIS, L. E. (1979a) "Job design: future directions," in L. E. Davis and J. C. Taylor (eds.) Design of Jobs. Santa Monica, CA: Goodyear.

—— (1979b) "Job design: historical overview," in L. E. Davis and J. C. Taylor (eds.) Design of Jobs. Santa Monica, CA: Goodyear.

—— (1977) "Job design: overview and future direction." Journal of Contemporary Business, 6, 2: 85-102.

ELDEN, J. M. (1981) "Political efficacy at work: the connection between more autonomous forms of workplace organizations and amore participatory politics." American Political Science Review 75: 43-58.

EMERY, F. E. (1978) The Fifth Kondradieff Wave. Canberra: Center for Continuing Education, Australian National University.

—— and E. L. TRIST (1965) "The causal texture of organizational. environments." Human Relations 18: 21-32.

ETZIONI, A. (1979) "Work in the American future: reindustrialization or quality of life," in C. Kerr and J. M. Rosow (eds.) Work in America: The Decade Ahead. New York: Van Nostrand Reinhold.

FRIEDLANDER, F. and L. D. BROWN (1974) "Organization deveopment," in R. Rosenzweig and L. W. Porter (eds.) Annual Review of Psychology, Vol. 25. Palo Alto, Ca: Annual Reviews.

GUSTAVSEN, B. and G. HUNNIUS (1981) New Patterns of Work Reform: The Case of Norway. Oslo: Universitets-forlaget.

HACKMAN, J. R. and G. OLDHAM (1980) Work Redesign. Reading, MA: Addison-Wesley.

HERBST, P. G. (1975) "The product of work is people," in L. E. Davis and A. B. Cherns (eds.) The Quality of Working Life. New York: Free Press.

—— (1966) "Socio-technical unit design." Document T.899. Tavistock Institute of Human Relations.

HILL, P. (1971) Towards a New Philosophy of Management. New York: Barnes and Noble.

KATZ, D. and R. L. KAHN (1978) The Social Psychology of Organizations. New York: McGraw-Hill.

KATZELL, R. A., D. YANKELOVICH, M. FEIN, D. A. ORNATI, and A. NASH (1975) Work, Productivity and Job Satisfaction. New York: Psychological Corporation.

KERR, C. (1979) "Industrialism with a human face," in C. Kerr and J. M. Rosow (eds.) Work in America: The Decade Ahead. New York: Van Nostrand Reinhold.

KORNHAUSER, A. (1965) Mental Health of the Industrial Worker. New York: John Wiley.

MARKUS, M. L. (1983) "Socio-technical systems: concepts and applications,"in T. Connolly (ed.) Scientists, Engineers, and Organizations. Monterey, CA: Brooks/Cole.

MILLER, E. J. and A. K. RICE (1967) Systems of Organization, the Control of Task and Sentient Boundaries. London: Tavistock.

PASMORE, W. and J. SHERWOOD (n.d.) Sociotechnical Systems and the Quality of Work Life. West Lafayette, IN: Organizational Consultants.

PASMORE, W., S. SRIVASTVA, and J. SHERWOOD (1978) "Social relationships and organizational performance: a sociotask approach," in W. Pasmore and J. Sherwood (eds.) Sociotechnical Systems: A Sourcebook. San Diego, CA: University Associates.

PASMORE, W., A. SHANI, J. HALDEMAN, and J. MIETUS (1982a) "Technological change and work organization in the U.S. Army: A field experiment," in G. O. Mensch and R. J. Niehaus (eds.) Work Organization and Technological Change. New York: Plenum.

PASMORE, W., C. FRANCIS, J. HALDEMAN, and A. SHANI (1982b) "Sociotechnical systems: a North American reflection on empirical studies of the seventies." Human Relations 32: 1179-1204.

PASMORE, W., A. SHANI, J. HALDEMAN, and C. FRANCIS (1980) Model for Sociotechnical Intervention. Cleveland: Department of Organizational Behavior, Case Western Reserve University.

POZA, E. J. and M. L. MARKUS (1980) "Success story: the team approach to work restructuring." Organizational Dynamics (Winter): 3-25.

President's Commission on the Accident at Three Mile Island (1979) The Need for Change: The Legacy of TMI. Washington, DC: Government Printing Office.

SCHUMACHER, E. F. (1973) Small Is Beautiful. New York: Harper & Row.

SKINNER, W. (1979) "The impact of changing technology on the working environment," in C. Kerr and J. M. Rosow (eds.) Work in America: The Decade Ahead. New York: Van Nostrand Reinhold.

SRIVASTVA, S., P. SALIPANTE, T. G. CUMMINGS, and W. NOTZ (1975) Job Satisfaction and Productivity. Cleveland: Case Western Reserve University.

STAINES, G. L. and R. P. QUINN (1979) "American workers evaluate the quality of their jobs." Monthly Labor Review (January): 3-12.

TAYLOR, J. C. (1979) "Job design criteria twenty years later," in L. E. Davis and J. C. Taylor (eds.) Design of Jobs. Santa Monica: Goodyear.

——— (1975) "The human side of work: the socio-technical approach to work system design." Personnel Review 4: 17-22.

——— and D. BOWERS (1972) The Survey of Organizations. Ann Arbor: Institute for Social Research, University of Michigan.

TOFLER, A. (1980) The Third Wave. New York: Bantam.

TRIST, E. L. (1981) "The evolution of socio-technical systems." Occasional Paper 2. Ontario Quality of Working Life Center.

——— (1976) "Toward a post-industrial culture," in R. Dubin (ed.) Handbook of Work, Organization and Socity. Skokie, IL: Rand McNally.

——— (1973) Organizations and technical change." Tavistock Institute of Human Relations.

——— G. W. HIGGEN, H. MURRAY, and A. B. POLLACK (1963) Organizational Choice. London: Tavistock.

TUTTLE, T. C. (1983) "Organizational productivity: a challenge for psychologists." American Psychologist 38: 479-486.

VAILL, P. B. (1967) "Industrial engineering and socio-technical systems." Journal of Industrial Engineering (September): 530-538.

WALTON, R. E. (1979) "Work innovations in the United States." Harvard Business Review (July/August): 88-98.

———— (1972) "How to counter alienation in the plant." Harvard Business Review (November/December): 70-81.

YANKELOVICH, D. (1974) "The meaning of work," in J. M. Rosow (eds.) The Worker and the Job. Englewood Cliffs, NJ: Prentice-Hall.

ZIEGENFUSS, J. T. (1983) Patients' Rights and Organizational Models: Sociotechnical Systems Research on Mental Health Programs. Lanham, MD: University Press of America.

NAME INDEX

SUBJECT INDEX

ABOUT THE AUTHORS

Rupert F. Chisholm is Associate Professor in the Master of Public Administration Program at the Pennsylvania State University, Capitol Campus. He also serves as Director of the Quality of Working Life Center at the campus. He holds a doctorate in organizational behavior from Case Western Reserve University and a master's degree in industrial relations from Cornell University. His major research interests are in the areas of job and workplace design, employee reactions to a crisis situation, and QWL issues. He is completing an extensive study of nuclear workers' reactions to the Three Mile Island accident. His consulting and research clients include the Agency for International Development (U.S. State Department), Alcoa, the Milton S. Hershey Medical Center, and M&M Mars, Inc. His work has appeared in such scholarly journals as the *Academy of Management Journal, Journal of Political and Military Sociology, Journal of Occupational Behavior,* and *Public Productivity Review.*

Raymond M. Duch (B.A., University of Manitoba, 1975; Ph.D., University of Rochester, 1982) is undertaking research on industrial policy in Europe and North America. He has written on French subsidy policies and on comparative evaluations of industrial policies for the telecommunications industries. He is currently writing a book on international telecommunications policies. He has also served as an expert witness before the Federal Communications Commission and as a consultant to a number of major telecommunications firms.

Irwin Feller is Professor of Economics and Director of the Institute for Policy Research and Evaluation, Pennsylvania State University. His research interests focus on the economics of technological change, the diffusion of innovations in the public sector, the utilization of scientific and technological innovation in public policy decisions, and university relationships with the public sector. His current research activities include state high-technology development programs, the transfer of agricultural technology, and university relationships with state governments.

Steve Godwin is currently a staff member for the study of the costs and benefits of the 55 mph speed limit being conducted by the Transportation Research Board, National Academy of Sciences. Since receiving his master's degree in regional planning from the University of North Carolina at Chapel Hill in 1980, he has contributed to numerous policy studies. In addition to being one of the coauthors of the U.S. Department of Housing and Urban Development's evaluation of the UDAG program, he coauthored research papers on urban infrastructure while a member of the Public Finance Center of the Urban Institute, Washington, D.C.

Marc Holzer is the founder and Director of the National Center for Public Productivity, as well as Professor of Government and Public Administration, at the John Jay College of Criminal Justice, City University of New York. He is Editor-in-Chief of the *Public Productivity Review* and the editor or coauthor of several volumes on public sector productivity, including *Productivity in Public Organizations, Productivity Management Workbook,* and the *Resource Guide for Public Sector Productivity.* He has contributed articles on productivity to the *Public Administration Review,* the *Bureaucrat,* the *Productivity Handbook for State and Local Government,* and other publications. He has directed or advised productivity improvement projects for federal, state, and local units of government. He currently serves on the National Council of the American Society for Public Administration, and has previously served the Society as Chair of the Section on Management Science and in other leadership capacities.

Irene Johnston is Coordinator, Grants and Contracts, College of the Liberal Arts, Pennsylvania State University. She received an M.A. in economics from Pennsylvania State University in 1982. Her research has focused upon the adoption of innovations in the public sector, organizational influences in the adoption decision-making process, and the economics of technological change. She is currently participating in a USDA-sponsored study, "The Transfer of Agricultural and Food Related Technologies," and is conducting evaluation research with PLN Associates in New Orleans.

Howard M. Leichter is Associate Professor of Political Science at Linfield College in McMinnville, Oregon. He received his Ph.D from the University of Wisconsin at Madison. He is the author of *Political Regime and Public Policy, A Comparative Approach to Policy Analysis,* and coauthor of *American Public Policy In A Comparative Perspective.* He is also the author of numerous scholarly articles on comparative public policy and policy analysis.

Daniel J.B. Mitchell is Professor at the Graduate School of Management, UCLA, and director of the UCLA Institute of Industrial Relations. He holds a Ph.D. in economics from the Massachusetts Institute of Technology and a bachelor's degree from Columbia College. He joined the UCLA faculty in 1968. In 1972-1973, he served as chief economist of the federal Pay Board, the agency that administered Phase II wage controls during the Nixon administration. During 1978-1979, he was a senior fellow of the

Brookings Institution. He has written extensively in the areas of wage determination and other labor-market matters.

Stuart S. Nagel is Professor of Political Science at the University of Illinois, a member of the Illinois bar, and the secretary-treasurer/publications coordinator for the Policy Studies Organization. He is the author of *Public Policy: Goals, Means, and Methods* (St. Martin's, 1983); *Policy Evaluation: Making Optimum Decisions* (Praeger, 1982); and *Policy Analysis: In Social Science Research* (Sage, 1979). He has been attorney to the U.S. Senate Subcommittee on Adminstrative Practice and Procedure and a contract/grant recipient from the Departments of Justice, Labor, HUD, Energy, Agriculture, Transportation, Education, and HHS.

Eli M. Noam is Associate Professor at the Columbia Business School and the director of its Research Program in Telecommunications and Information Policy. He has also taught at the Columbia Law School and has been Visiting Professor at Princeton and Stanford. His teaching and research combine economics and law in the analysis of regulation, centering on telecommunications and federal/state relations. He has received fellowships for the study of telecommunications from the German Marshall Fund and the National Science Foundation, and has been member of the organizing committee for the Annual Telecommunications Policy Research Conference. Among his publications are articles in the *Journal of Political Economy* and the *Quarterly Journal of Economics* and articles in law reviews and interdisciplinary journals. He received an A.B. in 1970 from Harvard, and a Ph. D. in economics and a J D degree from the same university in 1975.

Kathleen Peroff is Deputy Director of the Division of Policy Studies, Office of Policy Development and Research, U.S. Department of Housing and Urban Development. While in that position, she has coordinated several studies on such housing and urban economic development issues as an evaluation of the Urban Development Action Grant program, an evaluation of the federal New Communities program, and a stock management study of the public housing inventory. Her research interests and publications focus on a wide range of policy issues in the areas of health, welfare, and housing policy. She holds a Ph. D. in political science from the University of Wisconsin.

F. Stevens Redburn is a Senior Analyst in the Division of Policy Studies, Office of Policy Development and Research, U.S. Department of Housing and Urban Development. Since 1979, he has helped to design and manage a series of national studies addressing current housing and community development policy problems. His most recent book, coauthored with Terry Buss, is *Mass Unemployment: Plant Closings and Community Mental Health* (Sage). His other publications have dealt with economic development, industrial policy, and a broad range of issues in urban policy and public administration. He holds a Ph.D. in political science from the University of North Carolina.

Ellen Doree Rosen is Associate Professor of Government and Public Administration at John Jay College of Criminal Justice, City University of New York, and Associate Director of the National Center for Public Productivity. A political scientist by training, she specializes in open systems theory and the quantification of social phenomena. She has taught productivity in the Master of Public Administration Program and in workshops for in-service personnel. In addition to writing on the subject and serving on the editorial board of *Public Productivity Review,* she has conducted applied productivity measurement and improvement projects for federal, state, and local governmental agencies. Most recently, she was responsible for organizing the Second National Public Sector Productivity Conference—"Putting Productivity to Work"—and is editing the *Proceedings* of that conference for publication.

Alexander Rosenberg is Professor of Philosophy and Social Science at Syracuse University. He is the author of *Microeconomic Laws* (Pittsburg University Press, 1976), *Sociobiology and the Preemption of Social Science* (Johns Hopkins Press, 1980), and coauthor of *Hume and the Problem of Causation* (Oxford University Press, 1981).

David Sears is a planner, researcher, and urban analyst, currently working in the Division of Policy Studies, Office of Policy Development and Research, U.S. Department of Housing and Urban Development. Over the past three years, he has served as a senior analyst on major studies of public housing and urban development programs. Prior to his current position, he held both academic and public sector positions. His Ph.D. in regional planning is from Cornell. His publications cover a broad range of urban issues, including housing, health care, and recreation.

Jeffrey D. Straussman is Associate Professor of Public Administration, and Research Associate, Metropolitan Studies Program, the Maxwell School, Syracuse University. He specializes in public budgeting and urban management and has contributed articles in both areas to several professional journals. He is the author of *The Limits of Technocratic Politics* (Transaction, 1978) and coeditor of *New Directions in Public Administration* (Brooks/Cole, 1984).